TRAVELLING TO
New Zealand

TRAVELLING TO
New Zealand

AN OXFORD ANTHOLOGY

EDITED BY LYDIA WEVERS

OXFORD

UNIVERSITY PRESS

OXFORD
UNIVERSITY PRESS

540 Great South Road, Greenlane,
PO Box 11-149, Auckland, New Zealand

Oxford University Press is a department of the University of Oxford.
It furthers the University's objective of excellence in research, scholarship,
and education by publishing worldwide in

Oxford New York

Athens Auckland Bangkok Bogotá Buenos Aires Calcutta
Cape Town Chennai Dar es Salaam Delhi Florence Hong Kong Istanbul
Karachi Kuala Lumpur Madrid Melbourne Mexico City Mumbai Nairobi
Paris Port Moresby São Paulo Shanghai Singapore Taipei Tokyo Toronto Warsaw

with associated companies in Berlin Ibadan

OXFORD is a registered trade mark of Oxford University Press
in the UK and in certain other countries

ISBN 0 19 5584112

Edited by Cathryn Game
Cover and text design by David Constable
Typeset by David Constable
Printed by Kyodo Printing Co. (Singapore) Pte Ltd

Front cover picture: a steamer alongside a bank of the Wanganui River (photographer unknown; F-49536-1/2,
Field Collection); back cover picture: a passenger coach travelling along Buller Gorge, near Lyell, West Coast
Region, c. 1900 (G-626-10X8, Tyree Collection). Both pictures from Alexander Turnbull Library, National
Library of New Zealand/Te Puna Matauranga o Aotearoa, Wellington, NZ.

In memory of Joyce Rendall Spanjaard Wevers
1915–75

Contents

Contents

Contents

Part 4 Globetrotting

Contents

Illustrations

Introduction

ON 5 APRIL 1826 a 27-year-old sealer was in the crew of one of two boats landed from the *Elizabeth* at George Sound. Regarded by his crew mates as a 'regular scholard' for keeping a log, John Boultbee recorded his impressions of New Zealand and the events that occurred during the six months he spent there, on 'unusually rough, porous, handmade paper' with each gathering 'stitched to a thin strip of leather' and 'joined to a cover made by hand from a fragment of sailcloth'.[1]

Like many travellers in the nineteenth century, Boultbee thought of his reminiscences as written 'for the amusement of my relations and friends', not for a reading public. At the same time, as June Starke points out in her introduction to Boultbee's book, his 'urge to travel had been inspired by reading books by explorers and travellers which formed an integral part of a Regency family's library', a library that included Cook's journals, as Boultbee's frequent references to them make clear.

Travelling to New Zealand tries to give the flavour of travel and travel writing in New Zealand for almost two centuries. It begins in 1826 and finishes in 1996, but the focus is on the boom years of the last three decades of the nineteenth century and the early decades of the twentieth, when steamers, coaches, coasters, and Shanks's pony were the means by which you moved about, and everyone kept a travel diary or asked their families to preserve copious quantities of letters. Tourists flocked to the Hot Lakes in search of weird and wonderful sights or went south for grandeur. The food and accommodation varied wildly, and travellers were intensely conscious of themselves moving through the farthest outpost of the British Empire and observing a 'new' landscape and culture. Most of the early travel accounts are by people who arrived as settlers, although I have tried to avoid conflating settlers with travellers, or people who ended up in New Zealand as opportunists or adventurers, floating around the world, like Boultbee, keeping a log 'of all that is going on' for his own diverse reasons.

Edward Markham is another peripatetic traveller. Markham arrived in Australia in 1833 and spent time in Van Diemen's Land socialising, buying horses, and visiting whaling stations until boredom set in: 'Time went by in the usual Monotonous way Till February when I decided on going down to New Zealand.' In the introduction to his edition of Markham's journal, *New Zealand or Recollections of It*, Eric McCormick comments that Markham has nothing to say on his reasons for going anywhere: '[P]erhaps the spirit of adventure induced him to cross the Tasman, or merely perhaps his acknowledged boredom.'[2] Markham's account of being in New Zealand reflects this restless spirit. He roamed and worked around the top of the North Island for eight and a half months, and left an opinionated and vivid account of what he did, who he saw, and what he thought. His idiosyncratic text demonstrates, as McCormick observes, that 'few persons not actually illiterate could ever have been so poorly qualified for authorship',[3] but the formal deficiencies of Markham's writing impart a lively authenticity, giving the impression of an unmediated personal response to the New Zealand he encountered.

Some of the descriptions of early New Zealand are retrospective, like those of J.C. Crawford and Sir John Gorst, but I have included them in the chronological sequence according to when they took place rather than when they were written, as the difference between New Zealand in 1839, when Crawford crossed Cook Strait in an open boat, and 1880, when he published his *Recollections of Travel*, is profound. The accounts of travelling to New Zealand by early settlers, such as Alfred Fell and William Kennaway, give an idea of the conditions on sailing ships, and the arduousness and terrors of the journey are generally conveyed in the descriptions of ship life until the 1870s. Indeed, the mere idea of travelling for pleasure as a tourist distinguishes later travellers from the poor souls of the 1840s and 1850s, who packed up their lives and possessions and left their homes forever, braving first the storms, wrecks, mutinies, bad food, sickness, and boredom of sailing ships and then the rigours and disappointments of a new land.

The experience of a working-class immigrant such as Henry Wouldon in 1841 was obviously very different from that of an urbane well-endowed traveller such as Alexander Marjoribanks. Marjoribanks' attitude of amused interest marks him as a spectator, whereas Wouldon's cautious and practical assessments of his situation are a sign of his commitment to what he has done. Marjoribanks' observations on Maori, a consuming point of interest and self-reflexivity for all travellers, are substantively different from Wouldon's. Driving Wouldon's remarks is the implicit negotiation of a contested environment: there is a 'slopp of war in our harber' and '30 solgers to take care of us' because other tribes might kill and eat 'our tribe', who are 'quiett people' and from whom Wouldon can buy produce. Marjoribanks' observation that he is an 'object of attraction' to the 'natives' on account of his size (15 stone) develops into a playful attitude of amiable cultural superiority: 'Previous to this I used sometimes to regret being so stout as I then was, but my New Zealand friends have thrown quite a new light upon the subject, and I readily bow to their authority, as they are well known to be people of taste in all matters of that sort.'[4]

After the Land Wars

At the end of the 1860s, when the Land Wars were over and steam succeeded sail as a mode of transport, travel changed its focus from immigration to recreation. New Zealand took its place on a round-the-world route that began in Europe, crossed North America, moved down through Australia, and travelled back to the northern hemisphere via Asia, a route reproduced in countless frontispiece maps with a red line snaking around the world. A new class of travel writing emerges, the result of strong European interest in travel and travel writing which since the eighteenth century had established a profitable market for travel books. Many of these accounts were the product of leisured recreational travellers seeing the world and writing letters home about it, but travel writing also became a professional occupation, taken up by a number of women, such as Isabella Bird and Constance Gordon Cumming, as well as writers of guidebooks and travel manuals. When Anthony Trollope published *Australia and New Zealand* in 1873 he claimed that four hundred books had already been written about New Zealand. By the 1880s travel had become modish, and New Zealand was experiencing a tourist boom. In the Prefatory Remarks to her guidebook, *The New Guide to the Lakes and Hot Springs* (1882), Thorpe Talbot cries: 'Fifty or sixty volumes of travel and description have I waded through, skipped through, laughed through, cried through (cried because the authors hadn't died before they learned to write); been bored by, interested by, edified by, and deceived by; and now I say unto everyone: Never mind the books … but go and see the wonders for yourself.'[5]

Such celebrated novelists, historians, and politicians as Anthony Trollope, Rudyard Kipling, Mark Twain, Sir Charles Dilke, and James Anthony Froude wrote about travelling to New Zealand, and some also gave lecture tours, which attracted large crowds. Local populations were (and are) keen to hear what travellers thought about them. As Edward Wakefield commented in his review of Froude's *Oceana*,[6] the most widely read travel book about New Zealand, '[W]hen any famous writer undertakes to give the world an account of the colonies from his own observation, all good colonists await the publication of his book with feverish impatience, and when it appears, each of them takes his praise or blame as personal to himself.'[7] However, Wakefield thought Froude had spent too much time on 'trivial occurrences' and was wildly inaccurate: 'He swallowed everything he was told holus bolus, and probably imagined or invented as much as he was told.' In an interesting glimpse of colonial etiquette, Wakefield attacked Froude for the amount of time he spent describing life on the steamer, which was, according to Wakefield, a subject 'strictly tabooed': '… pretty nearly everyone has made several sea voyages … [T]o dilate upon it is to betray a "new chum".'[8]

One of the interests of nineteenth-century travel writing to a modern reader, however, is the physical detail of travel, and the quality of accommodation, the food they ate, the roads they travelled, the coaches, coastal steamers, and trains they took, certainly preoccupied many tourists. Paul Carter has noted the 'double aspect of travelling—an experience that … required places to rest as much as roads'.[9] Very few travellers were so indifferent to the places where they rested, waited for coaches, or waited for the weather to change that they didn't record their impressions of them, and it is the personal narratives describing the irritability and pleasure of the traveller that allows us to imagine what it was like. Alexander Marjoribanks commented in 1845:

There is one thing connected with a sea life which I have seen noticed only by one author, and that is, the effect produced upon the temper,—those with good tempers on shore, becoming often irritable at sea. This author asserts, that too close a conjunction of human beings without relaxation, tends to beget selfishness; and states his conviction, that if twenty philosophers were shut up in one cabin during a six months' voyage, they would all come to hate one another by the end of it.[10]

Travelling for health

Many tourists travelled for health reasons—famously the Victorian traveller and writer Isabella Bird—but many others as well. The section on 'Medical Aspects of the Voyage' in the *Orient Line Guide* for 1888 noted that only some illnesses would benefit from a sea voyage; for consumption, an early sea voyage 'is often of incalculable benefit' whereas patients with advanced cardiac disease 'should avoid going to sea', but few 'can benefit more than the really over-taxed and over-worried brain-worker'.[11]

New Zealand's inverse seasons were attractive to the European health-traveller wanting to avoid the winter, and its thermal springs developed a reputation for health resorts almost as quickly as for being natural wonders. A number of travel accounts of Rotorua were written by consumptives as letters to their families and were published posthumously in more than one case. Frank Henley's *Bright Memories* (1887) is a case in point. A devout Wesleyan, Henley embarked on a voyage to the Antipodes in 1884 after 'several attacks of haemorrhage' and died at Sandhurst at the end of the following year. His account of Tarawera is interesting for his description of the Maori school run by Mr Hazard, the teacher who died in the eruption of 1886.

The travel industry

Alongside the travel accounts of individual travellers came a huge increase in travel guides. Steamship companies, such as the Orient-Pacific, the Union Steam Ship Company, and the NZ Steam Ship Company, published guides and manuals to their ships, the routes they took around the world, and the sights travellers would encounter. Travel became much more organised. There were schedules of fees, and ships advertised their menus, facilities, and onward routes. The costs of excursions—from Auckland to Rotomahana, for instance—were estimated in guide-books, and many tourists from the mid 1870s on refer to such well-known books as Froude's *Oceana* or Sir Charles Dilke's *Greater Britain*, agreeing or disagreeing with what had been said.

The majority of tourists were British, and came from such a narrow social field that they often knew each other or of each other. When J. Ernest Tinne arrives in Napier in the early 1870s he is tapped on the shoulder by 'a nice looking young fellow whose face I had some difficulty at first in recalling. It was N—, a pupil of the same tutor as myself at Eton.'[12] The same meeting is recounted from the other side in *A Chequered Career* (1881), anonymously published by H.W. Nesfield, who ran out of money in New Zealand and did a variety of manual jobs, including driving a cab for hire in Napier. As Tinne notes: 'Most of the residents knew his history, and looked upon the whole affair rather as a joke than otherwise; so much so that they did not hesitate to offer him their hospitality, and ladies would always bow on meeting him, unless he was actually on the box driving.'[13]

Several travel writers refer to the numbers of Australians who came to visit the Pink and White Terraces and the Rotorua lakes; Froude talks of 'Australians with long purses and easy temper',[14] who spoil the market for everyone else. However, with some exceptions (for instance James Hingston, who toured the world in 1871, William Senior, an Englishman living in Queensland, the flower-hunter Mrs Rowan, or the mountaineer Marie Byles) they seem not to have written books about it in the prolific way of British travellers. The travel-writing archive includes some Americans, French, and Germans, a Prussian count, and (in the twentieth century) visitors from Czechoslovakia, India, and Vietnam. The overwhelming majority, however, are British, confirming a view perhaps of New Zealand as a place where British travellers felt particularly comfortable and 'at home', but also of Britain and its culture as mobile, assertive, and textual. A fifth of the travel accounts are by women, but this does not represent the huge quantity of unpublished writing by women—especially letters and diaries—which remained private and provides a quite different picture of the engagement of women in recording and documenting travel experience.

Travel writing as this collection represents it is a public and semi-professional activity, ranging from those writers who explicitly set out to write descriptive and explicatory accounts of New Zealand for an established audience eager for such writing—Trollope, Dilke, and Froude fall into this category—or others who were professional travellers—such as Bird and Gordon Cumming—or travelled with their profession, such as David Kennedy and his family of singers, who wrote an account of their tour through the British colonies, singing the 'songs of Scotland around the world'.

A number of writers are already well known—Kipling, Mark Twain, George Augustus Sala, J.B. Priestley, Paul Theroux—and part of their interest lies in their response to New Zealand as famous writers. However, many more in this collection have never been reprinted. This bulk of uncollected and largely unread travel writing was a discovery for me when I began to research the travel archive. From its volume and variety, as well as from the significant repetitions of this writing, it is possible to build up a picture of what it was like to move around New Zealand in the nineteenth century: where travellers went, what facilities existed for them, what they noticed, liked, and disliked, what kind of country they thought they were in, and how it revealed their own acculturation, their prejudices, assumptions, and judgments.

Visiting the Terraces

One of the points of emphasis of this collection is the mechanics of travel: accommodation, modes of travel, food. Another is the 'cluster' points where most writers congregated: the 'hot' travel locations, the Cold Lakes, the Hot Lakes, the West Coast Sounds, including Milford. Another emphasis is the cross-cultural encounter with Maori, which assumes different forms and degrees of intensity over the almost two hundred years from start to finish. As a whole, *Travelling to New Zealand* suggests a cultural geography, a shifting, nuanced, diverse, and reflexive record of how New Zealand and its inhabitants were perceived, received, and transmitted. It is also a book full of narratives.

Each traveller has a story to tell, and together their stories knit into a much larger narrative, which could have a variety of subtitles: Victorians Abroad, European Prejudice, the Hierarchy of Race, Assumptions of Colonisation, Weird Sights, Shipboard Life, Walking the Track, and so on.

Travellers were also very aware of other tourists, especially around Rotorua and the Pink and White Terraces. James Froude, arriving at Ohinemutu, noted: 'Tourists were lounging about by dozens at the hotel doors as we drove up; some come for amusement and curiosity, some to reside for the water-cure. Parties were arriving hourly from Cambridge by the route which we had taken, from Tauranga on the sea, or overland from Wellington. The carriages which brought the new arrivals returned with a back load of those who had exhausted the wonders.'[15] The volume of tourists to the Terraces caused problems in themselves. The painter Charles Blomfield estimated in the summer of 1885–86 that between ten and thirty tourists came to the Terraces every week day, 'mostly moneyed people from all parts of the world'.[16]

Many tourists comment about how much it costs them to get to the Terraces. As Charles Morton Ollivier reported in 1871:

> The natives of Kariri have settled among themselves, or passed a law, that any party visiting Rota Mahana in a canoe from that pa, shall employ and take with them two Maoris for each white man forming the party, and shall pay five shillings per diem for the canoe, and a similar amount to each native. To this rule the natives adhere most rigidly … The Maories also demand a fee of £2 sterling, if they take the canoe up the creek between Tarawera and Rota Mahana. This charge is only demanded when the creek is taputapu and the £2 is supposed to have a magical effect upon this superstitious practice of theirs.[17]

In 1884 a schedule of fees for boat transport to the Terraces was approved by the Minister of Native Affairs, William Rolleston, and travel guides, such as Thorpe Talbot's *New Guide to the Lakes and Hot Springs* (1882), told tourists what to pay. Talbot says that the round tour—Tauranga, Rotorua, Rotomahana—'need not occupy more than four clear days, nor cost more than £10. The natives charge £2 for rowing one person across Tarawera to Rotomahana, and for every additional passenger 5s more.' A guide's fee was 10s, and the canoe fare across Rotomahana was also 10s. 'For permission to see the Terraces, there is another charge of 2s 6d for each tourist. This land belongs to the Wairoa natives, and they have learned from the pakeha to charge for admission to their show—small blame to them!'[18]

Haggling over costs emphasised the racist attitudes held by virtually all tourists. The *Handbook to the Bay of Plenty* advises in 1875 that travellers may safely calculate on the cost not exceeding 15s *per diem* and and then diverges to a racist caricature of the Maori who tourists will meet at Ohinemutu, as if paying to visit the Terraces is the same as giving money to a fraudulent beggar:

> There, may be seen in perfection the Maori Lord of the Soil in all his pristine glory, affable to a fault, and suffering from a chronic impecuniosity, which his instinct leads him to relieve at the expense of any confiding stranger who will part with a shilling on the strength of shaking hands with a *soi disant* Rangatira, who will manufacture for the occasion a genealogical descent from the Maori Noah—a much more respectable old gentleman, by the way, than ours of vine-growing proclivities.[19]

Racist stereotypes about Maori as childlike, dirty, lazy, and mercenary, somehow illegitimately exploiting the legitimate desire of travellers to see natural wonders, circulate through all nineteenth-century travel writing to a greater or lesser extent. Even those who are well disposed towards Maori always speak of them as people on the other side of an unpassable boundary of civilisation. A tiny example is from the Kennedy singing family, riding in the Hutt, who are greeted with waves by two Maori women 'dressed in bright dyed matting, and with coloured cloth bands around their heads ... not to be outdone in politeness by savages [we] returned them quite a windmill salute with our arms'.[20]

At the Hot Lakes, the experience of seeing the Pink and White Terraces was dependent on the services of the local Maori, and every tourist comments on Sophia Hinerangi and Kate Middlemass, best known of the Native Guides. George Augustus Sala said Sophia was a 'very remarkable Belle Sauvage', and Kate's claim to have eight husbands was disbelieved by Froude. The effort of getting to Rotomahana and the conditions of staying there, literally at home among Maori, was represented by many tourists as a chance to 'go native' in a mild way, suggested in the illustrations from the *Graphic* (see page 146) showing European men naked in hot pools or wandering around clad only in a 'plaid'. But travel writing generally insists on the maintenance of an implacable boundary between travellers and the 'lords of the soil'; a 'pigheaded people', as James Edge Partington put it, spoilt by 'our conciliatory treatment' of them.[21]

To get to Rotomahana you either took the coastal steamer to Tauranga or drove there by coach from Cambridge or Ohinemutu through Tikitapu bush, mentioned in every account as bush of exceptional beauty. Thorpe Talbot took the steamer on a wild and stormy night:

> we ... poured out our woes on the midnight air, and wished we hadn't eaten so much dinner, for then had there been fewer woes to pour. The green-and-yellow melancholy caused us to look on Tauranga with a jaundiced eye, when early in the dim grey morning we struggled on deck and saw

the little town through a dense grey mist of rain ... We waded up the pier through the rain, we breakfasted dismally at an hotel. We climbed in silent melancholy to the box seat of the coach and so set out for Rotorua.[22]

A usual prelude to the Terraces was the performance of a haka at a shilling per performer. James Edge Partington thought the 'haka-haka ... but a poor performance' after the 'mekes of Fiji and the sivas of Samoa'.[23] When Froude was offered a performance, he was told gentlemen usually preferred the haka 'complete with its indecencies' for £3 10s. His comments were stern: 'Tourists, it seems, do encourage these things, and the miserable people are encouraged to disgrace themselves, that they may have a drunken orgie afterwards. The tourists, I presume, wish to teach the poor savage "the blessings of civilisation".'[24]

Arrival at Te Tarata, the White Terrace, produced flights of descriptive prose in almost everyone. Fortunately the Terraces were extensively photographed and painted before their destruction in the eruption of 10 June 1886, but painting and photography were also a source of contention between local Maori and tourists. The Maori issued a printed notice saying no one could take photographs without paying. In 1881 Miss Gordon Cumming was involved in a tussle over her sketches and watercolours as the Maori thought she should pay them a larger sum than for photographs as the coloured drawings 'give a truer idea of the place, and must therefore be more valuable'. The Maori repeatedly asked her to pay £5 for her portfolio of drawings, which caused her to become outraged and obstinate. In an undignified episode she hid her portfolio in a bundle of plaids and pillows, and sent it out of Te Wairoa under cover of a large party of tourists. Five years later a French tourist, Emile Wenz, also expressed outrage that he had to pay for photographing, and attempted to explain to the chief that in civilised countries it was photographers who were paid.

Something that horrified many tourists—and almost every travel writer commented on it—was the extent of the indelible graffiti on the Terraces. The artist E.W. Payton said:

> There is one feature about the Pink Terrace which is a disgrace to English tourists. The buttresses are covered with hundreds of names of people who probably thought the only way of letting the world know of their existence would be to write their names on this terrace—a piece of Nature's handiwork about which it has been written, and truly, 'anything so exquisite does not exist elsewhere in nature'.[25]

George Augustus Sala's friends were outraged by the scribblers and wanted a 'Ranger of the Terrace to be appointed, and the offence of wall-scribbling made punishable by fine and imprisonment'. However, Sala was fascinated by the fresh appearance of the writing. Climbing the White Terrace, he noticed one 'boldly pencilled, it looked so fresh and shiningly black that at first I thought the crumb of a penny loaf would have rubbed the writing out. But what do you think was the date? 1869!'[26]

A year later Tarawera erupted, and the Terraces were gone. With their disappearance the tourist flow to the region (and to New Zealand) diminished for a while, although the English illustrated papers had a field day with 'before and after' engravings from photographs. Some travellers went to see the destruction. J.L. Lambe visited in 1888, and where the favourite cry of travel writers before 1886 had been that no words could describe the glories of the Terraces, Lambe wrote: '[N]o words can describe the scene of desolation which now opened on our view, for on every side as far as the eye could see there was nothing but mud and ashes.'[27]

The mechanics of travel

Although New Zealand as a place of interest had become visible to Victorian travellers moving around the world for many reasons, including the huge interest in travel and information about travel that are products of imperialism, it is thanks to the Pink and White Terraces and the Wonderland of the Antipodes that such a wealth of travel writing exists from the 1870s and 1880s.

As a result of these accounts it is possible to reconstruct the mechanics of travel: what it was actually like to be a traveller in the late nineteenth century in a developing colony, and as a subject of the British Empire. Numbers of travellers talk about the food, and some transcribe entire menus. James Edge Partington, for example, exclaims over how cheap and extensive the bill of fare is in Kumara: 'Imagine a town at home, only five years old, giving you the following Menu: Kidney soup. Salmon. Roast: Lamb and mint sauce; beef. Boiled: Loin of mutton and caper sauce. Pickled Pork. Stewed steak and olives. Vegetables: cabbage, potatoes, carrots, peas. Marmalade roley-poley, apple pie, baked custard, black currant tarts, stewed apples, custard. Cheese. And all for half a crown!'[28] The Kennedys too remarked on the liberality of the table at Ohinemutu in the mid 1870s, which was so remote that they went there on horseback:

> the white man has only put his face in as yet to the extent of a store and two small wooden hotels
> … but the table … though not first class, as might have been expected in such an outlandish place,
> was very liberally supplied—steak, chops and preserved meat in lumps figuring at every meal. There
> was never any appearance of milk or eggs; but then we had failed to get these in some of the most
> rural parts of the colonies.[29]

Bradshaw's *New Zealand As It Is* (1883), a descriptive guide for emigrants and travellers, found that in Christchurch

> the better-class hotels are cheap and numerous. The usual charge is ten shillings a day, including sit-
> ting room. Food is plentiful and excellent. Soup, fish, poultry, beef, and mutton, vegetables, tarts
> with bread and butter of the very best quality ought to satisfy all grumblers … Those in an inter-
> mediate position will find at the smaller hotels or lodging houses, which everywhere abound, beds

at about two shillings a night, one shilling being charged for each meal. Under such circumstances a person can calculate to a nicety what he is spending.

The hotel landscape as humorously described by George Augustus Sala in Wellington brings to life a network of hotels and boarding houses that hardly varied through the Empire: the Victorian version of Hilton and McDonald's, suggesting that most travellers preferred the differences from home to be kept at a distance and definitely outside the living arrangements. Trollope's comments on New Zealand's social and political development were liberally interspersed with complaints about his accommodation or the state of the roads. Count Fritz von Hochberg said irritably of his hotel at Waiouru that 'the worst shed I've ever been in pompously calls itself an hotel. Cabin-like, small, low rooms with—one could hardly call them beds—and such thin partitions that you partake of the most private conversations.'[30]

The discomforts and dangers of travelling are constantly described. Making their way through New Zealand the Kennedys experience the full rigours of accommodation and coach travel. While crossing the Waitaki their ferryman and horse were swept away, although fortunately not fatally, leaving the coach 'arrested on the brink of a hidden terrace' until he managed to get back to them: 'We would advise no one with weak nerves to ford a swollen river in New Zealand. A few days after, a number of passengers were fording this same Waitaki, when their coach upset and a "female magician" was drowned. We afterwards saw, in the Christchurch cemetery, many graves of persons who had perished while crossing rivers.'[31]

John MacGregor observes: 'Do you know anything about the box seat? Then you have never travelled in New Zealand.'[32] Many travellers refer repeatedly to the desirability of the box seat when travelling in a coach and describe the competition to achieve this desirable outdoor position. Travelling companions also come in for a great deal of scrutiny. Differences of race and class are always noted, and there is strong anti-semitism, as von Hochberg, a Prussian who toured New Zealand in the early 1900s, demonstrates. Class distinctions are of necessity harder to maintain when you are travelling in a colony with rudimentary facilities, and many tourists commented on social conjunctions. Major S.E.G. Ponder thought his bedroom at the Wairakei hotel in the mid 1930s should have belonged to a 'tweeny maid at home' as the wallpaper, which revolted him, would have sent her into 'ecstasies of pleasure'.[33] C.R. Sail's account of an excursion to the West Coast Sounds typecasts his fellow passengers on No. 4 boat in the manner of a Victorian comic novel, and Mrs Rowan's social attitudes are entirely clear from her description of one of her travelling companions in 1890 as a 'tall English gentleman, a splendid specimen of the old-time squatter, one of those who have helped to make Australia what it is'.[34] Almost everyone complained about the state of the roads or railways, had horror stories about mountain passes or hotel food, was rained out on the Milford Track, marvelled at thermal wonders, had bad experiences on coastal steamers, and was intensely aware of their social and racial groupings.

Scenic New Zealand

Although the Tarawera eruption removed the Pink and White Terraces as a tourist attraction, Rotorua and other thermal locations remain a primary destination for travellers. After the 1880s, however, interest in other places, particularly the Wanganui River and the West Coast Sounds, increased perceptibly. Steamer excursions ran from Bluff, and numbers of tourists came to walk the Milford Track and see the more spectacular parts of the West Coast. Around the turn of the nineteenth century numbers of travellers ventured up the Wanganui River on special steamer excursions, and most found the accommodation and boats primitive. Alys Lowth's *Emerald Hours* complained of a 'very wretched third-rate boarding house' and perpetual rain, but even so tourists agreed that the scenery was spectacular and 'made up for all these annoyances'.[35] Blanche Baughan's collection of essays *Studies in New Zealand Scenery* (1916) featured the Wanganui River as one of the great sights of New Zealand, and Beatrice Grimshaw's 1907 account of travelling the river seemed to her like striking out 'into the early nineteenth century', although full of twentieth-century contrasts.[36]

Specialised travellers who came to climb mountains, fish, and hunt increased steadily through the early part of the twentieth century, precursors of adventure tourism and 'wilderness' backpackers. What they found was often a far cry from what they expected, as Frances Ahl's account of her visit to Manapouri illustrates, or Marie Byles who embarked on the Finest Walk in the World, and rechristened it the Wettest Walk in the World. After the Second World War there are not as many private travellers who write travel books about New Zealand. Travellers who write are more likely to be writing a travel book with an angle, for example, Tom Houston's account of circling the world on a £5 note, or to be engaged in some specialist activity. Quite large categories of travellers in the twentieth century make only a fleeting appearance in this collection: sailors and travelling professional sports people, for instance, or humorous accounts of working holidays such as Sarah Mussen's. At the same time it is possible to see a process of evolution from the professional travel writer of the 1950s, who is really producing a guide with a loose autobiographical narrative, such as Ray Dorien, usually sponsored by the New Zealand Tourist Board or equivalent organisation, to the confessional narrative of a practised cultural historian and observer such as Paul Theroux, whose *Happy Isles of Oceania* annoyed New Zealanders when it appeared. Noel O'Hare, reviewing Theroux's book for the *Listener*, commented that his journey had begun with Theroux in 'a thoroughly bad mood' in Auckland.[37] There are more books by professional writers such as Kate Llewellyn and no books intended for 'Private Circulation', the favoured publication mode of the nineteenth-century writer of letters or diaries.

Seeing New Zealand through the eyes of non-Anglo-Saxon visitors makes available a different set of reactions and comparisons. The sight of brown and parched Canterbury plains transports the Indian academic and travel writer A.S. Wadia back to his 'native India', and

Bohumil Posipil's litany of the fine cheap food he consumes in New Zealand is suggestive about Czechoslovakia in the 1930s depression. Trinh Khanh Tuoc's letters home to Vietnam when he arrives as a student in Wellington in the early 1960s give a bleak impression of what it was like to be a foreigner being processed through a strange country: 'We were taken to the External Aid Division where we were told of life in New Zealand for more than an hour. But the speaker was shouting so fast that I did not catch much. I can only remember him saying: "You must learn to eat mutton." '

Of course all travel accounts represent New Zealand as a place and a society coloured by the writer's expectations and knowledge. Nineteenth-century travel writing is overt about its frame of reference. New Zealand was a colony with interesting but primitive indigenous people, poor infrastructure, beautiful scenery, and unsophisticated inhabitants. Most Victorian travellers thought New Zealand had no cultural history or life, and that many of its natural and human features were wonderful or picturesque but should be tamed and utilised by the forward energies of European imperialism. Nineteenth-century tourists took travelling seriously. They equipped themselves with gear suitable for varieties of colonial climates, they reported their impressions and observations to a waiting audience at home, and they (especially the male travellers) published their findings. When Constance Gordon Cumming came to New Zealand as companion to the wife of the Governor of Fiji, Lady Hamilton Gordon, and governess to the Hamilton Gordons' children, she set off intrepidly to see the sights, on horseback much of the way:

> we had to keep up a hard swinging gallop and (being as yet a novice in the arts of bush-travelling, in a land where there are no patient coolies ever ready to run miles and miles with luggage) I was encumbered with a heavy travelling-bag insecurely strapped to the pommel—sketching materials ditto—opera-glasses keeping time against my side, and a large umbrella, which I dared not open, though the sun was burning. Having to hold on to all of these, and keep up our unflagging pace, was to me desperately fatiguing.[38]

Female travellers, although they often noticed and reported on different things, also displayed unshakeable cultural assumptions, such as Gordon Cumming's determination not to pay Maori for her watercolours, which were then exhibited in London. Leonard Bell has estimated that 'her paintings were probably seen by more people … than the work of any other female artist of the period' owing to the large quanity of her pictures exhibited at the Colonial and Indian Exhibitions in London and Glasgow in 1886.[39] The immense interest taken by the Victorian public in the British Empire, travel, and travel writing is evidenced both physically, in the increasing numbers of tourists landing at New Zealand ports in the course of a world voyage, and textually. The English illustrated papers ran feature articles on travellers, their exploits, and the places they visited, reviewed the travel literature, and ran advertisements for travel equipment. Travel books were a staple item on publishers' lists, and well-known travel writers commanded good sales and became public figures.

Why read travel writing?

Travel writing works in at least two directions, which has been a large part of its fascination for me while working on *Travelling to New Zealand*. It is an important cultural dimension of Victorian imperialism. As the expansionist push of Europeans into the rest of the world reached its physical limits, it was followed by the wave of colonisation and settlement that made it possible for the traveller who was not an explorer or adventurer to move around the planet and yet in some senses stay at home. As the travel environment became safer and more accessible, it became increasingly attractive, and the flow of tourists helped to develop travel facilities and networks. Their accounts of what they did, the places they visited, what they thought, how they got there, why they went, who they saw, and what they read give a complex picture of Victorians abroad and at home: the reactions and responses of tourists are like signals from a vanished metropolis. At the same time the travel literature, ranging as it does from the sophisticated and reflective texts of prominent intellectuals to largely unedited diaries for private circulation to family and friends, gives diverse glimpses of what New Zealand might have looked, smelled, and tasted like to a visitor in another time or from another place. The windy empty grey streets of 1960s Wellington to a boy from Vietnam or the sudden sight of a huia threaded by its beak through the ear of a Maori man in 1870s Tauranga seem to open a space in which we see our past or ourselves in sudden sharp focus. The travel archive offers a patchwork, a panorama, a sketchbook of thousands of views of a landscape, and a history that we think we know.

In the twentieth century there was a perceptible decrease in travel writing, which probably reflects a decline in letter-writing and diary-keeping. There has been a shift away from the amateur travel narrative written for a personal audience to the professional writer or specialised travel writer commanding huge audiences, a form of travel writing that has become very popular since the 1980s. Modern mass travel is a routine experience for many people, destinations are increasingly similar, physical hardships are minimised, and the sense of arriving in an exotic new world that propelled the Victorian tourist to his or her pen is harder to reproduce, although the huge growth in backpacking and adventure travel suggests ways in which the world is freshly experienced. But for most of today's travellers home is an email or a phone call away, the world is crammed with tourists and well supplied with guidebooks, which might be why reading narratives recounting the anxiety and excitement of nineteenth-century passengers as they glimpsed a line of land on the horizon or ploughed axle-deep through the muddy tracks of New Zealand is like getting a blast of air and light from another place and time.

Notes

1 John Boultbee, *The Journal of a Rambler* (ed. June Starke), Oxford University Press, Auckland, 1986, introduction, p. xx.
2 Edward Markham, *New Zealand or Recollections of It* (ed. E.H. McCormick), R.E. Owen, Government Printer, Wellington, 1963, p. 22.
3 Markham, p. 27.
4 Alexander Marjoribanks, *Travels in New Zealand*, Smith, Elder & Co., London, 1845; republished Capper Press, Christchurch, 1973, p. 25.
5 Thorpe Talbot, *The New Guide to the Lakes and Hot Springs*, Wilson & Horton, Printers, Auckland, 1882, p. v.
6 J.A. Froude, *Oceana, or, England and Her Colonies*, Longmans, Green, London, 1886.
7 Edward Wakefield, 'New Zealand and Mr Froude', *Nineteenth Century*, August 1886.
8 Ibid.
9 Paul Carter, *The Road to Botany Bay: An Essay in Spatial History*, Faber & Faber, London and Boston, 1987, p. 232.
10 Marjoribanks, p. 23.
11 Orient Line Guide, 1888, p. 23.
12 J. Ernest Tinne, *The Wonderland of the Antipodes*, Sampson Low, Marston, Low & Searle, London, 1873, p. 39.
13 Ibid.
14 Froude, p. 262.
15 Froude, pp. 270–1.
16 Blomfield's unpublished diaries, quoted in S.B. Reggett, 'The Tarawera eruption and its effects on the tourist industry', unpublished MA thesis in geography, University of Otago, 1972, p. 37.
17 C.M. Ollivier, *A Visit to the Boiling Springs of New Zealand*, John Hughes, Christchurch, 1871, p. 19.
18 Talbot, pp. 4–5.
19 *Handbook to the Bay of Plenty*, Langridge & Edgecumbe, Tauranga, 1875, p. 11.
20 David Kennedy Jnr, *Kennedy's Colonial Travel*, Edinburgh Publishing Company, Edinburgh, 1876, p. 216.
21 James Edge Partington, *Random Rot*, For Private Circulation, Altrincham, 1883, p. 366.
22 Talbot, p. 5.
23 Partington, p. 366.
24 Froude, p. 283.
25 E.W. Payton, *Round About New Zealand*, Chapman & Hall, London, 1888, pp. 128–9.
26 G.A. Sala, *The Land of the Golden Fleece* (ed. Robert Dingley), Mulini Press, Canberra, 1995, p. 178.
27 J.L. Lambe, *Twelve Months of Travel*, Printed for Private Circulation, 1888, p. 121.
28 Partington, p. 338.
29 Kennedy, pp. 258–61.
30 Count Fritz von Hochberg, *An Eastern Voyage*, J.M. Dent & Sons, London, 1910, p. 82.
31 Kennedy, p. 193.
32 John MacGregor, *Toil and Travel*, T. Fisher Unwin, London, 1892, p. 55.
33 S.E.G. Ponder, *Sun on Summer Seas*, Stanley Paul & Co., London, 1936, p. 103.
34 Mrs Rowan, *A Flower Hunter in Queensland and New Zealand*, Angus & Robertson, Sydney, 1898, p. 196.
35 Alys Lowth, *Emerald Hours in New Zealand*, Whitcomb & Tombs, Christchurch, 1907, p. 38.
36 Beatrice Grimshaw, *In the Strange South Seas*, Hutchinson & Co., London, 1907.
37 Noel O'Hare, 'Living out of Theroux's suitcase', *Listener*, 10 October 1992, pp. 52–3.
38 C. F. Gordon Cumming, *At Home in Fiji*, William Blackwood & Sons, Edinburgh and London, 1881, p. 181.
39 Leonard Bell, 'Travel art and its complications: Constance Frederica Gordon Cumming's 1877 visit to New Zealand and the Colonial and Indian Exhibition of 1886', *Bulletin of NZ Art History*, vol. 16, 1995, p. 30.

PART 1
Early arrivals

PASSING THROUGH A SWAMP IN NEW ZEALAND.

Henry Williams, 'Passing through a swamp in New Zealand', 1836. (F-325-1/4-MNZ, ATL)

Shoes on the beach (1826)

JOHN BOULTBEE

John Boultbee accompanied his brother Edwin to Van Diemen's Land in 1823 and in 1826 joined sealers heading for New Zealand. He spent two years around Foveaux Strait, working with Jack Price, a sealer, and the Maori people of Murihuku. Boultbee's family donated his journal of his time in New Zealand to the Alexander Turnbull Library in the 1970s.

Charles D. Barraud, George Sound, 1860s? (A-029-045, ATL)

WHEN WE HAD BEEN OUT 3 WEEKS, we saw the high land of New Zealand, near Thompson's Sound. Its appearance was remarkable from it's bold, uneven surface, and a huge mountain called Saddle Mountain, and one large bluff like an immense molehill, forming one of the heads of Thomson's Sound.—The distant range of mountains were tipped with snow.

On the 5th April, we anchored in a cove called George's Harbour. It is a deep inlet, surrounded by high mountains covered with trees and where we anchored, at the head of the cove, we could barely see the sun above two hours in the day; so that the air was cold and chilly. All our boats and crews were landed here, and the provisions for 6 months for 2 boats' crews, who were stationed *here* with orders to range the coast for 200 miles. The boat to which I belonged, took 6 weeks provisions, 3 muskets, a dog and our clothes, and went about 100 miles to the Northward; the vessel taking one boat to Dusky Bay, a distance of 100 miles to the Southward, where she was to land 6 months provisions, and where on our return from the Northward, we were to join her.

Our Captain advised the Boatsteerer to take 6 muskets, but he refused, saying 3 were sufficient, and more, would be only lumbering the boat up too much. We had a keg of gunpowder, 2 or 300 balls, etc. the Boatsteerer said we might by chance fall in with natives, and therefore it would be as well to make a few cartridges.—On the first day of our departure, we arrived at Milford Haven, so called by Sealers, a distance of 30 miles where we hauled the boat up, and went into a hut, made by sealers, and slept for the night. Milford Haven is a wild romantic looking place, abounding in high mountains, and intermediate deep vallies, the woods are abundantly supplied with game, as woodhens, green birds, emus etc—these birds are of large size, they lay their eggs in the holes in the ground and in hollow trees and as they cannot fly, they are easily overtaken with dogs.

On the lefthand side of this place is a deep and narrow passage between two tier of mountains which we called the flue, and through which the wind blows at times with great violence.

On our way, we had occasion to haul up at different places along the coast, and amongst the rest, at Cascade Beach, mentioned in Cook's voyages; the cliffs here are high and of a clay red colour, and from them are ejected 2 considerable falls of water, the beach here is covered with large pebble stones, and care is therefore required to prevent the boats from being stove in hauling them up. During this time we did not see any traces of natives, till we came to Open Bay, where on the beach we saw a broken spear and a pair of old porraras, (a kind of sandal made of flax). Cascade is the South Head of Open Bay, its distance from the North Head is nearly 40 miles, and from these heads the land forms a semicircle; at 3 miles distance from the nearest shore, and halfway between the 2 Heads is a small low island covered with a species of low shrubby bamboo. The Bay itself is very picturesque, the scenery, various, from gentle rises and vallies to high bluff mountains which lay a distance in the background; and the coast appears to be more convenient for the natives than any part we had seen, the land we had before passed being too high to admit of people travelling. We staid a night in a Cove to the S. end of this bay, and got some woodhens; these birds are in colour and size, like a pheasant, but they cannot fly, so that we easily knocked them down with sticks when they came out on the beach at night, in search of food; they are very spirited and will show fight at a bundle of feathers tied at the end of a stick and shook at them.—We hauled up our boat, on Open Bay island and a most difficult task we had, the place being steep and broken rocks, and at high water the surf beating against the boat so as to endanger her: however we had strong wooden rollers which we placed under her and by dint of lifting and launching together we got her up safe, one hand standing by the tackle, to hold on all the strain of the boat as we moved her.

On going into an old hut, we found a bag of flour and a bucket of sugar, with a note from the Master of a vessel to his boats' crew, informing them he had been there, and not finding anyone on the island, had left them what he could spare, and was on his way to Sydney. He mentioned that he had lost his mate, but how, he could not say, as he was on shore near Arnitt's River, and it was supposed by some that he was drowned.

John Boultbee, *The Journal of a Rambler*, pp. 36–40.

Chasing the French (1832)

FREDERICK MONTRÉSOR

Leaves from Memory's Logbook was compiled and edited by C.A. Montrésor, a nephew of the author. Frederick Montrésor joined the Royal Navy as a midshipman on the Cambridge *as a schoolboy. He left for South America and eventually went to Sydney, where he shipped in HMS* Zebra *for New Zealand in 1832 to see off the French corvette* La Favorite. *His journal 'jottings' became the narrative account published in 1884.*

Nov. 16th.—We had scarcely been three days in Sydney before a report was current that the French corvette *La Favorite*, had been cruising about New Zealand, and that she had at length landed a party there, hoisted the tri-colour, and taken possession in the name of La Grande Nation; the consequence was that everybody was up in arms. Books, parchments, in fact everything which contained the name of New Zealand, were searched, to find out if it had not already been taken possession of in the name of His Britannic Majesty, by Captain Cook. This was finally proved to have been the case. The papers immediately commenced an attack upon the acting Governor (Colonel Sydney), offering their advice, and recommending

Edmond François Paris, '*La Favorite* franchissant la Passe de Kororareka', 1835. (PUBL-0133-067, ATL)

beyond everything bold measures. 'How fortunate,' they said, 'that a man of war, the *Zebra*, has arrived at this crisis. We should recommend the Governor to dispatch her immediately in search of the French corvette, to demand the meaning of this attempt at claiming an island already under the protection of His Britannic Majesty, and should fair means fail in effecting the desired end, let the *Zebra* have orders to make use of the only alternative, that of force. We are fully aware,' continued the Editor, 'that this is a very delicate affair for an acting Governor to undertake, more especially one who may be superseded in a few days; but let the Colonel consider what his countrymen at home may think of his acting tamely on such an occasion; and even should the affair between the two ships end in a quarrel between their respective nations, it may easily be explained by attributing it to the too ready "Zeal" in the acting Governor—A fault easily forgiven.'

Whether the Governor listened to these words of wisdom, or whether he really had heard more than was publicly known, I cannot pretend to say; but anyhow we were ordered to prepare for sea instantaneously, and a few days after receiving our orders, we were on our way to New Zealand.

Standing in to the anchorage we observed an English whaler at anchor, the Captain came on board and told us that *La Favorite* had sailed some days ago for Valparaiso; that the report of the French having attempted to settle was quite unfounded, and had they done so, they would never have been allowed to land.

He said (with how much truth I do not know), that some years ago, a party of Frenchmen, sixty in number, were murdered by the natives: something of the sort must have happened, for it appears that nothing would induce them to go on board, and when the Frenchmen attempted to make a survey of the harbour, the natives hauled down their landmarks and interrupted them in every way, so that finally they were obliged to depart. After gleaning all the news we could from the whaler, we made sail and proceeded to the Inner Harbour. In running along the land I was very much pleased with its appearance.

New Zealand, I think, if cultivated, would be highly productive, far superior to the land about Swan River.

We had not anchored above a few minutes when we were surrounded by canoes, the natives all anxious to see King William's ship; we, however, chose to be 'not at home' till this morning, when we were favoured by a visit from several of the Chiefs.

Not one of them could speak English; but, as Paddy would say, they all asked for tobacco. Pipes and tobacco were soon provided, at which they seemed much pleased, and commenced smoking. It was a curious sight to see His Majesty's Quarter Deck, our grand Parade, covered with savages, spitting about it too, unconcernedly, as if our much feared, and much revered pennant were only a bit of red bunting!

We were all much surprised at the immense size of the men. The Chief, Tamiar, was, I should think, six feet four or five inches, and with limbs which would have made an English prize fighter look a mere pigmy. They came on board dressed in a blanket, thrown over them like a cloak, over which they had a kind of mat made of fine grass, and over this again a cloak of goat skin; these two last were, however, mere badges of state, and were thrown off as soon as the ceremony of shaking hands was over: the blanket showed to great advantage the immense strength and symmetry of their limbs.

Tamiar, if his face had not been disfigured by the tattoo, would have been a good-looking man; one of our Lieutenants said he reminded him of the pictures one often sees in the school Pantheon of Hercules; and I do not know anything else that would give a better idea of him.

Several of the officers made the natives presents of jackets, shirts, &c., and they were invited to the gun-room to eat *à la mode Anglaise*. They all accepted wine, grog, &c., but none of them asked for more, nor did any one of them get the least tipsy; they seemed to be extremely honest, taking nothing unless it was made quite clear to them by repeated signs that it was the wish of the officers they should do so; they have not been converted to the Christian Faith, preferring their own road to the other world.

The day after the Chiefs' visit, women crowded on board of us; they were dressed (being slaves) much in the fashion of Mother Eve. They certainly were no beauties; but still much better looking than Indian women; in the evening they favoured us, in the middle of a shower of rain, with a dance, which was extremely amusing; they sang to their own movements, and kept time by beating their hands. What lungs they had!

Among other oddities I think it worth relating that our caterer offered them three rolls of tobacco, weighing altogether about a quarter of a pound, for a sucking pig. His offer, after a little palaver, was refused. While he was consulting with somebody whether he should offer more, for he was afraid of spoiling the market by giving too much, he was cut out by one of the men, who, like an extravagant spendthrift as he was, gave five lumps of tobacco for the little beast.

Frederick Montrésor, *Leaves from Memory's Logbook*, pp. 61–4.

Original tattooed gentlemen (1834)

EDWARD MARKHAM

Markham, son of the Dean of York, spent his early manhood at sea before he left the East India Company in 1827. He sailed for Van Diemen's Land in 1833 aged 32, and arrived in the Bay of Islands the following year. His account of his eight months in New Zealand survived as an illustrated manuscript, which was bought by Alexander Turnbull in 1904. Markham returned to England in 1835.

NEW ZEALAND OR THE NORTHERN ISLAND, as there are three, is known to the Natives by the name of Eaheinomawe.

Feby 18th 1834. Crossed Hokianga Bar, in the Brig Brazil Packet Captain Crow, having left Hobart town in Van diemans [Diemen's] land on the 7th of Feby at Noon. Fellow Passengers Mr Oakes and Son (N B will be a sad scamp) Mr Rogers, and a Mr Phillips. At noon on the 18th MacLean [McLean] came on board and Piloted her across the Bar. There is a rise of 16 Feet at Spring Tides but the Breakers extend for three quarters of a Mile up, when there is any wind to speak of, and renders it a dangerous Bar. Six Ships have been lost there, but now they do not use you worse on the Northern end of New Zealand, than they would on the Coast of Cornwall. As they only plunder your Ship, and formerly they killed and eat the Crew. They have some odd Ideas on this subject, but I shall touch on that on some future occasion.

The moment you pass the Bar, there is deep Water. MacLean went out some ten years ago as Carpenter when a New Zealand company was formed in England, and they bought land which is theirs at this moment. They sent out numbers of people, under Capt Hird [Herd] but with what object I can not tell. Martin the regular Pilot had gone up the River with a Vessel the day before. The Currency Lass. At 3 pm came to an Anchor at Parkinneigh [Pakanae] a Village and had I suppose 150 Natives on board and a par [pa] or Fort about 12 miles from the heads. 12 Fathoms water and pretty close to the Rocks. The Mouth of the River is a good land mark as the Heads are high. The Southern side is high Bluff land 300 feet or so, and dark from being covered with Fern or Brackens. The Northern is not quite so high but is quite white from being covered with Sand. When the Bar was crossed Canoes or in the Native Mourie [Maori] Tongue, Walker [waka] Mouries, or native Boats, boarded us, and Moyterra [Moetara] as the Europeans called him came on board and rubbed Noses with Captain Crow and Oakes and greeted all the Men, as the Vessel had been there the Voyage before, or properly speaking she was there now for the second time. Numbers came on board in the course of the day. Mr Oakes (brother to the Coll Oakes who hired the Casa Felicaja [Filicaja] Piazza d'ogni Santi [Piazza Ognissanti] after the Turtons gave it up) called Moyterra aft, and presented him, with a Sword, Cloak and Letter from Coll Arthur the Governor of Vandiemans land. The substance of which was to thank him for his Bravery on a late Occasion, when he had gone in force to rescue property plundered from the Schooner Fortitude belonging to Clindon [Clendon] J Stepenson when an action had taken place and each party lost eleven Chiefs, 22 being killed in half an hour. The Chief Moyterra cried out 'How you now' [Heoi ano!] or enough, but this will lead to further details on the same subject.

A very Original set of Tattooed Gentlemen cam aft and there was a grand Corrirow [korero] or Talk on the occasion, great Joy was depicted on all their Countenances, and they seemed to be making up for lost time in their Corrirow or Talk, as I am credibly informed that they had no representatives at Babel at the confusion of Tongues. Moyterra was very dignified on the occasion, he sent back two large Pigs, and a Cacahow [kakahu], mat, in return to Col Arthur, and said he should report this to his People and Friends at the time he gave his Sharkatty or Harkatty [hakari], meaning a Feast, which he was making preparations for, and did not get drunk till Evening which showed rather an Aristocratic feeling. N B. he got very drunk, and laid with his bottom bare. The Dog hearing him snore thought he was growling at him, and caught him by the part that was thus exposed, the consequence was that he covered himself with his Cacarhow or Native Cloak, and next morning, called us all to him and gave us occular demonstration by exposing the part affected on the Breakfast Table. The Cabin boy counted 7 Teeth marks and the Hout [utu] or Compensation money was 8 Figs of Tobacco. Crow made all hands of the Natives (or Tangata Mouries) give us some of their Dances. I thought the Decks would have been stove in, and I never saw Fifty Men dance and move together better. No troops seemed so well drilled as these and the Yells and contortions

Edward Markham, Maori man, 1834. (C-19342-1/2, ATL)

of these people were quite terrific. In the Evening we had a second edition with variations as about 20 Young Ladies joined the dance before the house of Maclean and Nimmou [Nimmo]. There I found Mr Chand [Shand?] a Scotch man, well educated and doing the most menial Offices about the Establishment, as he would do any thing for drink, and if Grog was to be had, he would have no scruples if he could but get it but a man who had been articled as a writer to the Cygnet [Signet] in Edinburgh. Oh this is a Wicked World and full of Drink!! Oakes had brought an old Mare and a Foal for the Chief Moyterra and when she was landed the number of people looking at, and touching her, made her Savage; she kicked one, bit an other and played the Devil; she has thrown some of them repeatedly, but they can now manage her. All the Village (Kanger [*kainga*] Mourie) turned out to see the Horse rode, they call it (Karradie [*kararehe*] nui nui) or Big dog as they have no words to express it in their Language, as the only Animal a native of the Island is a Lizard (Dueterra) [*tuatara*]. Cats are imported, Dogs they seem to have a Native breed of but I believe they are not indigenous to

23

the Island but obtained from some Ships that have touched there. They must have come from the South Sea Islands. All the Europeans in the River were glad that the Governor had rewarded Moyterra, as they said it was the first time that a Governor of a Colony had taken any notice of a New Zealand Chief and they thought it would have a very beneficial effect on the minds of the people shewing them that we can reward as well as punish. Mr Butler was Interpreter on the occasion, he speaks the Language perfectly like a native, being the Son of one of the first Missionaries in the island, and can turn it any way. He is badly off, and no one knows how he exists, but that is his Affair. We were anxious to get up the River as Oakes and Crow had quarrelled, ergo he was not in good odour on board. He went the first day and took most of his Household affairs, but he was only taken down on Condition that he did not land his Investment till one Month after their arrival in New Zealand, so as not to interfere with Crow and he was obliged to abide by It, as he had made Crow his Enemy from want of Commercial Knowledge, and of Consistancy of Character. Oakes, his Son, Rogers, and the dogs, went up with what they could carry in the Boat of the Brig, but she was too full.

I went up the day after with Crow & Maclean in Captain Youngs boat taking Venus. The River is a fine, wide, and considerable body of Water, and the place I wanted to be put on shore at was about 30 miles from Parkinniegh. Ships of 400 Tons have gone thirty seven miles up above the last mentioned place. On the left about eleven miles up Maclean showed us the remains of his House and Saw pits and sheds, that had been burnt by the enraged Relatives of the Chiefs that were killed at that place. Every Goat, Dog, Fowl (and fence burned) was killed, and every Log of Timber burned and then Tabbooed or Tappooed (rendered Sacred) [i.e., *tapu*] the place is called Mouta Coudy [Motukauri]. About half way up the River on the left, the River narrows and turns to the Left, found a conical Hill and 17 fms Water there. The Scenery begins from this place to be beautiful, before it was only open but then you get Woods on both sides of you and the River much broader, and although there are deep Water Channels all the way up, yet there are Sands dry at low water, and it requires to go up and down the River, several times before you become acquainted with the sands. We came to the House of a Trader and Sawyer, named Fishwick a Yorkshireman and had a Lunch of Pork and Potatoes and a glass of Rum, and got up the Coko, or Coho [Kohu] meaning Fog in the Mouri language. The place where Oakes told me he had a beautiful House there was such a Scene awaiting me. Eight men, Europeans, drinking Oakes's Hollands, and only one sitting room and bedroom with bed places built up like a Packet, we called them Standing Bed Places, and I was hungry, but they had possession of the Table, and what was worse the Pork and Grog, and Potatoes; they turned out and fought and I tucked in at the Pork, Potatoes and grog, and when I had dined I found my Temper much better. As before, I wished the Sawyers to serve each other as the cats at Kilkenny, who eat each other up and left nothing but the tips of their Tails. I got my things into the House and took possession of a bed place, as six of us were to sleep in the narrow slip the whole not 10 feet long.

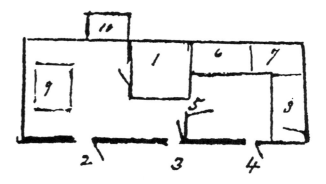

1 Pantry
2 and 4 Windows
3 Door into the House
5 Door of the bed room
6, 7 and 8 standing bed places one over another
9 Table
10 Fire place put up after.

The Above is the plan of little boarded Cottage or House, no Glass, no Lining. I went out and did not care who was licked, but looked on with perfect indifference. They were all fighting at once. I told young Oakes to put up the Pork and Hollands as I wished to get rid of the Visitors, and in the Course of the Evening they all paddled off, and I was not sorry to find them gone. But soon after the Natives mustered in great numbers about the House and became very troublesome, as they blocked up the Passages and stunk abominably, spitting every where, and always smoking; for some time, Three weeks I was very uncomfortable. The Fellows thieve so. You can not trust your own Servants. I found them one day melting our Pewter spoons to make Musket balls of, and the first Volume of my Voltaires, 'Louis 14. et 15.' torn up and made Cartridges of them. It may be conceived how angry I was, and I made them so too, for I caught up a Stick from the Fire and threw it among the Cartridges. Up they jumped as if the Devil kicked them, and most of them went off with some noise. Oakes decided on building a Ware house as in hot weather the Pork did not smell at all pleasant, and I decided on building a room at the end of it for my self nine feet square, which in due time I completed.

Edward Markham, *New Zealand or Recollections of It*, pp. 29–32.

To Queen Charlotte's Sound (1839)

J.C. CRAWFORD

James Coutts Crawford arrived in Sydney in 1838 and left for New Zealand just over a year later after hearing about the New Zealand Company. He built the first tunnel in New Zealand, established a farm on the Miramar Peninsula, and was a member of the Legislative Council and an active scientist and explorer.

Engraving of Captain Cook's chart of Cook's Strait, 1773, by John Ryland. (M-P 422-1773-CT, ATL)

As THERE WAS NO APPEARANCE of the 'Success' in the harbour, and as I had left my belongings in the safe keeping of a person on board, I determined to return to Porirua, and proceed to the South Island, so as to lose no time in seeing as much of the country as possible during my visit. Our party, therefore, returned to Korohewa on the following day, and I proceeded across the Straits with Hugh Sinclair, in an open boat belonging to Mr Arthur Elmslie. Had I known the dangers of the tide rips, I should probably have hesitated before I committed my life to the custody of this frail bark. Luckily we had light winds and fine weather, although in passing a tide rip near 'The Brothers' we nearly filled, and for a few minutes were in considerable danger of swamping, as the sea washed in a most aggravating manner over each gunwale in succession. We quickly ran out of the turmoil, however, into smooth water, entered the fair waters of Queen Charlotte's Sound, and towards evening arrived at the bay of Te Anahou, the next bay to the north of 'Ship's Cove', the favourite refitting anchorage of Captain Cook. Here we landed and found a considerable Maori village, the chief house in which being that occupied by Mr Arthur Elmslie. I had here an opportunity of seeing the way in which the whalers enjoyed themselves during the recess, when, that is, the whales were out of season, or rather, had left the coast. Most of the whalers I found had Maori wives, and used to spend the summer in such domestic felicity as they could find, probably in the village of the tribe of their bride. At Te Anahou there may have been a population of one hundred souls, most of whom were congregated in Mr Elmslie's house, where a bright fire was now blazing, and 'Eura,' the prettiest Maori woman I ever saw, was busy preparing the supper. After the news had been sufficiently talked over, Mr Elmslie managed to clear the house of all but a few of the principal chiefs, and we had our supper of pork and potatoes in peace. Strolling round the village afterwards, we found the Maoris collected in groups round numerous fires, and very busy sending messages to each other on slates. The art of writing had just been introduced, and the Maoris seemed to have acquired a *furor* for it. They wrote everywhere, on all occasions and on all substances, on slates, on paper, on leaves of flax, and with a good, firm, decided hand.

On the following day we saw a fine sight. A squadron of large canoes arrived from the north with Ngatiawa returning from the fight at Waikanae. The canoes were all under sail and well handled. On landing there was a great 'tangi' and feed.

The Bay of Anahou, like all the bays of Queen Charlotte's Sound, contains a triangular space of level land, backed by very steep hills forming into narrow ridges at the top. The hills are covered with forest, and the cultivations are in the small valley flats. I did not visit 'Ship Cove', but was informed that the stumps of the trees which had been cut by Captain Cook's people were still visible.

J.C. Crawford, *Recollections of Travel in New Zealand and Australia*, pp. 30–2.

An object of attraction (1840)

ALEXANDER MARJORIBANKS

Marjoribanks arrived in Wellington in 1840 on the Bengal Merchant *as part of the first Scottish colony to New Zealand. He wrote an account of New Zealand for emigrants in which he gave graphic descriptions of events and Maori customs and behaviour. He moved on to Australia after a year.*

ON FIRST LANDING, I observed that I was rather more an object of attraction amongst the natives than most of my friends; and this, I afterwards discovered, arose from my size, as I then weighed fifteen stone, though the hot suns of Australia reduced me to thirteen within a twelve month afterwards. It was amusing to see the delight with which they gazed on me; and, when I walked along the beach, two of them, a young man and a young woman, insisted on accompanying me, and taking hold of my arm. Had I been twenty stone instead of fifteen, I actually believe they would have worshipped me as a deity. Previous to this I used sometimes to regret being so stout as I then was, but my New Zealand friends have thrown quite a new light upon the subject, and I readily bow to their authority, as they are well known to be people of taste in all matters of that sort. The Chinese, in like manner, consider those amongst the male sex the most handsome who are the most bulky, though they are no great admirers of fat women.

When searching for lodgings after leaving the vessel, I fortunately procured them in the hut or hotel of a countryman of my own, of the name of George Rose, from the county of Banff, in Scotland; who, in personal appearance, was a sort of giant, being six feet six in height.

George was living quietly in Sydney, when he got notice of the grand project of the colonization of New Zealand; and like a true Scotchman, never for one moment losing sight of the main chance, when he heard of lord's sons, and of baronet's sons, flocking there, he naturally considered that it would be a good field for his own operations, and that it was his duty to hasten to that land of promise, in order to do justice to himself by relieving the first settlers of every sixpence he could legitimately appropriate to his own use,—a praiseworthy act, no doubt, on his part. He had accordingly been there some months before us, in order that he might have a proper start.

When I waited on him, he received me very kindly, and told me that he would share with me what he had, and give me the best accommodation which his hotel afforded; though he confessed it was somewhat open, having neither door nor window, and admitting both wind and rain, and native dogs. He promised, however, to give me a whole bale of blankets to cover

From *Album of an Officer* (artist unknown), Lambton Quay and the Terrace from Wellington Harbour, c. 1865.
(A-277-035, ATL)

me at night, if I required them, as he had them for sale in his store, and they would be nothing the worse of it; and I daresay you will think that I was pretty well baled up, when I mention that I had no less than eight pair upon me, so that though the rain occasionally came through one or two of them, it never penetrated through the whole. George had neither a table nor a chair in his hotel; but as he kept a store, we converted an old tea-chest into a table, and an old soap-box into a chair; and one knife and fork served us both, as we used them alternately, or time about, as they say in Scotland. We contrived, however, to fare more sumptuously than most of our neighbours, and it arose from this, that in addition to mine host's numerous other callings of store-keeper, publican, auctioneer, boat-builder, boat-hirer, hotel-keeper, commission-agent, &c. he added what, in a new colony, is more important than them all, namely, a butcher. To be sure there were nothing but pigs then to be had in the 'earthly paradise' of the far famed Mr Montefiore; but by putting two or three pigs' heads into the pot at once, we had excellent Scotch broth every day, and George always treated me to a glass of brandy or hollands after dinner, in case the strong pork of New Zealand should disagree with my delicate stomach; so that, upon the whole, I rather got fat under my worthy landlord's care. The only evil attending the butchering department of his extensive business, was that it attracted the native dogs during the night; as he brought whatever meat was unsold into the house, and the dogs crept through some of the holes in the hotel, in order to have a share of what was going. Instead, however, of blocking up the openings through which they entered, which he could have done in hour, he had a loaded gun all night by his bed side, and kept up a sort of running fire upon them, which disturbed my sleep very much. I think he must have been a very bad marksman, as amidst all the platoons which he fired, I am not aware that a single individual amongst his uninvited guests suffered in the cause.

Alexander Marjoribanks, *Travels in New Zealand*, pp. 24–7.

Divine worship at sea (1841)

ALFRED FELL

When he was 24 Alfred Fell joined the New Zealand Company's settlers, who left for Nelson in 1841 in the Lord Auckland. *His diary describes the voyage. After eighteen years Fell returned to England with his family, a prosperous man.*

Sunday, October 24th. This is our fifth Sunday on board. The wind the same, but there is so little of it that we are not going more than two miles an hour. The sea is as calm as a mirror; there is scarcely a ripple upon its surface, and the sun's rays make it sparkle like gold. It is beginning to be very hot, and we are all in our white dresses, and with our straw hats look like anything but a lot of Englishmen. We were agreeably surprised this morning by an awning extending from the main to the mizzen masts and completely protecting the deck from the fierce rays of the sun. It is all very well, or we should soon have been so tanned that it would have been impossible to have told whether we came from a northern or a southern clime. Under this awning was a most picturesque and interesting sight: at 11 o'clock all of us assembled for divine worship. The capstan, covered with a large Union Jack in the centre, served for a reading desk. The cabin passengers and officers of the ship were seated around it on chairs, whilst in front the steerage passengers and the sailors were seated upon the hencoops, arranged in rows and covered with flags to hide their appearance. All listened attentively whilst the captain read the beautiful service of the Church of England, and an appropriate sermon afterwards, and the utmost decorum prevailed. It was one of the most striking and interesting scenes I have ever seen: 200 people sending up their devotions to the Most High from the wide ocean, the strange picturesque appearance of the people, the calmness of the day, the delicious climate, and the sun shining down upon us so gloriously, made an impression upon my mind it would be difficult to forget. The latter part of the day was spent as usual, eating and drinking, I think, forming the greatest item in it. I am afraid we shall take but poorly to our salt pork in New Zealand after the sumptuous dinners we have on board. By far the greatest inconvenience we have is the want of fresh water; we have only a pint each day allowed us for washing and everything, and that stinks so that to drink any is out of the question. I have a string to my jug and so send it out of the porthole, and have a good souse in salt water. It is better than a thimble full of the other, only that you cannot wash clean, and it leaves an unpleasant roughness on the skin, even with the much talked of Marine soap. When we left Gravesend we had 95 tons of fresh water; each ton, I think, they say contains 247 gallons; but then there are so many of us, and so much is used in cooking, besides in case of emergency it

From *Album of an Officer* (artist unknown), 'Divine (?) service, ship *Pegasus*', 1865. (A-277-020, ATL)

is expected to last us the whole of the voyage, although we expect to call somewhere about the Cape of Good Hope for a fresh supply; yet it cannot be depended upon.

There seems to be a strange opinion on board with regard to the natives of New Zealand and our treatment of them. One says that he will not go out without a gun over his arm, and another without a brace of pistols in his pocket, and that they will not scruple to use them. Now this seems to me the very worst principle. The natives must be either our friends or our foes, and that they had much better be the former no one is prepared to deny; but this can only be by kindness and confidence on our part, not viewing them as our foes, but as our friends; not as slaves, but on a par with our own labouring population; not treating them with jealousy or distrust, apprehension or alarm, but with *openness, candour* and *boldness*. If force is used on their part, then and then only would I repel it with force, and not even then until every argument which reason and sophistry suggested had been used in vain, then only would I resort to the argument of the bullet. One single individual act of one hot-headed fellow may make them all our direst foes; and if they are treacherous, as some say, why unkindness and coercion will not make them less so, but rather, I opine, the reverse. These are my views, and I shall prepare an article for our Journal advocating them.

Alfred Fell, *A Colonist's Voyage to New Zealand*, pp. 26–8.

Harty and weel (1841)

HENRY WOULDEN

Two letters by Henry Woulden were published in Narrative of a Voyage from England to New Zealand in Letters from Mr Thomas Bevan and Another New Settler. *Woulden's first letter, giving a 'doleful account' of the state of things in Wellington, was written to the Rev. C.W. Saxton and is prefaced by a note signed J.N., which alleges that it was written to prevent Mr Saxton 'coming to the Island' as Woulden was letting out Saxton's town acre for his own benefit. Woulden's second letter to his father, in J.N.'s opinion, expresses his real sentiments: 'nothing can be more favourable than the last letter which evidently contains the truth of the matter'.*

Charles Emilius Gold, Wellington, 1847–60? (B-103-005, ATL)

January 28, 1841.

DEAR FARTHER,—i right thes few to you, hoping to find you all well as it leaves us at preasant. Thanks be to God, I have been harty and weel since i left home. I wass not sea sick at all; I wass coak to the Emagrants; I had £10 16s. in Ready money when i landed, that came in Jest the thing; my wife and chirldren was sea sick 5 week; Elizabeth caught the small pok, but she sone gott weel a gain, thoinks be to God, it is a pleasant country: we can see the tops of the mountains is coverd with snow: the ground is covered with Geranuems and myrtles and Fuccer Trees 40 foot hie; we have non of any kind of frutt, no oringes, nor coconuts; our frutts is wild Hogs and fish and birds. We had a very rouf passage from the Cape to New Zealand. We lost a gun throu the porthole, and one man and 2 boats. We had a fair wind when we went up Cook Straits, but jest as we wass about entrying the Harber, the winds sprung up, which it blew us out to sea gain, and we all thought we should be all lost; 8 times we wass served that way; 9 time we got in, and a moist beautifull harber it is; for it is surrounded with mountain, and we have pleanty of freash warter close to my Hut, which runs down from the mountains; we wera Trubbled very much with flies and grosshopers, for they eat up every thing as i plant out; it is very hot in the day time and cold nights; the winds blow very strong; the Naitive are set of quiett people; they are very stout and stroung; they are from 6 feet to 7 feet hie; the are of a copper couller; ther are got beautifull black long hair; ther is outher Tribs would like to be at war with them, onely they are freid of the shot gun; we have gott a slopp of war in our harber, and we have got 30 solgers ther to take care of us; for they a fread of the outher tribes comming down upon us, for if they cauch any of our tribe, they would kill them and eat them; our tribe is a couris set of men, for when they go out a shuting or Fishing, they tie a piece of Flax round ther body, and when they gets hungry, they tie it tite; they birn the ground till it is red, and then they rub them selves over with it to make them look smart; they stick Birds' Feathers in their hair; they will sell you a fat hog for a Blanket or some tobacco; they gro pumkins and India corn, and Potatos, thinks as they call Tallows; they are all Scotch Potatoos; they plant them in holes, and when they take them up, they leave one in the hole to grou a gain; so they are always gott plenty to eat; they are both laszey and loussey, for they will set down on the ground, and pick the lice of them and eat them, and they say it is good Kiki for a Mouri. We have plenty of shell fish of all sort; ther is 2 sorts of lobsters, fresh warter and salt warter we can catch them; ther was 6 men went to Reap Weat on the 30 January, but that was on a drifent part of the Ireland. I had Reaidishs for tea, and small sallet for tea on Christmas day, fir it wass as warm that day as it is in England. Labbor men gits 6s. a day, Tradsmen from 10s. to a pound, schuch as Carpinter or Boat Bilders, that is the time day. I shall never think of coming to England whiist I can git plenty of Pork, For you are wost of then our convicts, for they doant work half so hard as you do. Farther, Pray do come in the Next ship and I will look out for you, and mind and bring the children with you. Pleas to send me Plenty of Garden Seeds, for we cannot Gitt any seed ther. Pleas to send me some

Scarlet Runers, for they are £2 a quart; and Pleas to send me a 12 Rubbub Roots, for they only 2 upon the Ireland, and they wont sell them, and I will look out for you Farther, when the ships comes in; and if you don't come, Please take those Seeds to my Master, Revent M. Saxton; you can ast Thom Wyett were he lives, and he will tell you, We can see the Birning Mountains on the Ireland. Pleas to tell all young men and their wives to come to New Zealand, For they will soon gett fat as hogs. If you please to give love to my Uncle Cogger, and all my Enquire in friends. Tell them that i am happy as the days is long, and my wife and children, for they are got quite fat a Ready, Thanks be to God for every thing
HENRY WOULDON. ANN WOULDON.
Amen.

HENRY WOU.
EILZEBETH WOU.
SOPHIA WOU.

Father, I Have sent Letter to my Dear Brouther, James Wouldon. Pleas to Right to me sone as posible, for I long to her from you.

W. Wouldon. Gardener, Near the John Bull, Old Ford, Bow, Middlesex.

Henry Woulden, 'Henry Woulden's Letters', from Thomas Bevan,
Narrative of a Voyage from England to New Zealand, pp. 23–5.

Voyage in a whale-boat (1842)

R.G. JAMESON

R.G. Jameson sailed for South Australia in 1838 as Surgeon-Superintendent on the Surrey. *He visited New Zealand for business reasons the following year, and again in 1840 when he travelled widely, investigating New Zealand's resource potential as a colony.*

THE CLIMATE OF NEW ZEALAND is, throughout the winter, temperate and bracing. From May till September, during which period I resided in the Thames district, the weather was fine and clear. In the morning, thin pellicles of ice and a little hoar frost were occasionally to be seen, the sure indication of a warm forenoon; and the nights were uncommonly brilliant and starry. Indeed, in no part of the world, if I except Port Jackson, have I beheld more beautiful moonlight nights than in New Zealand, both in summer and in winter. Once every twelve or fourteen days, however, the serenity of the climate was interrupted by a strong gale from the eastward, during the continuance of which, heavy masses of clouds were borne onwards with great velocity, and the sea rolled into the Frith of the Thames with violence, causing a magnificent and formidable surf at every exposed part of the coast. The coming on of these gales is known during the calmest weather to the natives, by indications of the sky which are not perceptible to persons unacquainted with the peculiarities of the climate. Among other instances illustrative of the friendly disposition of the natives, it was related to me by Colonel Wakefield, that on one occasion, a chief of Cook's Straits travelled many miles to warn them that a gale would shortly set in, which would render the position of the ship a dangerous one, in consequence of which they stood out to sea time enough to escape its violence. These gales are usually accompanied with rain, and sometimes with thunder and lightning; and although most frequent and regular during the winter, they are said to accompany the changes of the moon throughout the year. They generally break up after forty-eight hours' continuance, the wind then hauling gradually round to the westward; whilst the sky resumes its serene and cloudless aspect.

After the cessation of a gale of this description, I resolved to start for the Aroha, a locality about forty miles up the Thames river, and consequently about ninety miles from Coromandel Harbour.

We in vain endeavoured to persuade a few natives to accompany us on this journey. They could not be tempted by the charms of blankets, or even of tobacco, to go so far from home; I was therefore under the necessity of departing in a whale-boat, accompanied only by Mr McInnes, a young gentleman of a mechanical bent of mind, who was desirous of ascertaining the extent to which the Phormium is spontaneously produced in the plain of the Thames, having, as he supposed, hit upon a mechanical invention, by which he hoped to be able to clean the flax for exportation at a paying rate.

Having caulked up an old whale-boat, 'rigged' two lug sails, and laid in a supply of potatoes, tea, sugar, tobacco, and pipes, the latter being intended as a means of procuring the assistance of the natives, besides a tent, an iron pot, an axe, and a few other utensils, we took our departure from Coromandel Harbour, and after contending for six hours against a head wind and tide, reached the little island of Rangipukea, precisely six miles distant from our starting place. It was evening—the sea outside of Rangipukea was rough, and the sky was gloomy. Moreover, a heavy swell and surf caused us to suspect that the gale was not yet over. We therefore determined to land upon this island, and tax the hospitality of its inhabitants for permission to sleep upon their beach, a more desirable bed, in our estimation, than the floor of a native hut, swarming with diminutive animalculae of various kinds.

The whole population of the island, (it was not above twenty acres in extent,) ran down to meet us, and the young of both sexes rushing into the water, hauled our whale boat far up upon the beach. We were soon surrounded by about sixty individuals, and whilst the old chief came up and saluted us, his tribe busied themselves in examining our goods and chattels; but when desired by my companion to refrain from touching anything, they complied, not without some reluctance, with his request. We were now joined by the chief's eldest son, a youth who spoke English, and was dressed in a new suit of clothing, comprising a round hat and a shooting jacket, in the ample pockets of which he ostentatiously rattled a few half-crowns. To him we explained that we had nothing to sell, and that we only required assistance in erecting a tent with our boat sails upon the beach. This being communicated by the monarch to his subjects, they proceeded, with the utmost alacrity, to carry our wishes into effect. The tent was set up, the fire lighted, and the potatoes boiled in less than half an hour; and whilst we enjoyed our very frugal fare, the natives squatted round us, and the old chief, whose language I *would not* understand, expressed the great pleasure that he would experience in obtaining possession of my boat cloak. He offered sundry large pigs in exchange for this, to me, indispensable article; and although we could hear the little bell summoning the people to their evening devotions, truth compels me to say, that one proposal of the old chief, as a means of obtaining possession of the cloak, was by no means consistent with the strictest morality, although it proved the absolute dominion which he held over his female slaves; at length, having exhausted his inventive powers, he took his departure in very bad humour. After a few hours of repose, we awoke, and resolved to pursue our voyage; and having, with the assistance of our friends, launched the whale-boat, we bade adieu to the whole population, among whom we distributed a pound of tobacco.

R.G. Jameson, *New Zealand, South Australia and New South Wales*, pp. 300–3.

Visiting the mission (1844)

[MARY DAVIS WALLIS]

Accompanying her husband to Fiji to procure a cargo of bêche-de-mer, the American Mary Davis Wallis arrived in the Bay of Islands on the barque Zotoff in 1844. She wrote a journal of her experiences to 'beguile the many lonely hours' and to entertain her friends.

THIS MORNING MR W. procured a boat and men, to take Mrs C. and myself across the harbor to a place called Pahia, where Rev. Mr Williams, one of the first missionaries to this place, is settled. Mr W. was absent. Mrs W., who is a fine, active woman, received us with apparent pleasure, and showed us about their premises. The mission buildings are situated in a little vale, at the foot of a lofty hill. They consist of a few dwelling houses, a chapel, and a printing office. They had gardens also, filled with the useful and ornamental. We had not been here

Henry Williams, Old Mission House at Paihia, 1843? (A-048-007, ATL)

long when Dr Ford and his wife came in. They had been to Mrs C.'s to call upon us, and learning where we were, had followed. I learned that Mr W. had been a missionary here about twenty-one years. As our time was limited, having engaged to meet Mr W. at Wapoa, I could not learn much of their doings.

It had commenced raining fast when we embarked in our little boat. We had a distance of three miles to sail, but the men rowed hard, and in due time we arrived at Wapoa, opposite the consulate. The consul and Mr W. met us at the landing, and we were conducted to the residence of the former. This fine mansion is situated on a small elevation, and commands a pleasant view in front. Roses, geraniums and many other beautiful flowers were blooming there, but no lady was to be found to grace so delightful a home. Its residents were not Benedicts, and although we found a handsome house, richly furnished, yet there appeared an air of solitariness, a want of something to perfect the whole. The consul favored us with music, and treated us with refreshments, after which, seeing no signs of pleasant weather, we took our leave, and after a sail of half an hour, arrived home.

23. It rained immoderately all day. As I was conversing with Mrs C. about the mission families, I inquired if there had ever been a family at that place of the name of Myers. She

replied that there had been a merchant of that name, but no missionary. My husband and myself were visiting, about two years since, in Salem, Mass., when a lady said to my husband, 'Is it true, Mr W., that when you were last at New Zealand, you gave my son a bottle and a dollar, and directed him to go on shore, to the store of a missionary, and purchase a bottle of brandy?' 'It is true,' replied he; 'I inquired of a man on board, who lived on shore where brandy was to be bought, and he said of Mr Myers, the missionary. Your son was directed thither; procured the article and brought it on board.' Mrs C. said that could be easily explained. The natives and loafers, who live along the shore, call every one who is not a heathen, a missionary; and use the word as we use the word, 'Christian'. We say that England and America are Christian lands, and their inhabitants are Christians, yet many are not, in the real sense of the word. So, they will say of any one here who is not a heathen, 'He missionary.' This brought to my recollection an incident which I heard Mr W. relate a short time previous. On a former voyage to Feejee, a 'Kanaka', who was in his service, wished to be discharged, giving as a reason, that he had found some relatives on shore, and he wished to go and live with them. 'But,' said Mr W., 'these persons live with the missionaries, and you cannot live with them.' 'Oh, yes I can,' he replied, 'cause I missionary too.' These facts will account for many of the unfavourable reports which come to us from the mission stations.

[Mary Davis Wallis], *Life in Feejee*, pp. 19–21.

PART 2

Coming out

From *Album of an Officer* (artist unknown), 'Reading on deck, HMS *Orontes* in the Atlantic, 1864'. (A-277-009, ATL)

The straggling village of Auckland (1846)

W. TYRONE POWER

William Tyrone Power came to New Zealand on board the Castor *in 1846 as Commissariat Officer for the British forces in the Hutt Valley and Wanganui.* Sketches in New Zealand *is an account of his experiences and the situation in New Zealand in the late 1840s.*

AFTER A COMFORTABLE VOYAGE of eleven days, we dropped anchor at the entrance of the river Thames, and ran in with the flood tide on the following morning. The appearance of the country is barren and uninteresting. It consists of low, rolling hills, covered with fern; Mount Eden, and one or two other black, scoria-covered, volcanic hills, are in the distance, but their sterile look does not make the landscape more inviting. How heart-chilling to the emigrant must be the first glance at his adopted country, where the eye wanders over such a bleak and dreary expanse, without one pleasant spot to rest upon!

Thomas Collinson, 'Town of Auckland from the head of the town valley', 1846. (F-69517-1/2, ATL)

We anchored opposite the town, or rather the straggling village, of Auckland, which, at first sight, has by no means a prepossessing appearance; an effect that is unluckily confirmed on a closer inspection. There is no wharf or landing-place but the muddy beach, on which I was put on shore from one of the 'Castor's' boats, and had to wade my way up to the barracks through a sea of mud.

On reporting myself, I found that I was destined to be sent off at once to the south, where there had been a fresh outbreak among the natives. Fortunately for me, the 'Castor' was under order to sail for Port Nicholson, to render what assistance she could; so that I was to go down in her, instead of in one of the miserable little coasters, to which I must otherwise have been consigned. There was very little time to become acquainted with Auckland, but I took a stroll through it, and saw nothing but a beggarly collection of poverty-stricken huts and wooden houses, without any of the bustle and briskness that betokens business and prosperity. This, however, could hardly be otherwise, as the colony was only just beginning to recover from six years of blundering experiments and maladministration.

Groups of Maories squatted about the sunny side of the street with pipes in their jowls, a few half-drunken loafers (beach-combers, as they are called here) hanging about the numerous pot-houses, here and there a sleepy-looking shopkeeper leaning against his own door-post in the vain hope of a customer, and one or two Maories going from house to house with loads of wood on their shoulders for sale, were the only symptoms of vitality at the seat of government. The streets and roads were unpaved, and, in some places, knee-deep in mud; and the whole town had a slatternly and neglected look, that reminded me of some of the ill-selected and deserted locations in the backwoods of America.

W. Tyrone Power, *Sketches in New Zealand*, pp. 2–4.

Maori in Auckland (1847)

G.C. MUNDY

Lieutenant-Colonel Godfrey Mundy held a military post in Sydney for five years from 1846, and visited New Zealand in 1847–48 on board the Inflexible. Our Antipodes *describes military action undertaken by Grey and others against Te Rauparaha as well as Mundy's impressions of New Zealand.*

THE ONLY CARRIAGE IN AUCKLAND, that of the officer commanding the 58th Regiment, was conveying its owners to the viceregal dinner, as their host and myself, both looking as if we had been in a smart skirmish—for I had had a roll in a bog—entered the town. Yes—there was a dinner to twenty-four guests in the clinker-built palace of the Governor of New Zealand; and not a bad dinner either—with wines from France and Germany, from the Tagus, (and the Thames, no doubt!) There were some very pretty faces there too; and some good-looking fellows moreover, most of them culled from the garrison and ships in harbour. There was on many of the fair cheeks a freshness and a bloom which are rarely to be seen in Sydney, especially in the hot weather. The flush of the heated ball-room is a very different thing; for music and exercise, and soft nonsense, and gratified vanity will bring transient colour to the palest face, but it fades with the cause of excitement. In New Zealand the rose is not merely a night-blowing flower—it is permanent. The climate indeed appears—(it is proved by medical statistics)—to be singularly suitable to the English constitution. This was wonderfully proved in the New Zealand campaigns, for there lie in the pigeon-holes of my office numerous documents, showing that however great the hardships the troops were exposed to during the war—however wretched the sheds or huts they lived in—although their clothing was in rags, their boots soleless, and their beds nothing better than a tattered blanket on a heap of damp fern—happy when the latter was attainable;—never was any large body of men so perfectly free from malady of any kind. I sincerely hope (and shall be curious to ascertain the fact) that at no future day may these fine fellows suffer from the exposure and privations they endured unscathed while their 'blood was up;' but I know so well the physical idiocracy of the soldier, and have so often found him, as well as the rural labourer, old before his time by rheumatism and other complaints arising from habitual exposure, that I cannot feel sure that the germ of these maladies of the old campaigner may not be contracted in this country as well as in others—latent, although unfelt at the time.

New Zealand has indeed a rough but healthy climate, a rough but fruitful soil, and a rough people—yet capable, I think, of being made useful subjects and members of society, if they may be spared the ordinary fate of the Savage on the approach of the White—first demoralization, then extinction.

I have mentioned the smallness of the Auckland dwelling-houses. Their apartments are indeed what the French call *modest* in the extreme. Nevertheless this peculiarity in the reception-rooms of the New Zealand metropolis appears to operate as no hindrance to the sociability of the inhabitants. I attended more than one quadrille party in saloons 12 feet by 10—while four whist-playing seniors were stowed immovably in a closet off the dancing-room—the table being slewed so as to wedge a player into each of the four corners. Verandahs, and tents, and sails, and bunting were called into play to furnish forth supper-rooms; and I did not remark that the guests danced, played, ate, drank, talked, laughed, or flirted with less spirit and zest than they would have done had they had more room to do all this in.

William Strutt, 'A group I once saw in Maori Land', New Plymouth, 1856. (E-453-f-005, ATL)

One evening a very gay little ball was given by the Sheriff at his pretty cottage about two miles out of town. There being, as I have said, only one carriage—in the genteel acceptation of the term—belonging to Auckland, it is needless to say that all the ladies were not conveyed to the festive scene on springs, however many of them might have travelled there on wheels. As for me, I found myself part of an equestrian escort to a detachment of young ladies, whose vehicle was the sheriff's cart carpeted with a feather-bed. They were too light-hearted to admit a doubt as to whether their equipage had on former occasions assisted in the more melancholy functions of its owner's dread office—a suspicion that certainly crossed my own mind; suffice that it played its part well in the present instance. On reaching its destination, the back-board being removed and the cart tilted, its fair freight was shot out in safety at the door, and about daybreak the same vehicle reconveyed them, without coughs or colds, to their home.

During the progress of this ball, several natives, attracted by the sound of music, entered the grounds, walked boldly up to the open French windows of the dancing-room, and seemed rapt in astonishment at the scene within. Perhaps the enormous amount of labour thrown into one of the favourite pastimes of the richer English surprised them. It is possible that while contemplating the vigour and earnestness with which valse and polka were executed, these naked philosophers may have formed the conclusion that a race so energetic in a dance must be invincible in fight; that the unflinching fortitude which carried young and old; light and heavy, through the herculean labours of Sir Roger de Coverley, must sweep all before it when the conquest of a country became the object in question! Oriental and southern nations have difficulty in understanding that our daily recreation as well as our daily bread is to be earned in the sweat of the brow. I have myself heard a Mussulman magnate express his surprise that the great men of a great nation should condescend to do such things—and that their women should be permitted to do them. 'We always keep dancers and singers, or hire them, when we want to be amused in that way!' is the maxim of the 'gorgeous East'. There appears to me a good deal of Orientalism in the character of the Maori, very strikingly different to that of the Australian aboriginal. The latter is quick, light, almost quadrumanous in his activity. I cannot fancy the massive form of the Maori darting up the stem of a slippery gum-tree to cut out an opossum from his hole! I rather picture him to myself sitting in the sun at the mouth of his warree smoking his pipe, with his half-shut eyes just above a fold of his mat. Although brave and warlike, there is, too, something of the Lazzaroni about his nature. His language, moreover, resembles in character the 'soft bastard Latin,' as Byron calls it, of the modern Roman.

I was standing with some officers on the lawn near a window opening to the ground, when a tall Maori, in a blanket and Brutus crop, 'thrust in,' and made one of us without apology or remark. An officer asked the intruder, in military Maori, whether he admired the white ladies, and which of them most. He instantly pointed out the object of his preference, thereby showing that his own standard of taste did not greatly differ from that of many of the Pakeha gentlemen present; and he clenched the compliment by averring that he would give a 'hickapenny' for her, which, measuring his regard by the price, was more liberal than might at first sight appear; for it was his *all*! His blanket, his Brutus, and sixpence in hard cash (tied up in a corner of the former) was 'all the store' of this noble savage. And indeed I have rarely met a finer looking creature. Full six feet high, erect and well-proportioned, he had a handsome oval face, a clear skin, scarcely darker than that of the southern European, was neither tattooed nor bearded—for he seemed quite young; and his black hair, curling back from his high brow, fell round his ears and poll in the most picturesque style. His only ornament was a flower of scarlet geranium, stuck behind one ear.

The residence of our host for this night is a fair specimen of those of the English gentry in the vicinity of Auckland. The house is placed at the end of a wooded ravine falling towards the sea, a site usually chosen in this part of the island, for there is little timber except on the sides and bottoms of the gullies by which it is liberally intersected. The chief justice and the attorney-general have located themselves somewhat in the same manner. Gardens, useful and ornamental, surround the dwellings, and the soil shows a capacity for growing the productions of a wonderfully wide range of climate. But the prettiest place and best garden I visited, were those of the Reverend Mr Lawrie, Wesleyan Missionary. The luxuriant hedges, covered with the climbing rose and passiflora, the arched avenue of fruit-trees, and the perfectly snug seclusion of the dwelling, although well nigh in the midst of the town, are remarkable proofs of taste and skill—if not of self-denial.

This zealous divine had lately returned from a voyage to the Figi Islands, whence he had imported a large collection of native curiosities. These, during my stay at Auckland, were exposed for sale at a bazaar held in aid of the expenses for the erection of a chapel for the Aborigines;—clubs, spears, bows and arrows, fishing-nets, hooks and lines neatly constructed; necklaces of teeth or shells; ladies' full dresses of flax, sea-weed or feathers, remarkable for their simplicity and suitableness for 'light marching order;' cannibal knives and forks, warranted to have been used at several feasts; and other goods 'too numerous to mention.' This is just the alluring but useless sort of gear with which every traveller encumbers himself, as a matter of course. He drags the accumulated hoard with infinite trouble, anxiety and expense round the world, and on arrival at home consigns it to dust and oblivion in some dark closet or lumber-room, where the treasures lie hidden till his notable wife persuades him that they are of no use, that there is no room for them, that they are a nuisance, that the children *will* play with the poisoned arrows; and the owner, actuated more by the desire to get rid of 'the whole confounded thing' than by any feeling of public spirit, at length makes a virtue of necessity, and devotes them to their best end, by presenting them to a Museum. Deeply impressed and convinced by long experience of the causes and effects above noted, need I add that I carried away from the bazaar half a cart-load of these savage treasures? Among them, by-the-bye, is a sling, that most ancient weapon, made precisely on the pattern of those used by English school-boys. It is formed entirely of hemp, and there is attached to it a pouch of pebbles, some of them of agate, ground into an oval shape, pointed at both ends.

December 19th.—This day, a chief from the Taupo Lake, 200 miles hence inland, came into Auckland to see the Governor. Te Hao-Hao is, I believe, the degenerate son, for he is a little fellow, of the gigantic chief of the Boiling Water tribes, described by Wakefield and Bidwill. This old man of the mountain—for he deserved this title if any man ever did—claimed his classic descent from Tongariro, the Mont Blanc of New Zealand, at whose feet he dwelt, and by a landslip of which, a slice of his ancestor, he was recently killed. The late Te Hao-Hao was brave in fight, unequalled in personal might, eloquent in council, generous in his gifts, and hospitable to all strangers. But he had two forbidden matters, as rigorous as Bluebeard's *one.* He would permit no attempts to convert him to Christianity, nor any one to desecrate his forefather, monarch of mountains, by walking up his back. My friend, Mr Bidwill, however, (and I will not say he did well in so doing,) excited by ambition and a botanical mania, stole a march upon the mountain as well as upon its human descendant, thereby breaking the 'tapu' and scarcely escaping the dire vengeance of the old chief. The present chief has taken the embargo off his ancestor Tongariro, but continues as good a heathen as his father. He is a pitiful fellow with only a couple of wives, whereas the old 'Boiling Water' man had eight. The present tepid representative of *the* Hao-hao came on board the *Inflexible* with three inferior attendants. None of these men had ever before left their own wild mountain home, and they seemed astounded at all the wonderful things they saw on board. Yet they appeared to attach no particular interest to any object except such as were applicable to warfare. The chief himself gauged the calibre of the huge 84lb. gun on the quarter deck, by thrusting into the muzzle his head and as much of his body as he could; and he took accurate measurement of the deck in length and breadth, by causing the longest of his slaves to prostrate himself, and thus using him as a six-foot rule. He looked over my shoulder as I was sketching Auckland from the seaward; and recognised the prominent features with great quickness and seeming pleasure.

G.C. Mundy, *Our Antipodes*, pp. 262–7.

My dearest K (1848)

THOMAS ARNOLD

Son of the famous headmaster of Rugby and brother of Matthew Arnold, Thomas Arnold the younger came to New Zealand as a prospective colonist with the New Zealand Company. He spent two years in Wellington and Nelson before moving to Hobart in 1850.

WELLINGTON IS A MOST BEAUTIFUL PLACE; far more so than I had expected. From my window in Mr Cole's house, which is high up above the rest of the town, the view, on a fine day, across the beautiful lake-like harbour, to the mountain ranges which rise beyond it, tier above tier, then to the low and level Hutt valley farther to the left, and behind that again, far inland to the lofty Tara-rua chain, the backbone of the island, is really more beautiful than I can describe. Since I have been here, we have had several calm and brilliant days, on which the sun shone with a power which he seldom has in England in June; yet this is our November. The town of Wellington is principally built on two level pieces of land backed by hills, called Thorndon flat and Te-Aro flat. These flats are about a mile from each other, and for that distance there is barely room for one row of houses between the sea and the hills. Our town-acres are on pretty steeply sloping ground close to Thorndon flat; and very near to Government House; and I believe they are likely to be valuable in process of time. I have been to-day over to the Makara valley to look at the country sections, or rather at one of them. For about 5 miles there is a cart road, though a most infamous one, leading to the end of what is called the Karori district; thence a very good bridle path, recently cut, conducts you over a pass in the hills about 2 miles down into the Makara valley, and stops about half a mile from our section No. 19. I ascertained however that from one point in this path, a path equally good might be cut right to the middle of our section which would only need to be 20 chains (¹/₄ of a mile) in length, and which I could get done for £5. There are many clearings in the Karori district, and the huge pine logs and the charred blackened stumps lie about, just as they are described to do in the American backwoods. The land is very much parcelled out among small proprietors, so that one sees a great many small wooden cottages, and children running about, and every-where the saw and the axe are busily at work, for it is from Karori that Wellington is principally supplied with sawn timber. But after leaving the Karori road and entering upon the bridle path, you plunge at once into the unbroken solitude of the forest. The path gradually ascends, winding a good deal, for about a mile, when you find yourself at the top of a hawse in a high range of hills, with the Makara valley, one mass of waving wood, deep down beneath you to the west, while to the North you see part of Cook's Straits, near where the River Makara empties itself. Descending by many Zig Zag turns, for the hill is very steep, and always thro' wood, you find yourself at last in a native clearing at the bottom of the valley. Here at present, the bridle path ends. But my guide struck the line originally cut by the surveyors between the sections, and led me on through the bush to a place where XIX was rudely cut in the bark of a tree. Here then was our section. The Makara, a pretty little clear stream, somewhat less than the Scandale beck, runs thro' a good part of it. You will understand its position better by this little plan.

The dotted line is the bridle path. Thus you see, I had to go right down into the native clearing, and then back again along the line between the sections, to get at No. 19, and you may observe how much it would save, if a path were cut along the *pencilled* line. Most part of our section seems to be level, as far as one can judge in such a thick bush. The timber is not very heavy, nor therefore would the price of clearing be. No. 14 is ours also, but I had not time to go and examine it. Altogether I was pleased with the aspect of things. The greatest drawback is that horrid Karori road, which is the only approach to Makara from Wellington. Oh for another General Wade! I think those lazy lobsters the soldiers, of whom there are 500 here, ought to be employed in road making, for they are of no earthly use else.

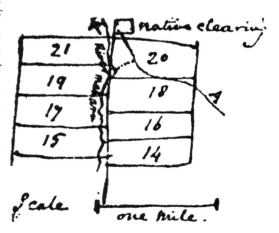

Thomas Arnold, *New Zealand Letters of Thomas Arnold the Younger*, pp. 47–8.

The shore of New Zealand (1851)

WILLIAM KENNAWAY

William Kennaway emigrated to the Canterbury Settlement in 1851 with his younger brother Laurence. Their shipboard journal was written when they were 18 and 17 respectively.

October 16 1851. Since yesterday night I can imagine how glad you would all be could you know that at about 2 o'clock on this eventful day we obtained our first view of The Shore of New Zealand. But it will be at least 4 or 5 months before you will be able to hear this news which will be of comfort and a cause of rejoicing to you all. But I must remember that we are not yet on terra firma, nor count on the chicken before the eggs are hatched. When we came on deck in the morning before breakfast the captain and those experienced in discerning distant coast could see what they call the loom of land, but of course we (inexperienced landsmen) could make nothing out of it. All the morning many anxious eyes were directed towards the west in the hope of catching a glimpse of the distant cliffs, but nothing could be plainly seen. So at last the dinner called us from the deck, consisting of our frugal fare of peas pudding, Pork and dumplings, to which we were extravagent enough to add a little of porter. But

John Pearse, 'How the water was caught in cabin!!!', 1851. (E-455-f-008-03, ATL)

48

John Pearse, 'The dry or comfortable side of the cabin', 1851. (E-455-f-008-07, ATL)

I know you will excuse this when you hear that this beverage is very useful in keeping us from a very painful and troublesome rising called sea boils which this diet makes you very liable to. (But I am forgetting my account.) After dinner the cry of 'land' soon called us upon deck and our delighted eyes saw at last the long grey and hilly part of the Southern port of New Zealand which you will find marked on the map as Otago point. The formerly much deserted poop was alive with people the whole afternoon. We all walked up and down the deck with that kind of contented feeling which I cannot describe to you. At length the evening closed in with a most beautiful sunset and, the clouds clearing off, the long and irregular range of hills was thrown out in fine and bold relief against the clear sky. I took a rough sketch of the shore, knowing that these little drawings are as interesting as any description can be. All the emigrants are now making merry over a good allowance of punch. We shall (*Deo volente*) cast anchor in a day or two but it is impossible to fix a time, as coasting is sometimes very long and tiresome work. The wind changed from the West to North East scince 3 o'clock so the ship's head is obliged to be put towards the East. These circumstances of course delay us, but we shall land in good time and there the best plan is to wait with patience. How I am looking forward to see the beach, the pebles, the trees, houses and all those objects which we have missed for so long a time.

William Kennaway, *Biscuit and Butter: A Colonist's Shipboard Fare*, pp. 96–8.

Sailors' Home (1852)

JOHN ROCHFORT

Rochfort arrived at Lyttelton in 1852, working as a surveyor for a time at the 'bad pay of a stingy Government'. He was the first European to walk cross-country from Rangitikei to Hawkes Bay. He left for the Australian goldfields after six months but returned to New Zealand, and from the early 1860s he was involved in important surveying and engineering work.

On the following day we dined with him, accompanied by Captain K…y. we met a pleasant company, consisting of a countryman of the Baron's and his wife; Mr W…e, a regimental doctor; Mr H…t, and several others, whose names I do not remember. The Baron amused us with a curious anecdote. He began by telling us that the natives were very fond of tattooing their hinder quarters, and, when the ship he came out in arrived in Port Nicholson, several Maorie chiefs came on board and walked round the decks curiously examining everything. Some of the lady passengers naturally enough had the curiosity to look at them: they misinterpreted this, and thought the ladies were admiring their tattoo; so one of the chiefs, willing to gratify them, strutted up to a fair one, and deliberately turned the ornamented portion of his person round for her examination, at the same time shouting *Kaupi!! Kaupi!!!* (good!! good!!!). We discussed politics over the Baron's wine (which by the bye he took great pride in having good) till a late hour. When the party broke up, we retired, and tried to wake up some of the sleepy publicans, but without success, and were just thinking of turning ghosts and wandering about till daylight, when we fortunately met a watchman, who volunteered to guide us to what he described as a 'remarkably quiet and genteel private boarding-house.' He led the way to a small house, with Sailors' Home inscribed in large letters over the door. As we preferred sleeping anywhere to wandering about till dawn, we rapped with our knuckles, and the landlord, Mr Boodle, himself deigned to open the door, dressed simply in his shirt, and grasping a tallow candle. His face showed the unmistakable remains of two very black eyes; while his wife's nutcrack, lantern-jaw visage, bearing a great resemblance to his own, especially about the eyes, was peering at us from the half-open door of his dormitory. He led us up stairs, where we threw ourselves, undressed, on the straw beds which were ranged up and down like a hospital ward, and were shortly lulled to sleep by the heavy breathing of several sailors, who had evidently just come home from a 'spree'.

At daylight in the morning we were up and stirring. Going down stairs we paid Mr Boodle for his excellent accommodation, and were on the point of quitting, when who should come

Samuel Brees, Barrett's Hotel, Wellington, 1847. (A-109-027, ATL)

in but the sailor who ran away in Port Cooper? He was coolly smoking his pipe, but, on see-ing us, looked quite taken aback; nevertheless before the captain could articulate, 'Halloa, Mr George! I've got you now,' the said George was getting out of the back parlour window. 'Landlord,' says Captain K...y, 'go and fetch a policeman.'—'Couldn't, sir, at the price; I should lose all my customers,—unless,' he added, pausing, 'I had five pounds for my trouble.' In the mean time George was over the garden wall and far way, and six or seven stout sailors barred the passage till our runaway had got a good 'offing', when we were allowed to depart in peace. 'Never mind,' says the captain, 'I'll give him three months yet, if it costs me twenty pounds out of my own pocket; I shall catch him when he least expects it.' And so he did, a few months after, when he came into port unexpectedly.

We went aboard to dinner with the captain, and then brought our luggage, which amoun-ted to several tons, ashore. Here let me caution the reader against taking out a large and expen-sive outfit. I took out one which cost me about £60, and found almost everything was useless to me; nearly the whole is lying untouched in Wellington. Suitable clothes may be bought in the colony for little money, by doing which you save the cost of moving and storing them: this is a very general mistake amongst emigrants.

Mr H…t recommended us to a boarding-house in Willis Street, Te Ara flat, kept by a Mr Edwards, where we were 'taken in and done for' at a pound per week; we made ourselves at home, and were soon on good terms with our four fellow-boarders. Mr W……h was a young man of about five-and-twenty, studying for a clergyman. He expects to be ordained in two years by the Bishop of New Zealand at Auckland. Mr S…l was a tall peculiar man, rather too fond of drinking, quite the opposite of Mr W……h; he was noisy and quarrelsome: he held a good appointment under government, but was always in debt, and shortly after ran away to the diggings, leaving his salary heavily mortgaged. The other two were brothers of the name of H…l, who had just finished their 'cadetship,' that is, they had been learning sheep-farming under a settler, and were waiting for a remittance from their friends in England to begin on their own account.

John Rochfort, *The Adventures of a Surveyor in New Zealand*, pp. 18–20.

Travelling to Napier (early 1850s)

EDWARD WILSON

Edward Wilson's sketches are described as written by a colonist for the amusement or information of other colonists. Wilson lived in Australia for twenty years and visited New Zealand in the early 1850s on his way to Britain.

IN VISITING AUCKLAND it was my intention to have struck through the heart of the northern island, and after inspecting the very interesting districts of the hot springs, to have made my way down one of the principal rivers to Wellington, at the other end of the island. But I found this a more formidable undertaking than I calculated upon. There are few facilities of communication through the interior; the frequent occurrence of creeks, rivers, and swamps renders progress on horseback impossible; the climate necessitates the carrying a tent, and you have to depend almost entirely upon the co-operation of the Maories to get on at all. As few of them speak our language, and as, on the best-known routes, contact with the whites has developed a good deal of the natural covetousness of the race, it is at once a disagreeable, slow, laborious, and rather expensive undertaking to venture across the country, particularly alone. Except when getting up or down a river in a native canoe, you have to perform almost the entire journey on foot, and to subsist mainly on the omnipresent potato; and to this sort of life you have to reconcile yourself for a month, or perhaps six weeks, the time being dependent upon the zeal and moderation, or indolence and spirit of extortion, of the natives. I

View of some ship masts, Napier, 1860s–70s, by an unknown photographer. (F-120788-1/2, C.G. Coxhead Collection, ATL)

attempted to inveigle a very intelligent scientific gentleman, with whom I had the pleasure of sailing from Sydney, into accompanying me on this expedition; but as neither his leisure nor his state of health admitted of his entertaining my proposition, and as no other eligible companion presented himself, I had to arrange other schemes for seeing something more of New Zealand and its inhabitants.

After some delay, I took my passage in a little schooner of 40 tons for Napier, in the district of Ahuriri, on the eastern coast, about 400 miles to the south of Auckland. You will easily imagine that this was not a very pleasant undertaking on a coast so liable to stormy weather as that of New Zealand; but I had no alternative. There is very little traffic between the several provinces, and Wellington is often a month without news from its more northern sister. Little as I relished the prospect of coasting this distance in a vessel of such insignificant proportions, whose cabin was little better than a cupboard, the only light and air for which were supplied through a small hatchway, the reality proved much worse than the anticipation. The little cockboat could not sail a bit, and, when it came to anything like beating against an unfavourable wind, her efforts were simply ridiculous. Her lee-way often actually exceeded her progress forward, and once or twice on a lee-shore, and with uncertain weather, we were in real danger. To do our skipper justice, however, he seemed thoroughly to distrust the sailing powers of his man-of-war; and in case of the weather looking threatening, he stood upon no ceremony whatever in putting his ship about and scudding for some one of the numerous ports of shelter with which the eastern coast of New Zealand is amply supplied. But the loss of time was terrible. For twelve mortal days was I condemned to drag out existence within the narrow bounds of this little cockle-shell; and although I bore the infliction as a philosopher should, I was never much better pleased in my life than when I found the little schooner sailing into the harbour of Napier.

Edward Wilson, Rambles at the Antipodes, pp. 83–5.

Ferry over the Rangatikei (1854)

J. L. C. RICHARDSON

Major J.L.C. Richardson visited New Zealand in the early 1850s, and spent the summer travelling through the lower North Island. He wrote a description of the colony interspersed with extracts from his journal of his experiences.

James Crawford, 'Daniell's Rangitikei—Te ara taumai', 1862. (A-229-055, ATL)

OUR FERRY MAN, a gigantic savage, informed us, that within a mile, by following the course of the river, we should find a house of accommodation. After due consultation we resolved to seek it, and rest and refresh ourselves. By some of those contretemps which occasionally mar the best devised plans, we missed the house, which fact we learned after making a detour of 3 miles and reaching the house of a recent settler. He kindly undertook to give our jaded horses a feed, while his good lady reinvigorated ourselves. It was near 3 o'clock, and we had to retrace our steps through sand hills, and worse still, on regaining the beach to get through 13 miles before we arrived at the river Rangitiki, on the right bank of which was an inn. We were advised to defer the prosecution of our journey, and accommodation was kindly pressed on us; but an advance was decided on. The sand hills which we endeavoured to cross diagonally, under the guidance of a Maori, tried us terribly, but in due course, the sun having long since bade us good night, we arrived on the banks of the river.

The night was pitchy dark, across we saw lights; we coo-eed vociferously, but the wind opposing, we met with no response. A dark rising cloud portended rain, so hastily consulting, we decided upon encamping for the night, or, colonially speaking, 'bushing' it. The ever-present flax soon furnished us with tethering ropes, and we were not long before a blanket provided a snug retreat for Mrs B. Not a tree was nigh, but a quantity of drift wood being at hand, and abundance of tall grass and flax, we doubted not that we should do well. Ere long the storm burst upon us in all its fury; we hastened to light our goodly pile, but the matches had got drenched on the road and the tinder-box was without tinder, so we took refuge under a Macintosh blanket, which, in addition to extending its fostering care over us, had to protect the saddles and carpet-bags. Wet up to the thighs, I occasionally snatched a few minutes' sleep, emerging now and then to assure myself that the horses had not broken away. Our Maori guide, instead of assisting us with his colonial experience in our novel and unpleasant position, hastened to convey himself away and to form a comfortable tent from the twisted flax and toi-toi. No pipe cheered the solitary hours, but we repined not. At 3, P. and I rose and hastened to the ferry, which was scarcely a mile distant, we coo-oo-ed with all the energy that remained in us, but a solitary cock alone responded to our appeal. Drooping, dripping, and desponding, we returned to our encampment. Happily, at this crisis, two Maoris, whom we had met on the preceding day, arrived, and in answer to our inquiry if they could procure a light, instantly produced a properly furnished tinder-box, and kindled at once our hopes and the fire. Encircling the blazing pile, our disasters were forgotten, and we managed to extract many a hearty laugh from the narration of our individual misfortunes. An homoepathic portion of bread and cheese revived and cheered us; our tent was struck, our horses saddled, and by sunrise we were standing as humble petitioners on the banks of the Rangatiki. With redoubled vigour coo-ee followed coo-ee, but in vain. Under the artistic hands of one of our new comrades a horn emerged from a flax bush and a merry blast poured across the water, but the silence remained undisturbed. Rapidly divesting himself of his dress, the younger of the two dashed into the stream and swam half across, but the coldness of the water, or some unpropitious circumstance, induced hesitation, and finally a return. Again a blazing fire rejoiced us, and we resolved to wait patiently until our opposite friends had satiated of sleep. We had not long to wait: the smoke and flame did more for us than our united efforts, and within an hour we were seated in a snug little room enjoying a most palatable breakfast.

J.L.C. Richardson, *A Summer's Excursion in New Zealand*, pp. 159–61.

At the ferry-house, Wairarapa (1850s)

C.R. CARTER

Charles Carter arrived in New Zealand in 1850 on the Eden *when he was 28. He was a builder responsible for many early buildings and reclamation works in Wellington before developing the Wairarapa, where Carterton is named after him. He was a noted bibliophile and writer.*

IN THE AFTERNOON I left the *station* of my considerate host, and after walking over the length of the sand spit, I crossed the outlet of the lake in the ferry-boat; I noticed at this time that myriads of wild ducks were floating on the lake's surface. From the Ferry-house I walked over a plain up to my knees in natural grass, and soon arrived at Mr Kelly's station, *Turanganui*. Mr Kelly was a Scotchman, and an eccentric individual; he lived with a *Maori* woman, or, in colonial parlance, he had a *Maori* wife, and boasted of being a gentleman, and also of his having been educated at St Andrew's College, Aberdeen. As he was seldom sober, and used bad language, I could not understand how he could justly or rightly lay claim to the title of gentleman. I soon completed my business at his place, and as I desired to return to town quickly, I hired a horse at Mr Kelly's, and on horse-back returned to the Ferry-house, which, by the coast and across the heads, is about thirty-two miles from Wellington, and by the inland road, nearly seventy-five miles. The Ferry-house stood by the side of the lake. Such a house! It was made with old boards, pieces of timbers from wrecks, old fencing-poles from the bush, and was thatched in at the roof; it was a cross between a *Maori warre* and a rude-built labourer's cottage. It was the only public-house, inn, or accommodation house in the whole valley. It was kept by an Englishman, who lived with a stout, intelligent, good-looking, broken-English-speaking *Maori* wife, who played the cheerful, bustling coloured hostess remarkably well, considering her origin. She was dressed decently in English female costume, only she dispensed with shoes and stockings. She could make bread and bake it; she could wash and sew, and

William Hawkins, Ferry Inn, Ruamahanga River, 1867. (E-370-010-2, ATL)

cook eels, potatoes and pork for *my supper*, or that of any other traveller; so said the host, and so say I, for I watched her peel potatoes, then clean and wash them, and place them all over the bottom of a large camp oven;—she next placed some lumps of fat rancid pork over and between the potatoes, upon which latter she fixed a monster eel, coiled up, and so large as to cover all the potatoes, and nearly the diameter of the camp oven. The eel appeared to me to be about 2¹/₂-inches in diameter at its thickest part, and with its head in the centre of its coil and slightly raised, looked like a moderate sized serpent ready for a spring—in fact, it was not quite dead, for I saw it move, and to the best of my recollection it was unskinned. The lid was duly placed on the oven, the oven put over the fire, where the luscious Anglo-Maori compound fried, spluttered and steamed—till it was done.

My host, inn-keeper, landlord, and ferryman was named Mr H——y. He had been a sailor, a whaler, and a shepherd, and was now a publican and ferryman. He was a powerful and well made man, and in stature rather above the middle height; his head was large, and covered with a profusion of curly black hair, at least six inches in length; his face was in proportion to his head, squarely formed, of a ruddy hue and generally showing signs of good humour and natural intelligence. Sometimes it displayed the reverse of these qualities, when at times he felt called upon to put down a fray or a drunken brawl in his house, by the threatening display or by the *actual use* of a pair of large and formidable fists. My host was a trader as well as a ferry-man: he sold drapery slops to the natives, and exchanged gaudy prints, blue shirts and fustian trousers with them for pigs, potatoes and wheat,—which latter he ground (or made a *native* grind) in his own steel mill. More than this, with native assistance, he had built his own ferry-house, and he killed his own pigs. He was a wonderful man in his district, and in his way, if you could only put up with his accommodation.

It was at this Anglo-*Maori* hotel I had the distinguished honour of meeting with a knight, in search of adventures. No! not that, but in search of a snug, cheap and ready-made sheep-run. He was a real, live knight, above the middle-height, with a drab suit of clothes on his body, a drab complexion to his face, and a loose, semi-military scarlet cloak over his back and shoulders. He appeared to be about fifty years of age, and though not very bright in mind, he was shrewd and good-natured, and bore the name of *Sir Osborne Gibbs*. He, like myself, was doomed to remain all night at the *Ferry hotel*. Our first difficulty was to find something to eat for tea or supper; as for the *savory mess* in the camp oven, we could not touch that, so we partook of some dry bread and bottled beer, and went to bed early to sleep away our partial hunger and disappointment. We were not destined to sleep, there was company in the house that night. There were two or three shepherds on their way up the coast to their stations, nearly, they said—150 miles distant; they were staying here for the night and must have a spree. Besides these shepherds there were two other shepherds or farm labourers, who had been here over a week, drinking and spending the money they had been many months in earning. One of them, they called Sinclair, seemed half mad, and had been drinking for a fortnight, and was now begging for a glass of grog, as he said, to save him from dying; his beard had grown nearly half an inch in length, and looked as stiff as porcupine's quills. There he sat, his vision impaired, his reason muddled, his hair tangled and matted, his face long unwashed, and his body without a coat or waistcoat; yet this man, when he was in a sober state, was a good-natured, hard-working man; but sad to say, as too many do in the colonies—Ah! And elsewhere—this *naturally good-natured man* had fallen a victim to the demon of intemperance.

When in bed, we could not sleep. First there was a quarrel and scuffle amongst the shepherds in the kitchen—which our host by a vigorous use of his voice and of his bodily and fistic powers, soon quelled. Then all was quiet; the tipsy men had retired to rest. Oh dear no! Not that; they could not rest themselves, so they would not let any one else do so. Two of them tumbled out of bed, that is out of the *bunks*—bedsteads were not used at this hotel—Mr H——— appeared on the scene, and quickly bundled them into bed again. At last the long-wished for day-light came, and we (self and Sir O.) got up. Our appetites were amazingly good this morning, so much so, that we made a hearty breakfast off excellent potatoes, coarse bread, wild pig's liver, and boiled salted pork of fair quality. I was glad to leave the Ferry-house—Sir O. remained, thinking he would go further up the coast; he was sadly put out that the roads were not carriage roads, but nature's roads, and that the eating, drinking, and lodging were so bad. I crossed the outlet of the lake once more in a boat, my horse swimming after it, and as I held his head with a long rein, he puffed, snorted, and tried to swim close to the boat, as if he wished to place his fore feet in it, which, not being desirable, I kept him at a sufficient distance to prevent such an untoward accident. We landed, the boatmen scraped my horse, wiped him dry, and then saddled him, and I made the best of my way to the *Muku Muku rocks*.

The weather was stormy, and the sea rough and angrily lashing the shore with its waves, for the wind was south-east and blowing in-shore. My horse was a small, but a compact, *stock-horse*, used to the coast and cattle mustering. I arrived at the rocks at nearly low water, but the sea was running-in, breast high, against the first rock, which was about 5 feet high, and nearly perpendicular. I rashly rode into the surf—which at one moment was knee-deep and one or two minutes after as high as the five-foot rock—when a huge roller dashed in, and ran up the sides of the cliffs, and buried me and the horse for the space (I should say) of half a minute. I then saw nothing and, for the instant, I was half-blinded and smothered with foam and water, and also nearly washed out to sea by the reflux of waters. My little horse threw himself against the rock, and as it were clung to it, and when the sea receded for a moment he turned his head and quickly and safely brought me back to a high and dry part of the beach.

Being very anxious to continue my journey, I next mounted to the top of the rock, and rein in hand, I endeavoured to lead—by coaxing and threats—the horse round it; but he appeared so alarmed at the boiling surf about him that he would not move an inch. Just at this moment, another roller came fiercely in, burying the horse and immersing myself—where I was standing on the rock—up to my middle in spray and water. After this, I gave up any further attempts to pass the rocks, and made my way to Mr Matthews's station, where Mr M. kindly supplied me with dry clothes and warm food, and where I remained for the night. The next morning the wind was blowing hard, and the sea still up; I therefore remained where I was.

During the forenoon, Mr Matthews invited me to take a gallop with him over his run; I had been for a long time unaccustomed to riding on horse-back, and I already felt saddle-sore—partly from my riding exertions the day before—but I did not like to refuse the kindly-meant offer of Mr M. who was a good horseman. When we were fairly mounted, and but a few yards from the house, my friend put spurs to his horse, and cried out, 'Now, Carter! come on! follow me!' If I had wished *not* to 'come on,' or 'follow' *him*, I could not have done so; for I soon found out, when my horse heard the crack of the *stock whip* and saw the other horse gallop off, that he too had been a 'stock horse', and at a rapid pace he bore me onwards. There was no help for it, away we went at full gallop at first, then came a trot. Oh! that horrid trot! How my bones jarred—almost rattled—against each other, and how the sore place smarted; next came a canter, which was more pleasant, then a walk which was very acceptable to me; but it was too short: on we went again, now galloping over level ground, then up hill and down hill, next cantering over a sloppy bush road, where, if not careful, one's feet came in contact with the stumps of recently felled trees; but nothing stops us—still through swamps and streams we go, splashing and frightening the wild pigs on the adjoining fern-ridges, and the goats on the near hills, and the wild ducks on the reedy waters, when suddenly my horse stuck fast in the mire and mud of a swampy creek; he plunged and struggled, and plunged again, and finished by throwing me clean over his head, into the water and liquid mud:—the horse soon extricated himself, and I, unhurt from my *soft fall*, scrambled out after him. Thus ended our day's ride, and as it was raining fast, and blowing hard from New Zealand's *cold quarter*, the south east, we returned to the house by the shortest route. Here another change of clothes and a seat by the side of a large talking and laughing fire—a crackling and blazing wood fire on a huge hearth beneath a great chimney—and tea with rashers of bacon (wild pig), potatoes, bread and butter placed before us—of which we partook with a keen appetite—soon placed us in a state of comfort, and inward and outward satisfaction with ourselves and everybody else. We passed the evening away in telling stories, as they say in England, sitting round by the common hearth; Mr M.'s two assistants at shepherding and tilling the ground told stories about the natives and about the wild cattle they had seen in the bush, the pigs they had killed, the boars they had fought and slain, and the great eels they had caught—all of which was then new and strange to me.

C.R. Carter, Life and Recollections of a New Zealand Colonist, pp. 94–101.

Mutiny on the Red Jacket (1860)

J.E. GORST

Sir John Gorst came to New Zealand first in 1860 as a young man on the ship Red Jacket, *on which he experienced a mutiny. His account of this trip was published after his second trip to New Zealand with his daughter in 1906. He was Civil Commissioner of the Waikato District under Sir George Grey in 1860–63.*

WE ARE GETTING COOLER and a little more jovial. We've started evening concerts twice a week. Of course, among 500 people we got some good singing; all our music is vocal, and our programme improves every time.

'The concerts are productive of harmony in more senses than one. The jolliest of all the fellows connected with the ship is the chief mate; he is a tall and thin man with a long nose, and has not his equal at chaffing, nautical or otherwise, on whatever subject you choose to assail him. He generally stands on his watch at the end of the poop, with a crowd of children, big and little, round him, some getting ships rigged and others teasing him. Of course this is in the Trades where you can sail all day without stirring a brace. He is altogether a kind of nautical Mark Tapley.

'There was a great fight on Sunday between the crew and some foreigners, whom the crew amuse themselves by teasing. The chief mate knocked a sailor down in the most refreshing manner and then conveyed him aft, and put him in irons to cool. A German had his nose broken, and another sailor had his head cut open with an iron hook, and after a great deal of explanation and jabbering of English, German, and Italian the affair was healed up *pro tem.*, but the storm will break out afresh.'

'We are miserably becalmed and the heat is tremendous though the midday sun is 15° off being vertical. The day is passed in literally gasping for breath, but the nights are delicious, cool, with bright moonlight, and nothing but the vulgar necessity for sleep prevents your spending the night on deck. Yesterday we had a boat out and rowed round the ship, but the intense heat greatly interfered with the pleasure.'

'The calm ended yesterday morning and we had a jolly fresh breeze all day. The row on board has come at last with a vengeance, and in a more atrocious manner than I anticipated. Last night about eleven, I took a turn down the starboard gangway, just to look at the main deck, before turning in, and at the corner came upon a terrible row. The same sailor who was in irons for fighting the Germans had just been engaged at fisticuffs with another victim, and the captain, second mate and boatswain were trying to drag him aft from a crowd of sailors. After narrowly escaping braining by the legs of the passing madman, who was knocked on the head in time by the mate, we held the gangway against his comrades with the greatest difficulty. On the monkey poop the prisoner, who was deliriously drunk, behaved with frantic violence, but was at once securely ironed and tied down; they got another sailor aft and ironed him, then cutlasses, bayonets and revolvers were produced and twenty passengers were armed. The critical moment was twelve o'clock, when the next watch was called and the captain intended to secure two more of the crew, who were ringleaders of the mutiny. The watch came on the main deck and the captain and two mates, accompanied by five of us unarmed passengers, went down and ordered the men aft. They went quietly, but one made a most desperate resistance to being ironed and screamed to his comrades for help. They rushed up the port gangway, but were met by bayonets. The chief mate thrust at the foremost man and would probably have killed him but the captain parried the blow, and the weapon only went about four inches into the woodwork of the poop. The crew were beaten back and the gangways and front of poop manned by armed men. Then there was an awful pause, while the captain went down to load his revolver. You can have no idea how ludicrous the whole affair appeared to us, though the officers all thought it serious. I saw the doctor, who is a very meek man, armed with a cutlass, which he used as a walking-stick, making holes in the deck, and

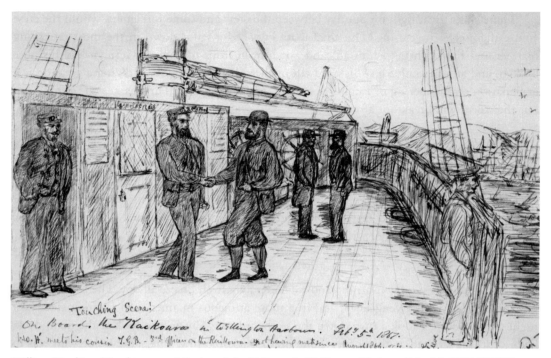

Touching Scene!
On Board, the *Kaikoura* in Wellington Harbour. Feb. 5th 1867.
W.W.H. meets his cousin T.G.B. – 3rd officer on the *Kaikoura* not having met since August 1864 or so.

William Hawkins, 'Touching scene! On board the *Kaikoura* in Wellington Harbour. Feb. 5th 1867. W.W.H. meets his cousin T.G.B. 3rd officer on the *Kaikoura*, not having previously met since August 1864 or so'. (E-370-005-1, ATL)

the chief officer took him in the wind, to our intense delight, as he passed. When the pistols were loaded the captain went down and ordered the watch to haul taut the main brace to test their obedience, and it was done. We kept watch and watch all night in the gangway with fixed bayonets, and there are four men in irons garnishing the monkey poop. To-day every arrangement is being made to keep armed watch. Indeed, this is necessary for our own safety and that of the ship.'

'The ship is getting into an orderly and secure state again. We had a meeting of passengers in the saloon yesterday and a document was drawn up and signed, reciting that in consequence of the mutinous conduct of the crew the captain had requested the passengers to form an armed watch to guard the poop, where the four prisoners were confined and agreeing to certain rules for our government. We have three watches of about twelve men each, which are on duty in rotation; it is very jolly fun now in fine weather, but will be anything but pleasant in the gales of the South Seas. The sentries are mounted in each of the gangways, armed with cutlasses and pistols, and two on the poop with revolvers during the night; the rest of the watch dispose themselves about the poop, quite ready to come if necessary. There is not much likelihood of a rescue being attempted on the bright nights we now enjoy—if it is tried at all, it will be on some squally night in the South Sea, but with the present precautions nothing is to be feared. The prisoners are always handcuffed; they are chained in pairs on the monkey poop all day, and sleep below the monkey poop where our luggage used to be, with their legs in a handsome pair of stocks all night. Yesterday we passed a homeward-bound American ship so close as to shake all his sails. He was, I am sorry to say, so exasperated as to use his speaking trumpet to swear at us through. The winds continue so light and weather so sultry, it is an exertion to write.'

J.E. Gorst, *New Zealand Revisited*, pp. 11–15.

PART 3

The tourist boom

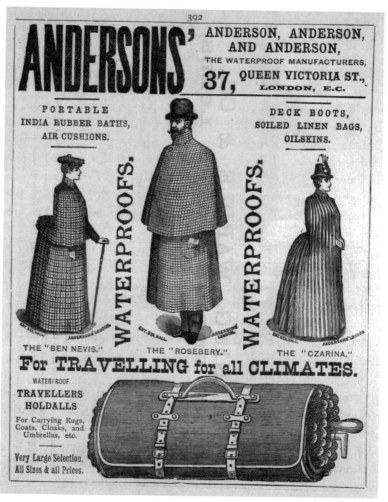

Andersons' 'For travelling for all climates': advertisement for waterproofs, holdalls, boots, and other items for travellers from the *Orient Line Guide*, 1890.

(B-K 402-392, ATL)

Hard up (1866)

HENRY W. NESFIELD

An Old Etonian, Nesfield emigrated to New Zealand in 1865 at the age of 19 and knocked around doing various kinds of work—shepherding, cab driving, working on a coastal steamer and acting—before moving to Melbourne six years later. A Chequered Career *describes his fifteen years in Australia and New Zealand.*

I DECIDED ON TRYING the west-coast diggings of the Middle Island. There happened to be a 'rush' on just then. The difficulty was how to get there, as the passage-money in the coasting schooners from the Manukau harbour was five pounds—I possessed only one! My stock of station clothes came in handy on this emergency. I selected a dirty pair of moleskin trousers, a cotton shirt, felt hat, and 'watertight' boots, and astonished my landlady by coming down to breakfast in that costume. I had gone to bed quite a swell. I explained to her that I was 'hard up', and intended looking for a billet. The kind-hearted old creature actually burst out crying. I had only known her for a week, but women are such puzzles! I walked over to the Orehunga office to see if I could engage to work my passage down to the diggings on board one of the coasters.

In applying for a situation a man should always endeavour to look fit for it. No one, for instance, would dream of engaging a man as gardener or groom if he looked like a barber's clerk, or a prince in disguise. I suppose I looked like work, for I succeeded in engaging as cook's mate for the run down, there being over thirty diggers as passengers, besides two or three in the cabin. The schooner was anchored near the heads, waiting to take in sawn timber from the mills. Having bade adieu to my pleasant landlady, I embarked that evening in an open boat, with two sailors, three or four diggers, and my sheep-dog 'Wattie'.

I took 'Wattie' with me because I had not the heart to leave him behind. He proved very useful to me at the diggings, and helped me to get my living. The distance from Orehunga (which is almost joined on to Auckland) to the Manukau Heads is about thirty miles. We had the tide against us when about half-way, so we stopped at a 'shanty' on the north shore, and 'spelled' for a couple of hours. I stuck to the bow-oar all the way, and 'Wattie' stuck between my legs, the motion causing him to behave in a manner that proved he had not much stomach for 'sailorising'. About two o'clock in the morning we got alongside the schooner, and I was not sorry. My hands were not as tough as they might have been, and the boat was not a Thames wherry. Having found a snug place for'ard for the dog, I looked about for a shakedown for myself. I had blankets and my valise, but the only place I could find to crawl into was the hold.

The cargo was not in—but she had a quantity of bricks in the bottom. Did you ever sleep on bricks at the bottom of a ship's hold? For the man who is *blasé* and disgusted to repletion with the pleasures of life, allow me to recommend them as a mattress. The bottom of a vessel being of a somewhat circular formation, the bricks were not as evenly arranged as I have observed them under different circumstances. I slept like a top. When I say that I felt just a trifle stiff and sore about those portions of my body that I reclined upon, you will understand it as the natural consequences of sleeping on a couch of such velvety softness. My slumbers were disturbed by a begrimed and dishevelled individual, who shook me violently by the shoulder.

'Are you the cook's mate, young un?'

'Yes,' I replied.

'Then just look "slippy," and come and give us a hand in the galley, there's a good lad. Have a nobbler?'

Therewith, my future mate pulled out a flask of a questionable mixture which he christened dark brandy. We imbibed. Our friendship was at once cemented, in the approved-of colonial manner. In four-and-twenty hours I was quite *au fait*, and as much at home peeling potatoes, scraping out pots and washing up, as if I had been at it all my life. As for my appearance—two hours after I commenced work I am sure my mother would not have known me.

During the passage to the Buller River, we encountered very heavy weather. This was rather an advantage to me, as all our digger passengers were in a state of utter prostration, and we had less cooking and messing about than if we had had a fine trip. I am never sea-sick, fortunately. I think that if anything could make a man ill, it would be the variety of smells in a cook's galley, on board a New Zealand coaster.

Most respected and respectable reader, let me explain to you, ere you follow me into positions even worse, perhaps, than cook's mate, that I have never 'gone to the dogs.' I have associated with plenty of men who have, and always managed to earn a living amongst that motley crowd that forms one of the most interesting phases of colonial society. It has often been a matter of regret to me that I could not get hold of a true tale of antipodeal vicissitudes, considering the number of clever men who have wasted the remnants of their lives in gaining such experiences. It is the fashion nowadays for people to take the colonies in the grand tour. They fly round the seven colonies, note-book in hand, and are home again within the twelve months. They write a book. The public read it as colonial experiences, and accept it as the truth. The statistics are probably correct, as they can be purchased for one shilling per volume; the impressions false; the anecdotes all lies, told to them in the smoking-room at the club, and jotted down at two a.m. in their bedrooms on the quiet. To vary the monotony of descriptions of places and scenery, authors invariably have recourse to 'anecdote.' Thus a great many things are written about the colonies that are utterly untrue.

Henry W. Nesfield, *A Chequered Career*, pp. 59–63.

Hokitika (1866–67)

C. W. DILKE

Sir Charles Wentworth Dilke, prominent nineteenth-century politician, member of Gladstone's cabinet, Privy Councillor, advocate of 'true imperialism', and writer, wrote his first and most popular book Greater Britain *after an extended tour of the 'English World' in 1866–67 when he was just 23.*

APPENDIX.

A MAORI DINNER.

For those who would make trial of Maori dishes, here is a native bill-of-fare, such as can be imitated in the South of England :—

HAKARI MAORI—A MAORI FEAST.

BILL-OF-FARE.

SOUP.

KOTA KOTA . . . . Any shell-fish.

FISH.

INANGA . . . . Whitebait (boiled in milk, with leeks).
PIHARAU . . . . Lamprey (stewed).
TUNA . . . . . Eels (steamed).

MADE-DISHES.

PUKÉKO . . . . . Moor-hen (steamed).
KOURA . . . . . Craw-fish (boiled).
TUI TUI . . . . . Thrush (roast).
KÉRÉRU . . . . . Pigeon (baked in clay).

ROAST.

POOKA . . . . . . Pork (*short* pig).

Part of a menu for a Maori dinner, from C.W. Dilke's *Greater Britain*, 1868.

(B-K 401, ATL)

PLACED IN THE VERY TRACK OF STORMS, and open to the sweep of rolling seas from every quarter, exposed to waves that run from pole to pole, or from South Africa to Cape Horn, the shores of New Zealand are famed for swell and surf, and her western rivers for the danger of their bars. Insurances at Melbourne are five times as high for the voyage to Hokitika as for the longer cruise to Brisbane.

In our little steamer of a hundred tons, built to cross the bars, we had reached the mouth of the Hokitika river soon after dark, but lay all night some ten miles to the south-west of the port. As we steamed in the early morning from our anchorage, there rose up on the east the finest sunrise view on which it has been my fortune to set eyes.

A hundred miles of the Southern Alps stood out upon a pale-blue sky in curves of a gloomy white that were just beginning to blush with pink, but ended to the southward in a cone of fire that stood up from the ocean: it was the snow-dome of Mount Cook struck by the rising sun. The evergreen bush, flaming with the crimson of the rata-blooms, hung upon the mountain-side, and covered the plain to the very margin of the narrow sands with a dense jungle. It was one of those sights that haunt men for years, like the eyes of Mary in Bellini's Milan picture.

On the bar, three ranks of waves appeared to stand fixed in walls of surf. These huge rollers are sad destroyers of the New Zealand coasting-ships: a steamer was lost here a week before my visit, and the harbour-master's whale-boat dashed in pieces, and two men drowned.

Lashing everything that was on deck, and battening down the hatches in case we should ground in crossing, we prepared to run the gauntlet. The steamers often ground for an instant while in the trough between the waves, and the second sea sweeps them from stem to stern, but carries them into the still water. Watching our time, we were borne on a great rolling white-capped wave into the quiet lakelet that forms the harbour, just as the sun, coming slowly up behind the range, was firing the Alps from north to south; but it was not till we had lain some minutes at the wharf that the sun rose to us poor mortals of the sea and plain. Hokitika Bay is strangely like the lower portion of the Lago Maggiore, but Mount Rosa is inferior to Mount Cook.

As I walked up from the quay to the town, looking for the 'Empire' Hotel, which I had heard was the best in Hokitika, I spied a boy carrying a bundle of some newspaper. It was the early edition for the up-country coaches, but I asked if he could spare me a copy. He put one into my hand. 'How much?' I asked. 'A snapper.' 'A snapper?' 'Ay—a tizzy.' Understanding this more familiar term, I gave him a shilling. Instead of 'change,' he cocked up his knee, slapt the shilling down on it, and said 'Cry!' I accordingly cried 'Woman!' and won, he loyally returning the coin, and walking off minus a paper.

When I reached that particular gin-palace which was known as *the* hotel, I found that all the rooms were occupied, but that I could, if I pleased, lie down on a deal side-table in the billiard-room. In our voyage down the coast from Nelson, we had brought for The Buller and for Hokitika a cabin full of cut flowers for bouquets, of which the diggers are extremely fond. The fact was pretty enough: the store set upon a single rose—'an English rosebud'—culled from a plant that had been brought from the old country in a clipper ship, was still more touching, but the flowers made sleep below impossible, and it had been blowing too hard for me to sleep on deck, so that I was glad to lie down upon my table for an hour's rest. The boards were rough and full of cracks, and I began to dream that, walking on the landing-stage, I ran against a man, who drew his revolver upon me. In wrenching it from him, I hurt my hand in the lock, and woke to find my fingers pinched in one of the chinks of the long table. Despairing of further sleep, I started to walk through Hokitika, and to explore the 'clearings' which the settlers are making in the bush.

C.W. Dilke, *Greater Britain*, pp. 330–2.

The Galatea in Auckland (1871)

[MASTER SMILES]

Samuel Smiles, famous author of the immensely influential Self Help, *edited this account of his youngest son's voyage around the world. The 'boy', who remains nameless, was sent on a long sea voyage at 16 after an inflammation of his lungs, and went to Melbourne in the summer of 1868–69. He stayed in Victoria for eighteen months and then went home by the Pacific route, via New Zealand. While at sea the boy kept a full log for his family.*

A FINE QUEEN'S SHIP was lying at anchor in the bay, which, on inquiry, we found to be the 'Galatea,' commanded by the Duke of Edinburgh. The 'Clio' also was anchored not far off. We were soon alongside the long wooden pier, to which were also moored several fine clipper ships, and made our way into the town. As the principal street continues straight in from the pier, we were shortly enabled to see all the principal buildings of the place.

Though a small shipping town, there seems to be a considerable amount of business doing at Auckland. There is a good market-place, some creditable bank buildings, and some three or four fine shops, but the streets are dirty and ill-paved. The Supreme Court and the Post Office—both fine buildings—lie off the principal street. The Governor's house, which occupies a hill to the right, commands a fine view of the bay, as well as of the lovely green valley behind it.

Auckland, like Sydney, being for the most part built upon high land, is divided by ravines, which open out towards the sea in little coves or bays—such as Mechanics' Bay, Commercial

The *Galatea* under anchor in Wellington Harbour. (G-533-1/1, W.J. Harding Collection, ATL)

Bay, and Official Bay. The buildings in Mechanics' Bay, as the name imports, are principally devoted to ship-building, boat-building, and rope-making. The shore of Commercial Bay is occupied by the store and shop-keeping people, while Official Bay is surrounded by the principal official buildings, the Government storehouses, and such like.

I have been told here that Auckland is completely out of place as the capital of the colony, being situated at the narrowest part of the island, far away from the principal seats of population, which are in Cook's Straits and even further south. The story is current that Auckland is due to an early job of Government officials, who combined to buy up the land about it, and when it had been fixed upon as the site of the capital, sold out their lots at fabulous prices, to the feathering of their own nests.

A great many natives, or Maoris, are hanging about the town. It seems that they are here in greater numbers than usual, their votes being wanted for the passing or confirmation of some land measure. Groups of them stand about the streets talking and gesticulating; a still greater number are hanging round the public-houses, which they enter from time to time to have a drink. I cannot say I like the look of the men; they look very ugly customers indeed—beetle-browed and down-looking, 'with foreheads villanous low'. Their appearance is all the more revolting by reason of the large blue circles of tattoo on their faces. Indeed, when the New Zealander is fully tattooed, which is the case with the old aristocrats, there is very little of his original face visible, excepting perhaps his nose and his bright black eyes.

Most of the men were dressed in the European costume, though some few were in their native blankets, which they wear with grace and even dignity. The men were of fine physique—tall, strong, and well-made—and, looking at their keen fierce eyes, I do not wonder that they have given our soldiers so much trouble. I could not help thinking, as I saw them hanging about the drinking-shops, some half drunk, that English drink will in the long run prove their conquerors far more than English rifles.

There were many Maori women mingled with the men. Some of them were good looking. Their skin is of a clear dark olive; their eyes dark brown or black; their noses small and their mouths large. But nearly all of them have a horrid blue tattoo mark on their lips, that serves to give them—at least to European eyes—a repulsive look.

Many of the women, as well as the men, wear a piece of native greenstone hanging from their ears, to which is attached a long piece of black ribbon. This stone is supposed by the Maoris to possess some magical virtue. Others of them—men, as well as girls—have sharks' teeth hanging from their ears and dangling about their faces,—the upper part of the teeth being covered with bright red wax.

Mixed with the Maoris were the sailors of the 'Galatea,' rolling about the streets, and, like them, frequent customers of the public-houses. In fact, the sailors and the Maoris seemed to form a considerable proportion of the population of the place.

[Master Smiles], *A Boy's Journey Around the World*, pp. 205–8.

Smells on board (1871)

[MASTER SMILES]

Master Smiles' visit to Auckland occurred as a stop on a voyage from Sydney to Honolulu. After leaving Auckland the trip to Honolulu took seventeen days. The monotony of life on board a steamer, with its regular progress and irritating passengers, was relieved by such activities as journal keeping. Master Smiles' table of the smells on board brings the steamer's physical character vividly to mind. The sentiments expressed by Master Smiles are offensively anti-semitic. I have included them to suggest something of the entrenched and distasteful attitudes of nineteenth-century travellers, which colour the world they reported.

THE FIRST NIGHT I slept on board I smelt something very disgusting as I got into my bunk; and at last I discovered that it arose from a dead rat in the wainscot of the ship. My nose being somewhat fastidious as yet, I moved to the other side of the cabin. But four kegs of strong smelling butter sent me quickly out of that. I then tried a bunk next to the German Jews, but I found proximity to them was the least endurable of all; and so after many changes, I at last came back and slept contentedly beside my unseen and most unsavoury companion, the dead rat.

But there are plenty of living and very lively rats too. One night a big fellow ran over my face, and in a fright I cried out. But use is everything, and in the course of a few more nights I got quite rid of my childish astonishment and fear at rats running over my face. Have you ever heard rats sing? I assure you they sing in a very lively chorus; though I confess I have heard much pleasanter music in my time.

Amidst all these little troubles, the ship went steadily on. During the second night, after leaving Auckland, the wind began to blow pretty fresh, and the hatch was closed. It felt very close and stuffy below, that night. The light went out, and the rats had it all their own way. On the following day, it was impossible to go on deck without getting wet through, so we were forced to stick down below. The rolling of the ship was also considerable.

Next day was fine, but hot. The temperature sensibly and even rapidly increases as we approach the Line. We see no land, though we have passed through amongst the Friendly Islands, with the Samoa or Navigator's Islands lying to the west. It is now a clear course to Honolulu. Not being able to go on deck in the heat of the day, at risk of sun-stroke, I wait until the sun has gone down, and then slip on deck with my rug and pillow, and enjoy a siesta under the stars. But sometimes I am disturbed by a squall, and have to take refuge below again.

As the heat increases, so do the smells on board. In passing from the deck to our cabin, I pass through seven distinct perfumes:—1st, the smell from the galley smoke; 2nd, the perfume of decaying vegetables stored on the upper deck; 3rd, fowls; 4th, dried fish; 5th, oil and steam from the engine-room; 6th, meat undergoing the process of cooking; 7th, the galley by which I pass; until I finally enter No. 8, our own sweet cabin, with the butter, the rats, and the German Jews.

[Master Smiles], *A Boy's Journey Around the World*, pp. 216–17.

Reception at the Ormonds (1872)

HENRY BROWN

Henry Brown's health was the reason for his decision to spend the summer and autumn of 1871–72 in Australia and New Zealand. His book is a diary that he posted home for his wife. Brown's friends and connections in New Zealand meant he spent time with pastoralists. He gives a glimpse of the social life in Hawkes Bay and the many links between rural New Zealand and the British upper class.

May 10*th*.—Lovely weather. Richardson took me down to the township, of six to eight hundred inhabitants, I should think; also to the Spit or shipping wharf, which is about a mile and a half from the township, introducing me to all and sundry, from the biggest wigs to the most insignificant in the place, taking me through all the Government offices as well, describing everything, and chaffing everybody in his usual amusing and humorous style, walking into people's offices and places of business, and chaffing them in the most cool manner possible, as if life here, whether in private business or Government Offices, was a kind of joke. He has got very stout, and promises fair to be a second edition of Brodie of Clairilaw, and, like most fat people, is very easy-going, jolly, amiable, and amusing. He is very fond of horses, and buys and sells in them largely, for the love of the thing as much as anything else, I think, and certainly does not look like a marrying man. Mrs Thomson is now sixty-nine, is a good deal aged since I last saw her, and has thinner cheeks, but, with very much the same old spirit, and is as interesting and amusing as ever; only, one can see that her coming to the Colony, and accepting its life, has not been to please or gratify herself, and, on the whole, has been looked upon as a mistake, even in spite of her daughter being comparatively so well off. She has no end of energy, and is very amusing with her Scotch, which is finer than ever, when she indulges in it, and which she speaks better than anyone I know of at home, by a long way, using words and expressions, which, for quaintness and originality, almost convulse one. Her whole heart and soul are in Hannah, Richardson, and the children, and to me she assumes the position of a mother *pro tem.*, just as of old; splendid chats we have together—Hannah, she, and I—on old days, friends, Scotch and London associations, &c., &c. Mrs Ormond is little changed, unless that she is much deafer, and hears only when one speaks very loudly. She is a very dutiful, busy housewife, and works hard with her children at their lessons, including Latin and music, her mother being as good as a head nurse to the establishment. Ladies do all sorts of household duties and work in the Colonies, and the two do not grudge putting out hands, although they have three servants, of the colonial class.

The Hon. J.D. Ormond, 1900. (B-094-022, ATL)

May 11*th*.—Weather lovely. Last night, Mrs Ormond had a reception in my honour, including the senior division of Hawkes Bay society. We began to receive at half-past seven o'clock, had music and conversation until ten, and wound up with a cold collation, fruit, wine, etc. The affair passed off most agreeably, and was thoroughly enjoyable—so many pleasant people, full of intelligence on things colonial, indeed, the *élite* of the town and province, including the old Bishop of Waiapu, his lady and daughters, Archdeacon Williams, the English clergyman and resident magistrate, with their wives, and also the leading settlers of the district and gentlemen of the township, with their wives and daughters, the honour of leading the way to the supper-room with the Bishop's lady having been accorded me. To-day, along with Mr Locke, the resident magistrate, Richardson, and little Geordie Ormond, a very sharp boy of twelve years, I rode out to a native pah, a distance of about twelve miles from Napier, where a transformation from the savage to the civilized Maori is taking place. The place is called Pakowhai, and is a settlement with a large tract of land attached, belonging to one of the tribes of Maoris, which, during the war, was a faithful ally of ours. There is here an English school with an English master, supported by Karaitiana the principal chief, sixty to seventy Maori boys attending it, and fast being taught to read and write English. He was from home, but we were received by his wife and brother, Henare Takamoana, a chief who distinguished himself more than any other in fighting the rebels, or Hau-Haus. We had a repast of roast pork, bread, butter, and preserved fruit, with brandy and water for a beverage, and were waited on by Karaitiana's wife and niece. Henare and I exchanged cards, and when he goes to England some day, with which prospect he is hard at work studying English, is to visit me. He promised to send me a Maori rug in return for a plaid I am to send him, and presented me with a specimen of Maori carving in wood, representing the neck of a calabash, also, a photograph of himself in uniform, with the sword in hand which was presented to him by Her Majesty the Queen of England, for his special bravery in the late war. [I may now mention here that he was as good as his word, and has sent me two beautiful specimens of Maori hand-made mats—our presents having crossed each other on the high seas.]

Sunday, May 12th.—Weather fine, and a quiet day. Morning at Scotch Church, evening at English.

May 13th.—Fine weather. Managed to extract a Maori Taiaha, or spear, from the resident magistrate, Mr Locke, one which was taken in 1869, at Waikare-Moana, from Te Waru, a Wairoa chief, and ally of Te Kooti during the great portion of Te Kooti's career. Locke has a very good collection of Maori trophies, and Richardson and I have exhausted every dodge to get some more of them from him, but, is very loath to part with them on any consideration whatever. Long walk, and made some calls with Mrs Ormond.

Henry Brown, *Diary During a Trip Round the World*, pp. 152–5.

Life on board the steamer (1872)

GEORGE CHAPMAN

George Thomson Chapman arrived in Port Chalmers in 1848 as a missionary for the Otago Association. He left again in the 1850s for the Victorian goldfields and returned to England. However, he came back to New Zealand in 1855, settling in Auckland, where he became a prominent bookseller and publisher, publishing about a hundred titles. He claimed his was the first guidebook to New Zealand and that it corrected 'no end of blunders' already published in 'almost every book' about New Zealand.

THERE IS SOMETIMES a good deal of amusement and fun on board the steamer, even sailing round the coast of New Zealand; for the wind does not always blow great guns; neither does the sea always jump mountains high. The weather for twelve or sometimes for twenty-four hours may be a little squally, and the sea may rise in beautifully crested waves or gentle ripples, just sufficient to make one feel inclined to sing 'I'm afloat,' &c.

The small steamers are particularly disagreeable; for should the wind blow, they will roll and tumble quite enough to frighten one. They bob up and down like a heavy cork, and make small progress, unless the wind, for sport, gets behind them. The saloons are straight and narrow, and as any number of passengers may be accommodated, these small steamers are never full; they seem to be licensed to carry all that come. The captain, purser, and steward try to please and accommodate everybody; should the cabins prove insufficient, there is room on the table, on the seats, or on the floor; and you are consoled with the soothing reflection—'It is only for a few days.' Sometimes, however, you will find these few days spent in a small, crowded, strong smelling steamer, to contain an allopathic dose of the concentrated essence of misery.

The large coasting steamers are more comfortable; in fact, unless you are fastidious, it is quite possible to be nearly happy, for no one will try to prevent you from enjoying yourself. You may have to complain of over-crowding; but this being such a common sin with these sons of salt water, they will appear perfectly shocked, that, in your opinion, there may be too many on board trying to be happy; and although the vessel may be rather full, one will still find room, more particularly in rough weather;—the passengers are then so quiet and gentle, one can do anything with them, but the greatest kindness one can confer is to let them alone.

In average weather one may grumble. This is expected. It begins about seven o'clock with, 'Steward, bring me a towel'; 'Steward, can you get me a cup of coffee,' &c.; it matters not, the steward is always ready and attentive; we have very seldom seen them uncivil or saucy. The bell or gong goes at half-past seven—notice to prepare for breakfast—at eight o'clock: sit down at table wherever one can find room. At noon the bell goes for lunch, at four for dinner, and at seven for tea; and at ten the cabin lights are—not always put out. So far, everything on board our favourite coasting steamers looks simple enough and straightforward. A passenger will have plenty to eat, and he may have as much drink as he pleases to call and pay for.

There is no place like 'a life on the ocean wave' to study character; newly-married couples, aye, and old hands too, how affectionate and attentive about each other's welfare. The young ladies, we beg pardon, we mean the young men, on their first excursion, are perfectly swellish, seem to know everything, and are so communicative. But the old bachelor, he is perfectly happy, give him just two hours in the morning to adjust his necktie.

One stage of the voyage round New Zealand we had Governor Sir George Bowen on board. It was Sunday, and a most beautiful day. Although sailors are not proverbial for an over-strict observance of one day in seven, landsmen when at sea, looking around, then feel that without an Almighty power to direct and guide the wind, the wave, and the little vessel, there would be no Sabbath peace or comfort. At breakfast the Governor did not appear, perhaps he was sick, and had breakfast in his cabin. It seemed to be generally expected that he would ask some of the passengers to engage in religious service, to show that at least we were professing Christians; but lunch time came, he sat down with us, and was very polite and pleasant; afterwards he went on deck, and walked and talked till dinner-time when he sat down by the captain, who, as usual, spun some stiff yarns. Two of his Yankee tales only we remember:—'A farmer in Los Angelos had a farm of 200 acres, which he dug with a spade, planted, and reaped, all by himself, and carried the produce to San Francisco!' 'One old woman, he knew her perfectly well, when she was a girl, 80 years ago, planted a vine cutting, it had never been pruned, and it now covered two or three acres of ground.' He was going to tell us how many tons of grapes it had yielded yearly, but the 'silver toned' voice of the Hon. Dillon Bell, addressing a gentleman at the adjoining table stopped the captain. 'I am the oldest civil servant in the Government, and as such, had a right to expect the highest honour the colony had at its disposal.'

G.T. Chapman, *Chapman's Travellers Guide through New Zealand*, pp. 93–5.

Dinner from a Maori oven (1872)

J. ERNEST TINNE

An Old Etonian and Oxford graduate, J. Ernest Tinne came to New Zealand to help his brother establish a flax mill in Northland. His visit to Rotorua and Rotomahana in 1872 is described partly to encourage sightseers and immigrants to come to these 'recently disaffected districts'. Tinne returned home via North America and gives advice about routes and modes of travel.

SHOOTING THE RAPIDS at precipitous speed, and amid intense excitement of all but the old steersman, who sat immovably at the stern, like a tattooed statue in bronze, we were soon floating on the broad bosom of Tarawera. We landed in one of the little bays, and after mooring our canoes under the shade of some gigantic pohutakawas, whose knotted arms make the best possible 'elbows and knees' for shipbuilders' work, we watched with some interest the preparation of our food in a genuine copu-maori, or native oven. This was done as follows: the women scraped a hole in the soft ground with their hands, and filled it with dry wood, to which they set a light. On the top of the blazing fire they placed stones about the size of a man's two fists, which became heated and dropped through as the fuel burnt out. Then having collected fish, potatoes, and a few squashes, which we found in the deserted settlement hard by, they brought a good-sized pannikin of fresh water, dashed it over the stones, and, before the steam had time to escape, filled the hole in with the provisions. On the top of these a clean kit, or hand-bag of woven native flax, was placed; then some armfuls of fresh-cut fern, and lastly a pretty thick layer of soft mould, which they patted down till there was no aperture by which the vapour could escape. In about twenty minutes the cooking was complete, and we sat down to a frugal but most delicious repast of steamed food, which I thought much superior to the usual boiled vegetables of an English cuisine. We coaxed some of the little children into friendship by letting them drink the oil from our sardine-tins when we had eaten the fish; but they evidently looked upon us as a kind of white-faced ogres, whom it was prudent to keep at a respectful distance. One little pickle of a fellow, with bright black eyes, who had quite overcome his terror, amused himself by creeping up behind the others, and frightening them by shouting in their ear, 'Nui pakeha, nui pakeha' (the big white man, the big white man) 'is coming'—meaning me; at which they would burst into tears and run like rabbits from the supposed cannibal—your humble servant. They had evidently been taught the same cock-and-bull stories that English nurses often inflict on their charges, of the giants that eat naughty children, only that here the case was reversed, and instead of the 'big black man' in the myths of our infancy, our pale-faces produced a similar effect on them.

We held a 'drawing-room' at Kariri that evening, in a small hut of 8 feet by 18, with a small aperture (misnamed a door), through which I could scarcely drag myself even when prostrate. Imagine the state of the atmosphere, with a smoky fire of green wood, no chimney, and about twenty Maori ladies and children all smoking furiously at their pipes, and nearly a hundred-weight of green tobacco steaming on the walls preparatory to use!

I had heard a good deal of the fresh-water cray-fish (goura) that are found in these lakes, and asked whether I could have some of them. My wish was soon gratified, but my equanimity was a good deal disturbed, for when a kit of them was produced, instead of letting me shell them myself, an old hag, with very dirty fingers, seated herself opposite to me and proffered her services. A sense of etiquette forbade me to decline, so I screwed up my courage and held out a biscuit for her to lay the first slippery morsel upon. It went down pretty easily, and when she had given us two or three dozen, like the Greek travellers of old, '*mensas etiam consumpsimus*,' we even ate our temporary plates as a finale to the repast.

J. Ernest Tinne, The Wonderland of the Antipodes, pp. 15–17.

Antipodean remoteness (1872)

ANTHONY TROLLOPE

The visit of eminent Victorian novelist Anthony Trollope to Australia and New Zealand in 1872 attracted large audiences and much publicity. His entertaining account of his travels was widely read and often referred to by other writers.

I FOUND MYSELF STRUCK, for a moment, with the peculiarity of being in New Zealand. To Australia generally I had easily reconciled myself, as being a part of the British Empire. Of New South Wales and Van Diemen's Land I had heard so early in life, as to have become quite used to them,—so that I did not think myself to be very far from home when I got there. But New Zealand had come up in my own days, and there still remained to me something of the feeling of awful distance with which at that time I regarded the young settlements at the Antipodes,—for New Zealand is, of all inhabited lands, the most absolutely Antipodean to Greenwich. I remembered the first appearance in public of the grim jokes attributed to Sydney Smith, as to the cold curate, and the hope expressed that Bishop Selwyn might disagree with the cannibal who should eat him. The colony still retained for me something of the mysterious vagueness with which it was enveloped in early days,—so that when landing at The Bluff I thought that I had done something in the way of travelling. Melbourne had been no more than New York, hardly more than Glasgow, certainly not so much as Vienna. But if I could find myself in a Maori pah,—then indeed the flavour of the dust of Pall Mall would for the time depart from me altogether. Most travellers have experienced the feeling,— have anticipated a certain strangeness which they have never quite achieved. But when I reached Invercargill, the capital of Southland, I felt exactly as I might have felt on getting out of a railway in some small English town, and by the time I had reached the inn, and gone through the customary battle as to bedrooms, a tub of cold water, and supper, all the feeling of mystery was gone. I began to inquire the price of tea and sugar, and the amounts of wages which men were earning;—but had no longer any appreciation for my Antipodean remoteness from the friends of my youth.

Anthony Trollope, *Australia and New Zealand*, pp. 321–2.

Travelling by winter in Otago (1872)

ANTHONY TROLLOPE

Trollope arrived at Bluff in 1872 after a year in Australia. On landing he 'immediately asked to be shown some Maoris' but was told they were scarce in Southland, and 'it seemed I might as well have asked for a Moa'. His sense of remoteness related to his historical contiguity with the establishment of New Zealand as a colony at the farthest point of the British Empire. Travelling from Queenstown to Dunedin, the intensity of Otago's winter climate surprised him.

CORRUGATED IRON DOES NOT make picturesque houses. Probably my readers all know the thin fluted material of which I speak, drawn out so fine that it can be cut like cloth with a pair of shears. It is very portable; very easily shaped; capable of quick construction; and it keeps out the rain. It is, however, subject to drawbacks. The rooms formed of it of course are small, and every word uttered in the house can be heard throughout it, as throughout a shed put up without divisions. And yet the owners and frequenters of these iron domiciles seem never to be aware of the fact. As I lay in bed in one of these metal inns of the road, I was constrained to hear the private conversation of my host and hostess who had retired for the night. 'So this is Mr Anthony Trollope,' said the host. The hostess assented, but I could gather clearly from her voice that she was thinking much more of her back hair than of her visitor. 'Well,' said the host, 'he must be a —— fool to come travelling in this country in such weather as this.' Perhaps, after all, the host was aware of the peculiarity of his house, and thought it well that I should know his opinion. He could not have spoken any words with which at that moment I should have been more prone to agree.

On the fifth day,—the worst of all, for the snow fell incessantly, the wretched horses could not drag us through the mud, so that I and the gentleman with me were forced to walk, and the twelve miles which we accomplished took us five hours,—we reached the town of Tuapika, whence we were assured there would run a well-appointed coach to Dunedin. Tuapika is otherwise called Lawrence,—and it may be as well here to remark that in this part of New Zealand all towns have two names. The colonists give one,—sometimes, as in the case of Taupika, taking that of the natives,—and the government gives another. We had come through Dunedin alias Clyde, through Teeviot alias Roxburgh, through Beaumont which had some other name which I have forgotten, and at last reached Tuapika alias Lawrence. The rivers and districts have been served in the same way, and as the different names are used miscellaneously, the difficulty which travellers always feel as to new localities is considerably enhanced. At Tuapika

A small tent hotel in the Taranaki district. (G-22156-1/2, ATL)

we found an excellent inn, and a very good dinner. In spite of the weather I went round the town, and visited the Athenaeum or reading-room. In all these towns there are libraries, and the books are strongly bound and well thumbed. Carlyle, Macaulay, and Dickens are certainly better known to small communities in New Zealand than they are to similar congregations of men and women at home. I should have liked Tuapika had it not snowed so bitterly on me when I was there.

On the following day we got on board the well-appointed coach at six in the morning. It certainly was a well-appointed coach, and was driven by as good a coachman as ever sat upon a box; but the first stage, which took us altogether six hours, was not memorable for good fortune. There was a lower new road and an upper old road. The former was supposed to be impracticable because of the last night's snow, and the nam decided on taking the hills. As far as I could see we were traversing a mountain-side without any track; but there was a track, for on a sudden, as we turned a corner, we found ourselves in a cutting, and we found also that the cutting was blocked with snow. The coach could not be turned, and the horses had plunged in so far that we could with difficulty extricate them from the traces and pole-straps.

The driver, however, decided on going on. Shovels were procured, and for two hours we all worked up to our hips in snow, and did at last get the coach through the cutting. But it was not practicable to drive the horses down the hill we had ascended, and we therefore took them out and brought it down by hand,—an operation which at any rate kept us warm. We had hardly settled into our seats after this performance, before one of the wheelers slipped into a miner's water-run, and pulled the other horse under the pole atop of him. The under horse was, as it were, packed into the gully and buried, with his brother over him, like a tombstone. So we went to work again with the shovels, and dug out first one animal and then the other. We were wet through, and therefore a good deal the worse for our task, but the horses did not seem to mind it. At last we reached the town of Tokomairiro, alias Milton, where comforts of all kinds awaited us. In the first place there was a made road into Dunedin, and a well-horsed coach to take us. We had descended below the level on which the snows were lying. My wife found a kind hostess who took her to a fire and comforted her with dry stockings, and I got some dinner and brandy-and-water. About eight in the evening we reached Dunedin, alive, in fair spirits,—but very tired, and more ready than ever to agree with that up-country inn-keeper who had thought but little of the wisdom of one who had come travelling by winter in Otago.

Anthony Trollope, *Australia and New Zealand*, pp. 335–8.

Bathing at the Pink Terraces (1872)

ANTHONY TROLLOPE

Trollope had heard a lot about the 'hot-water territory' before coming to New Zealand but was a comparatively early visitor to Rotorua and its region. There was no road to the 'Lake District' in 1872, and some of the route was on horseback along the beach from Tauranga to Maketu. After a complicated and tiring journey Trollope thought there was 'nothing pretty' at Ohinemutu, but he found that the Pink and White Terraces lived up to their reputation.

THE BATHER UNDRESSES on a piece of dry rock a few yards distant, and is in his bath in half a minute without the chance of hurting his feet,—for it is one of the properties of the stone flooring which has here been formed that it does not hurt. In the bath, when you strike your chest against it, it is soft to the touch,—you press yourself against it and it is smooth,—you lie about upon it and, though it is firm, it gives to you. You plunge against the sides, driving

People in the hot pools at the Pink Terraces, Rotomahana. (F-37712-1/2, ATL)

the water over with your body, but you do not bruise yourself. You go from one bath to another, trying the warmth of each. The water trickles from the one above to the one below, coming from the vast boiling pool at the top, and the lower therefore are less hot than the higher. The baths are shell-like in shape,—like vast open shells, the walls of which are concave and the lips of which ornamented in a thousand forms. Four or five may sport in one of them, each without feeling the presence of the other. I have never heard of other bathing like this in the world.

And from the pink terraces, as you lie in the water, you look down upon the lake which is close beneath you, and over upon the green broken hills which come down upon the lake. The scene here, from the pink terraces, is by far the lovelier, though the white terraces themselves are grander in their forms. It is a spot for intense sensual enjoyment, and there comes perhaps some addition to the feeling from the roughness you have encountered in reaching it;—a delight in dallying with it, from the roughness which you must encounter in leaving it. The time probably will soon come in which there will be a sprightly hotel at Roto Mahana, with a table d'hôte, and boats at so much an hour, and regular seasons for bathing. As I lay there, I framed the programme of such a hotel in my mind,—and I did so, fixing the appropriate spot as I squatted in the water, and calculating how much it would cost and what return it would give. I was somewhat troubled by the future bathing arrangements. To enclose the various basins would spoil them altogether to the eye. To dabble about in vestments arranged after some French fashion would spoil the bathing to the touch. And yet it must be open to men and women alike. The place lies so broad to the world's eye that I fear no arrangement as to hours, no morning for the gentlemen and evening for the ladies, would suffice. Alas, for the old Maori simplicity and perfect reliance on the royal adage! The ladies, indeed, might have the pink, and the men the white terraces; but the intervening lake would discourage social intercourse,—and there would be interlopers and intruders who might break through the 'tapu' of modern propriety. After bathing we went to the top, and walked round the hot spring from which the water descends. It has formed a lake about a quarter of a mile in circumference, the waters of which are constantly boiling, and are perfectly blue. In the centre it is said to be many feet deep. The colour is lovely, but in order to see it we had to get behind the wind, so that the steam should not be blown into our faces. As we came down we found parts of the crusted floor perfectly yellow with pure sulphur, and parts of the fretted stonework on the under curves of the rocks, where they were not exposed to the light, as perfectly green. Then there were huge masses brightly salmon-coloured, and here and there delicately-white fretwork, and the lips and sides of the baths were tinted with that delicate pink hue which we are apt to connect with soft luxury.

Anthony Trollope, *Australia and New Zealand*, pp. 483–5.

A pleasure trip (1872)

H.B. MORTON

Henry Morton emigrated to New Zealand in 1863 with the Albertland settlers in the Tyburnia. *He became a successful merchant, and was interested in New Zealand history and ethnology.* Notes of a New Zealand Tour *is the record of an overland journey to the Rotorua district in 1872.*

THE TIME AT MY DISPOSAL would not admit of my visiting Otago, so taking passage by the Rangatira for Wellington, we started about seven o'clock in the evening, and after exchanging hurrahs with the ship Lady Jocelyn, to sail the next morning for England, cleared Lyttelton Heads. It is impossible here to refrain from commenting for a moment upon the misery of the next 24 hours. The Rangatira was advertised for an excursion trip, and the fares reduced to one minimum rate throughout the ship. Notwithstanding this a number of gentlemen and

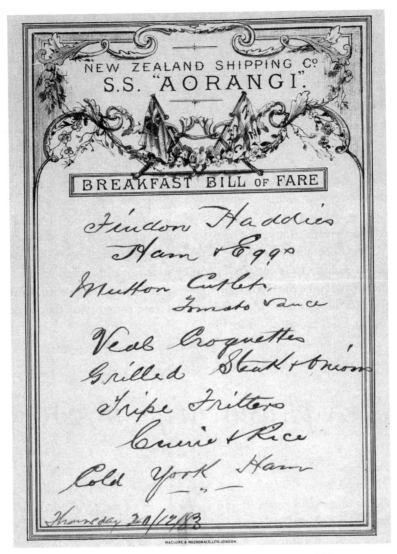

Breakfast menu from New Zealand Shipping Co.'s SS *Aorangi*, 1883.
(C-23433-1/2, ATL)

one or two ladies, with whom time was an object, were compelled to avail themselves of the opportunity of getting to Wellington. The maximum number of passengers the steamer is certificated to carry at sea is 56, but on this occasion there were over 70; and as these included several women of the lowest class and a number of roughs who practically monopolised the saloon, the discomfort that ensued was such as one might expect to find on a Fiji labor vessel, but certainly not on a certificated passenger vessel on the New Zealand coast. The filth and stink on all sides were insupportable, and these remarks are penned in deference to a general desire on the part of many of the passengers. The directors of the N.Z.S.S. Company deserve every credit for their enterprise in purchasing the *Taranaki*, and subsequently the other vessels of their fleet, but that enterprise has been abundantly rewarded. Their late dividends have been almost unprecedented, save in gold-mining companies; and now if they turn round and render the movements of their boats a matter of caprice, omit to advise their various agents when to expect them, and ignore the comfort of their passengers for the sake of a trifling gain, Nemesis will overtake them, and a well-organized opposition has only to be started in order to secure a firm footing on the coast. The longest lane has a turning, and so this miserable trip had a termination.

H.B. Morton, *Notes of a New Zealand Tour*, pp. 11–12.

Overland to Taranaki (1872)

H.B. MORTON

Morton's comments on the Native Land Courts—something a number of tourists comment on, especially around Rotorua and Tauranga—are interesting, especially his view of who attended them and his allegation that many of the Pakeha-Maoris were exploitative ex-convicts.

DECIDING TO PROCEED overland to Taranaki, I found that a coach left Wellington twice a week, and accomplished the journey, a distance of 270 miles, in four days. The first day's ride to Foxton lies through a country almost utterly devoid of interest, excepting a few miles of forest scenery at the commencement of the day. The remainder of the day is spent in traversing the sea beach or drifting sandhills, and the small fringe of level land from the base of the mountains to the sea appears to be of very little value. Now and then one comes upon a small cultivation; a veritable oasis in the desert; such, for instance, as the mission station at Otaki; but just outside this life ceases, and the coach-wheels are buried half way to the axles in hot sand. In passing I may remark that this drifting sand is causing much havoc all round the western coast of the North Island, and is continually encroaching upon good land, and rendering it useless. The little township of Foxton, situated in the Manawatu river, amidst the sand hills, showed signs of considerable liveliness on the night of our arrival. A Native Lands Court was sitting in the vicinity, and the hotel was thronged with Maories, accompanied by those white harpies who, known as pakeha-Maories, follow the natives on every side, drinking at their expense and filling their minds with all manner of evil counsel. At tea-time I observed an old gentleman of this class, who I afterwards learned had been forwarded to Australia many years ago under the auspices of the Imperial Government—I observed this old gentleman take up a roast fowl and pull it asunder with his hands. This led me to remark that his method of dividing poultry was unusual, as I did not remember to have seen it practised before. It was his way, he said; and on my replying that it was so much the worse for the person who was served after him, he merely said that he didn't care a naughty word for anybody; if they didn't like it, he would eat the lot, as he always paid twenty shillings in the pound. During the evening the Maories and their satellites became very much intoxicated, after which they discussed the events of the day with considerable vehemence. This was continued with variations till early next morning. Among other incidents of the evening, I remember there was a domestic squabble between our host and hostess. The old gentleman had an attack of *delirium tremens*, and the gentleman in the next bedroom, a Wesleyan local preacher, recited his prayers in a stentorian voice; various other gentlemen became inebriated, and burnt cork was used to improve their facial expression. The excitement continued the following morning. As the up-coach to Wellington was crossing the Manawatu river, at 5 o'clock, the horses suddenly became restive, and dashed off the punt into ten feet of water. The coach contained several lady passengers and young children, and loss of life appeared imminent; but by the promptitude of those on board the punt the whole of the passengers were rescued, apparently little the worse for their wetting.

H.B. Morton, *Notes of a New Zealand Tour*, pp. 13–15.

On the Nevada in a hurricane (1873)

ISABELLA BIRD

One of the most famous Victorian female travellers, Isabella Bird, later Mrs Bishop, began travelling in 1854 for health reasons. The Englishwoman in America, *based on her letters, provided the successful formula for her later books about Hawaii and Japan. She visited New Zealand briefly on her way up the Pacific to Hawaii in 1872–73.*

A WHITE, UNWINKING, SCINTILLATING SUN blazed down upon Auckland, New Zealand. Along the white glaring road from Onehunga, dusty trees and calla lilies drooped with the heat. Dusty thickets sheltered the cicada, whose triumphant din grated and rasped through the palpitating atmosphere. In dusty enclosures, supposed to be gardens, shrivelled geraniums scattered sparsely alone defied the heat. Flags drooped in the stifling air. Men on the verge of sunstroke plied their tasks mechanically, like automatons. Dogs, with flabby and protruding tongues, hid themselves away under archway shadows. The stones of the sidewalks and the brick of the houses radiated a furnace heat. All nature was limp, dusty, groaning, gasping. The day was the climax of a burning fortnight, of heat, draught, and dust, of baked, cracked, dewless land, and oily breezeless seas, of glaring days, passing through fierce fiery sunsets into stifling nights.

I only remained long enough in the capital to observe that it had a look of having seen better days, and that its business streets had an American impress, and, taking a boat at a wharf, in whose seams the pitch was melting, I went off to the steamer *Nevada*, which was anchored out in the bay, preferring to spend the night in her than in the unbearable heat on shore. She belongs to the Webb line, an independent mail adventure, now dying a natural death, undertaken by the New Zealand Government, as much probably out of jealousy of Victoria as anything else. She nearly foundered on her last voyage; her passengers unanimously signed a protest against her unseaworthy condition. She was condemned by the Government surveyor, and her mails were sent to Melbourne. She has, however, been patched up for this trip, and eight passengers, including myself, have trusted ourselves to her. She is a huge paddle-steamer, of the old-fashioned American type, deck above deck, balconies, a pilot-house abaft the foremast, two monstrous walking beams, and two masts which, possibly in case of need, might serve as jury masts.

Huge, airy, perfectly comfortable as she is, not a passenger stepped on board without breathing a more earnest prayer than usual that the voyage might end propitiously. The very first evening statements were whispered about to the effect that her state of disrepair is such that she has not been to her own port for nine months, and has been sailing for that time without a certificate; that her starboard shaft is partially fractured, and that to reduce the strain upon it the floats of her starboard wheel have been shortened five inches, the strain being further reduced by giving her a decided list to port; that her crank is 'bandaged', that she is leaky, that her mainmast is sprung, and that with only four hours' steaming many of her boiler tubes, even some of those put in at Auckland, had already given way. I cannot testify concerning the mainmast, though it certainly does comport itself like no other mainmast I ever saw; but the other statements and many more which might be added, are, I believe, substantially correct. That the caulking of the deck was in evil case we very soon had proof, for during heavy rain above, it was a smart shower in the saloon and state rooms, keeping four stewards employed with buckets and swabs, and compelling us to dine in waterproofs and rubber shoes.

In this dilapidated condition, when two days out from Auckland, we encountered a revolving South Sea hurricane, succinctly entered in the log of the day as 'Encountered a very severe

C & NZ mail steamer *Nevada*, 1870s? (B-089-003, ATL)

hurricane with a very heavy sea.' It began at eight in the morning, and never spent its fury till nine at night, and the wind changed its direction eleven times. The *Nevada* left Auckland two feet deeper in the water than she ought to have been, and laboured heavily. Seas struck her under the guards with a heavy, explosive *thud*, and she groaned and strained as if she would part asunder. It was a long weird day. We held no communication with each other, or with those who could form any rational estimate of the probabilities of our destiny; no officials appeared; the ordinary invariable routine of the steward department was suspended without notice; the sounds were tremendous, and a hot lurid obscurity filled the atmosphere. Soon after four the clamour increased, and the shock of a sea blowing up a part of the fore-guards made the groaning fabric reel and shiver throughout her whole huge bulk. At that time, by common consent, we assembled in the deck-house, which had windows looking in all directions, and sat there for five hours. Very few words were spoken, and very little fear was felt. We understood by intuition that if our crazy engines failed at any moment to keep the ship's head to the sea, her destruction would not occupy half-an-hour. It was all palpable. There was nothing which the most experienced seaman could explain to the merest novice. We hoped for the best, and there was no use in speaking about the worst. Nor, indeed, was speech possible, unless a human voice could have outshrieked the hurricane.

In this deck-house the strainings, sunderings, and groanings were hardly audible, or rather were overpowered by a sound which, in thirteen months' experience of the sea in all weathers, I have never heard, and hope never to hear again, unless in a staunch ship, one loud, awful, undying shriek, mingled with a prolonged relentless hiss. No gathering strength, no languid fainting into momentary lulls, but one protracted gigantic scream. And this was not the whistle of wind through cordage, but the actual sound of air travelling with tremendous velocity, carrying with it minute particles of water. Nor was the sea running mountains high, for the hurricane kept it down. Indeed during those fierce hours no sea was visible, for the whole surface was caught up and carried furiously into the air, like snow-drift on the prairies, sibilant, relentless. There was profound quiet on deck, the little life which existed being concentrated near the bow, where the captain was either lashed to the foremast, or in shelter in the pilot-house. Never a soul appeared on deck, the force of the hurricane being such that for four hours any man would have been carried off his feet. Through the swift strange evening our hopes rested on the engine, and amidst the uproar and din, and drifting spray, and shocks of pitiless seas, there was a sublime repose in the spectacle of the huge walking beams, alternately rising and falling, slowly, calmly, regularly, as if the *Nevada* were on a holiday trip within the Golden Gate. At eight in the evening we could hear each other speak, and a little later, through the great masses of hissing drift we discerned black water. At nine Captain Blethen appeared, smoking a cigar with nonchalance, and told us that the hurricane had nearly boxed the compass, and had been the most severe he had known for seventeen years. This grand old man, nearly the oldest captain in the Pacific, won our respect and confidence from the first, and his quiet and masterly handling of this dilapidated old ship is beyond all praise.

When the strain of apprehension was mitigated, we became aware that we had not had anything to eat since breakfast, a clean sweep having been made, not only of the lunch, but of all the glass in the racks above it; but all requests to the stewards were insufficient to procure even biscuits, and at eleven we retired supperless to bed, amidst a confusion of awful sounds, and were deprived of lights as well as food. When we asked for food or light, and made weak appeals on the ground of faintness, the one steward who seemed to dawdle about for the sole purpose of making himself disagreeable, always replied, 'you can't get anything, the stewards are on duty.' We were not accustomed to recognize that stewards had any other duty than that of feeding the passengers, but under the circumstances we meekly acquiesced. We were allowed to know that a part of the foreguards had been carried way, and that iron stanchions four inches thick had been gnarled and twisted like candy sticks, and the constant falling of the saloon casing of the mainmast, showed something wrong there. A heavy clang, heard at intervals by day and night, aroused some suspicions as to more serious damage, and these were afterwards confirmed. As the wind fell the sea rose, and for some hours realized every description I have read of the majesty and magnitude of the rollers of the South Pacific.

Isabella Bird, *The Hawaiian Archipelago*, pp. 6–11.

A wild new country (1873)

HENRY SCOTT

Henry Scott emigrated to New Zealand as a young man seized with wanderlust. He landed at Port Chalmers in 1873, and his lively Reminiscences *describe his early work and travels in Otago and Southland.*

Two days in Sydney and a fortnight in Melbourne elapsed before I could be sent across to New Zealand, but at last, after a beautiful passage of four and a half days in the S.S. Albion, whose bones now lie in Taylor's Bay, Sydney, with the genial companionship of Captain McLean (better known in those days as 'Hell-Fire Jock') and his officers, I landed in Port Chalmers on October 8th, 1873, with a few letters of introduction to business people and a burning desire for further adventures.

I had not to wait until I landed in New Zealand to find that some of the ideas of my new home, as assimilated from pamphlets obtained at the office of Shaw, Savill and Co., would have to be considerably modified. For instance, I learned from those valuable (?) publications that there was little or no snow in New Zealand, and behold! my first glimpse of land showed me a beautiful panorama of snow-capped mountains. I don't think I was much disappointed at that, but when I arrived at Port Chalmers and found I was to travel to Dunedin in a common, everyday railway train, a lot of the romance I had been indulging in about a wild, new country, where savages roamed the plains and skulked in the forests, and where I should carry my life in my hands day and night, said life to be desperately defended by means of a heavy Colt revolver strapped uncomfortably to my person (this weapon had been solemnly presented to me before leaving home, and was about the only thing I saved out of the wreck), began to dissolve within me, and a deep regret for the fate of a couple of suits of evening clothes lost in the destruction of the cabin on the Dallam Tower, began to overtake me.

Colt revolvers and dress suits are somewhat paradoxical, but while the former was presented to me for personal defence, I was instructed to take the latter because a lady friend of one of my lady friends resided at a place called Wellington, and as I was going to Dunedin I was to be sure and run over and dine with them on Sundays—'and you know, Harry, they always dress for dinner.' I promised, in the innocence of my heart, to do this impossible thing, but made excuses in my first letter Home.

Henry Scott, *Reminiscences of a New Chum in Otago in the Early Seventies*, pp. 11–12.

Rowing on the Avon (c. 1875)

W. LITTLE

A commercial traveller in farm supplies, W. Little described his account of his visit to North America, Australia, and New Zealand as a 'Collection of Notes of Impressions'. Round the World *is a mixture of business and sightseeing, and it gives a vivid impression of the life and attitudes of a 'Commercial' in the 1870s.*

MOUNTAINS ARE CLEARLY VISIBLE all round the plain on which Christchurch stands except on the sea-side to the north-east; the nearest are those which separate the town from Port Lyttleton and they are only about four miles distant. The land round the town varies in price from £8 to £40 per acre, according to its position, condition and nature. Town lots for building fetch £20 to £30 a section (quarter of an acre) and sales are continually going on: house property is also high in price and a really good house cannot be rented under £60 to £80 per annum. Money in the colonies has a very different value from what it has at home: eight per cent interest for a lengthened term of years may be got anywhere with absolute security; this is the general rate and every person I have spoken to on this subject assures me of the same thing. Ten per cent may be got with about the same security as six per cent at home. Money is wanted everywhere, I heard of many instances where money had been borrowed on landed property and the term of years having run out the land became the property of the lender being valued at three times the amount of the loan. Horses are very cheap. I was watching an auction of some at the Christchurch Tatersall's one morning and saw several sold at £20, handsome horses, which would if sound have made five times as much at home: for driving, gigs, dog-carts, broughams, barouches and buggies are chiefly used but I think the two first most. Bicycles are tolerably frequent too of the best makes. My intention on leaving Christchurch has been to cross the country with the coach to Hokatika on the west coast as the route lies through some of the finest scenery in the islands, but I gave it up with regret although I had telegraphed for a box seat for it is a costly journey and would not have been very profitable, besides, I had to risk catching a boat at Hokatika or having to remain there a week, so I contented myself with a run over the country with the railway to Amberley the last station on the line running over the plain to the north of Christchurch. On the Saturday evening Mr Dombrain suggested a row on the river so I went down with him to his lodging in the town for tea, and three of us started. Number three being a young man lodging in the house, by name Meadowcroft. We got a light pair oar at the boating club and were soon pulling down as picturesque a river as can be seen anywhere in a flat country; it winds about a good deal and there was some little stream running. Were it not for the narrow leaved flax plants growing on the banks it would be impossible to say that one was not on a river at home. Near the town it passes between gardens with little boat-houses on the water's edge and rows of weeping willows which give a beautiful effect: there were plenty of people on the water besides ourselves, some in family tubs with children, others pulling for their lives in out-riggers in jerseys and tights. The river is not broad but there is generally comfortable room for two eights to pass: further down the river opens out and it runs through meadows and agri-cultural country. It was a pleasant evening and we pulled a long way down getting more thirsty at every stroke. Meadowcroft knew of a public some miles down and we set to to reach it intending to return at once. On the way we came across a young retriever which had got fast in the mud and weeds at the side and the poor thing had evidently been struggling at that place for several hours for he was smothered with mud and nearly done: I pulled him out and let go of him but as he sank twice was obliged to take him into the boat again to land him when we arrived. After a long row we reached the little public at last and shandygaffs flowed steadily for some time: it was now rather late and on inquiry we found that it was only two miles further to New Brighton on the sea shore where there was a good Hotel. Meadowcroft did not want to go on as he was courting one of the landlady's daughters at the lodgings where he lived and was afraid she would be anxious about him: at the moment however, whilst we were discussing the propriety of returning, a stranger turned up who was going to the town on foot and promised to take a letter up with him. This settled we started again and in half-an-hour were at the landing stage of the Hotel: we pulled the boat up onto the bank taking the oars and skulls along with us. About half-a-mile from the stage down a sandy road stood a neat little Hotel right on the sea beach with sand all round it: the landlord relieved Meadowcroft of the oars and showed us into the sitting room where we soon settled down to a game of whist with him as a fourth as it was still early: his wife and niece soon came in and together with some whisky and a piano in the corner of the room we got very festive espe-cially my mates who having been long enough in the colonies to have mastered the art of guz-zling down an innumerable succession of drinks one after another, soon became somewhat elated and not being so highly educated as themselves in this respect and feeling too sleepy to sit and look at them I soon retired leaving them to their own devices. The Hotel like most others in this country had been built with a view to the future by some speculative genius: there are plenty of good bed rooms, a good entrance hall, and large rooms below. At present there is only one other house in the vicinity, but this spot will no doubt some day become a sea-side resort for the overworked Christchurchers of the future. We were all up early in the morning and had a bathe amongst the breakers on the flat shore which they call ninety mile beach on account of its length. When we had settled up with mine host and were in the boat again we did not turn her head up stream at once but rowed several miles down into the estu-ary till the water became so broken that we could not go further for fear of swamping the boat.

It was a long pull back again and we did not reach Christchurch till five o'clock in the evening, finding no one at the boat house to take the money or the boat. The whole way along we had come across wild duck in great numbers, some with families of half-a-dozen ducklings swiming amongst the reeds and all of them apparently as tame as the domestic variety: this was the closed time and I understand they do not remain in the river long when it is open again. I took a return ticket to Amberley, the next day, the last station on the line running northward of Christchurch, and intended some day to connect it with Blenheim in Marlborough. Amberley is situated under the northern range of mountains skirting the plain and is not far from the Marlborough boundary. The journey was one of two hours about and several hours to spend when I got there. There are only two classes on the New Zealand trains, most people travel first and only the agricultural community second: I took a second class ticket and sat next a Maori 'lady' with two children. All the natives in this island dress themselves in European toggery and when they happen to be of pure blood they occasionally present very ludicrous figures. My fellow passenger was a huge bony female as strong as a man; her face was not at all like that of a nigger but was a good sample of the Maori physiognomy: a long straight nose, small eyes, square forehead and large mouth and chin: she was dressed in a black stuff dress, small round black straw hat and with her head off had the appearance of a strong English servant: in a gold broach at her throat was the photo of some white gentleman of her acquaintance with blonde whiskers and hair parted in the middle; her children were not half-castes and had a greater resemblance to the African than their mamma, altogether she appeared to be good natured enough and was continually holding her children up to look out of the window, the latter were tolerably well dressed with clean linen bonnets on and looked like little black puppies dressed for a joke. The other passengers were either labourers, young girls, and small farmers.

W. Little, *Round the World*, pp. 90–3.

The first concert party in Popotunoa (1876)

DAVID KENNEDY JNR

Son of a professional singer, David Kennedy Jnr wrote regular articles for the Edinburgh papers during the Kennedy Family's tour singing songs of Scotland in the colonies in the early 1870s. The articles became Kennedy's Colonial Travel. *The book was republished with a memoir of David Kennedy in 1887 as* David Kennedy: The Scottish Singer.

WE HAD THE HONOUR of giving the first concert ever held in Popotunoa. The receipts went to help a young kirk. The 'hall' was the barn of a neighbouring sheep-station. The seats were planks laid upon bags of grain, and an open loft, filled with sacks of chaff, served as gallery. On the platform, which was a few boards covered with carpet, stood a table with a globe-lamp, and on our small travelling-piano bloomed a neat bouquet of flowers. The audience soon assembled. We saw the folks coming across the moorland, through the long grass—men, women, lads, lasses, mothers, children, shepherds, servants, and people on horseback. Every few moments we heard the far-off thud of hoofs—then a head would appear over the brow of a gentle declivity, and a man would dash up hurriedly to the door, with a sweating, hard-breathing horse. Every shepherd brought his 'collie' with him, so that the barn swarmed with dogs. The horses were hitched-up to railings, posts, and the wheels of drays. The barn was not very brilliantly lighted. Chandeliers were made of crossed pieces of wood, each with two holes, into which candles were placed. Perforated battens jutted out from the walls. At one end of the platform was a shaky door, leading to the shed which did duty as 'side-room'. In this door was a hole, apparently for the ingress and egress of cats, and it so chanced that during 'The Land o' the Leal' a poor dog jammed his head into the aperture. The melancholy howl that followed effectually banished sentiment. Then ensued fresh horror. The wooden chandeliers did not happen to be at all straight, and there was a strong draught, so the grease came drop-ping down. Icicles of grease hung on the walls—stearine stalactites drooped from the cande-labra. The lights guttered out one by one, till nothing was left but the dim globe-lamp. By ten o'clock the concert had concluded. When the audience went outside they found that the horses, alarmed either at the singing or the applause, had stampeded, and that a number were miss-ing. Walking back in the gloom we were suddenly met by a party of riders, who had been on

PROGRAMME

FOR

FRIDAY, 22ND FEBRUARY, 1884.

(LAST NIGHT BUT ONE.)

"ANITHER NICHT WI' BURNS."

"Rantin, Rovin Robin" (43)	MR. KENNEDY
"Duncan Gray" (31)	MR. KENNEDY
"Thou hast left me ever, Jamie" (47)—Trio	THE MISSES KENNEDY
"O my love is like a red, red rose"	MR. ROBERT KENNEDY
"John Anderson, my Jo" (16)	MISS HELEN KENNEDY
"Address to a Mouse"—Recitation	MR. KENNEDY
"Tam Glen" (4)	MISS MARJORY KENNEDY
"My Bonnie Mary" (27)	MR. ROBERT KENNEDY
"Scots wha ha'e wi' Wallace bled" (5)	MR. KENNEDY
"O wert thou in the cauld blast" (Mendelssohn)—Duet	
	MISS HELEN AND MAGGIE KENNEDY
Recitative—"My Arms" }	
Air—"Sound an Alarm" (Handel) }	MR. ROBERT KENNEDY
Jacobite Airs (pianoforte)—" Wha'ell be King but Charlie," "The Piper o' Dundee," "The Braes o' Killiecrankie," "The Hundred Pipers"	THE MISSES KENNEDY

MR. KENNEDY WILL RECITE

"TAM O' SHANTER."

"I'm ower young to marry yet"—Trio	THE MISSES KENNEDY
"My heart's in the Highlands"	MR. ROBERT KENNEDY
"Whistle ower the lave o't" (22)	MR. KENNEDY
FINALE	"AULD LANG SYNE" (48)

☞ *The figures refer to page in Song Book.*

POST TYP.

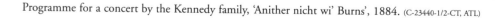

Programme for a concert by the Kennedy family, 'Anither nicht wi' Burns', 1884. (C-23440-1/2-CT, ATL)

97

the search for the animals. 'There's nine of them gone,' said a man in a big flapping cloak—'clean gone, and into the ranges, I'll bet.' We were really sorry for those poor fellows. The black sky—the moonbeams striking through the rents in the clouds, and sweeping round like so many aerial bulls' eyes—the strange shadows on the hills—the sound of the wind as it rustled the high grass—the sight of the dark range far away, where the horses were supposed to have strayed—increased our sympathy. Nothing ever impressed us with such a sense of hopeless search as this night-ride of those men. After plunging through some half-mile of tussocks and climbing six or seven fences, we reached the Manse, and next morning had the satisfaction of knowing that most of the horses had quietly cantered home to their respective stables.

David Kennedy Jnr, *Kennedy's Colonial Travel*, pp. 175–7.

Perilous fording of the Waitaki (1876)

DAVID KENNEDY JNR

The Kennedy family's progress through New Zealand in 1876 included many hair-raising episodes, such as their crossing of the Waitaki in flood. David Kennedy's vivid descriptions of coaches, hotels, horseback journeys, and concert venues supply detail and colour to ideas about colonial travel.

'THE WAITAKI IS UP!' was the news we received in Oamaru. We had to cross this river on our journey northward into the province of Canterbury. Word came that it was barely fordable, a hot wind having melted the snows on the Ranges, and swollen the mountain torrents. This river, one of the most important in the colony, is 120 miles long, and has its source in the Southern Alps, not far from Mount Cook, which is 13,000 feet high, and the monarch of New Zealand mountains. The first forty miles of the Waitaki lie through a deep gorge hemmed in by barren, perpetually snow-covered, precipitous mountains—after which the river flows in a commonplace manner through the Plains towards the sea. This Waitaki is also the boundary-line between Scotch Otago and English Canterbury, so that 'Both sides of the Waitaki' may in the course of time come to be as suggestive a phrase as 'Baith sides o' the Tweed.'

A drive of fourteen miles brought us to the river. What!—this the Waitaki?—this the famed, the terrible Waitaki?—impossible! Half-a-dozen small streams appeared to be pouring past us, covering a large extent of ground, so intersected was the channel by shallows and long

Thomas S. Cousins, 'A dramatic scene with Cobb and Co.'s coach crossing the Waimakariri', c. 1875. A writer in the *Illustrated New Zealand Herald* described it: 'The ferry man with a lifebelt is showing the way, as the fords shift in every flood … the river at the spot referred to consists of a number of streams, which in bad weather are sometimes quite impassable.' (F-643-1/4-MNZ, Making New Zealand Collection, ATL)

shingly spits. This was one of those New Zealand rivers that are never full-flowing save during a heavy 'fresh', and whose banks are simply floodmarks. We waited here three hours, watching through a glass one or two houses on the opposite shore, about a mile off, the Waitaki all the time growing more important in our eyes. At length a boat approached. The head ferryman, who was trying to discover a ford for the coach, came slowly across on horseback. He was a Norwegian named Müller—a big-built giant of a man, with a long red beard, flannel shirt, and tweed trousers. By his orders the luggage was taken out of the coach and put into the boat. Then, after my father, mother, and my two sisters had taken their places, one of the men waded up to his knees and shoved off the boat to the edge of a 'terrace', where it was caught by the rush of the deeper stream. It floated round the end of a spit, was hauled by the men along some shallow water, guided over a rapid current, dragged over another bed of shingle, and rowed across a second broad channel to the opposite shore.

The coach was not equally fortunate. Our driver, though sustained greatly by a dram he had taken at a cottage, was almost on the point of relinquishing the ford. Gideon was in great terror of water, for a brother of his had been drowned whilst crossing an Otago river. Had it not been that two of us went on the box as company, he would assuredly have thrown up the reins. It was certainly far from pleasant to see the grey current rolling past us at six knots an hour, and know that next minute we were to trust ourselves to its uncertain depths. The danger magnified every moment, though we had not long to think, for the Norwegian, riding into the river, called on us to follow. He was mounted on a bare-backed white horse, so as to be ready any moment for a swim. Gideon cracked his whip, and we splashed in, the rear being brought up by my two brothers on the saddle-horses. The stream widened out as we proceeded, while the water tore noisily through the wheels. A bank of shingle was reached. Then our guide took us some two hundred yards in an oblique direction down stream, which was the cause of a strange illusion; for the swifter speed of the current, combined with the grating of the wheels on the rough channel, made us appear to be going at a considerable speed backwards. We came to another branch of the river, and progressed cautiously. Plump!—the leaders sank over their knees; splash!—the wheelers swayed for a foothold, while their tails flowed on top of the stream; bump!—the coach went down over the axles. Farther in the pole disappeared—then the horses' legs—then the front wheels. The coach gave a severe pitch, and a substantial wave came over the box-seat, wetting two of us considerably, while Gideon threw his legs up in the air and thus escaped a ducking. The two on horseback had a bad time of it keeping their horses' heads up-stream. My brother, who rode a little black pony, was every moment expecting to be carried away; but he got at last under the lee of the large horse, and felt safer. Müller tied a rope to the leading horses, to guide us round some awkward places—a proceeding which kept us continually on the alert; for once or twice he turned us sharply on the 'lock' of the coach, and we felt the vehicle lifting for an overturn in the river, which, of course, made us gesticulate wildly, and cry out loudly to the ferryman.

Another shingle-spit was gained, and Müller again peered about for a ford, but the bottom was lost a few feet from the edge. We drove in at random, the Norwegian keeping close alongside our leading horses. All at once his white horse sank to the belly, and in a second the coach had crashed down to an equal depth. It was a most awing sight to see the solid mass of water moving past us—not foaming, but gliding swiftly; with every indication of a treacherous foothold. We had gone but a few yards farther when Müller suddenly threw up the leading-rope into the air, flung his hand back warningly, and sank with an ominous plunge, almost at our feet, into an unknown depth of water. Horse and rider were swept before our terrified gaze away down the river. Clutching the bridle firmly in his left hand, the ferryman made a lunge with his right, caught the mane, and held grimly on, while the horse swam strongly and brought him at last to a small point of land. The coach was left standing on the brink of a hidden terrace, with the current rushing round us. We trembled for the slightest movement of the horses, but luckily they stood like statues, despite the water surging up violently against their sides. Müller made his appearance again, all dripping but hopeful, and got us out of our predicament by a sharp turn of the coach—telling us afterwards, in proof of the shifting nature of the channel, that he had crossed easily, at this very place, only the day before. When we arrived on the shore we found an hour had been occupied in fording, an experience that cost us thirty shillings. The Norwegian, who treated the whole affair very coolly, told us he had been ten years at this ferry, had been swept off that same old white horse many and many a time, and had frequently to swim for his life. We would advise no one with weak nerves to ford a swollen river in New Zealand. A short time after, a number of passengers were fording this same Waitaki, when their coach upset, and a 'female magician' was drowned. We afterwards saw, in the Christchurch cemetery, many graves of persons who had perished while crossing rivers. The inscriptions, which came home to us in all their force, included such texts as 'A horse is counted but a vain thing to save a man.'

David Kennedy Jnr, *Kennedy's Colonial Travel*, pp. 191–3.

A *lady* traveller (1877)

C.F. GORDON CUMMING

Constance Gordon Cumming was a painter and experienced travel writer who visited New Zealand in 1877 with Lady Gordon, wife of the Governor of Fiji. The author of articles for English and American illustrated papers and several published books, Gordon Cumming set off alone to see New Zealand. She gives this portrait of herself encumbered with the essential equipment of a lady traveller.

As IT was, I wistfully turned away from the exquisite fern paradise and the dark *kauri* forests, and then commenced a long ride across uninteresting plains bounded by commonplace hills. Towards noon we overlooked the seaboard, and paused to learn our day's geography from the vast map outspread below us, the horses, meanwhile, feasting on a kind of veronica, a shrub with purple blossoms, evidently highly appreciated. We, too, were conscious of having breakfasted at an unwonted hour, but could find no cool shady spot where we could halt for luncheon, till we reached a Maori settlement on the sea-coast.

Thence our way for the last few miles lay along the beach, on broad beautiful sand, with the wavelets rippling right under the horses' feet. It would have been most enjoyable could we either have gone leisurely, or unburdened. But as it was, we had to hurry on, in order to cross

A portrait of Constance Gordon Cumming published in 1904. (B-K 403, ATL)

a wide tidal creek at low tide, and already the tide was on the turn. So we had to keep up a hard swinging gallop, and (being as yet a novice in the arts of bush-travelling, in a land where there are no patient coolies ever ready to run miles and miles with luggage) I was encumbered with a heavy travelling-bag insecurely strapped to the pommel—sketching materials ditto— opera-glasses keeping time against my side, and a large umbrella, which I dared not open, though the sun was burning. Having to hold on to all these, and keep up our unflagging pace, was to me desperately fatiguing, and after all, we reached the creek too late, and there was nothing for it but to wait patiently at the little lonely telegraph-station for a couple of hours, when Mr Field, the civil young clerk, offered to row us to our destination (four miles).

This proved fortunate, for the hard gallop in the sun had exhausted me, and all in a minute I turned giddy and unconscious, which would have been awkward had we been half-way across the wide, and at all times unpleasant, ford; as it was, I was all right in a few minutes, and Mr Field made me lie down in his wee room till it was time to start, when we had a lovely moonlight row, and landed here—all three, total strangers—to find that Arthur Fisher and our host and hostess were all alike absent. But we were most hospitably received by two sweet lady-like girls under thirteen, and five sons, the youngest a dear little fellow of four, with a kind good nurse. It had been intended that we should continue the ride to Tauranga to-day, but when I found it was forty miles, and no resting-place by the way, I cried off, and am going down the lake (twenty-five miles) by boat. Mr Allom and his daughter will return from here.

C.F. Gordon Cumming, *At Home in Fiji*, pp. 180–2.

The trouble with sketching (1877)

C . F . G O R D O N C U M M I N G

Constance Gordon Cumming's journey to Ohinemutu was over the 'very worst bush-road I ever saw'. An accomplished artist, she made a number of sketches and watercolours, especially of the Pink and White Terraces, and ran foul of the local Maori over charges for her water-colours. She thought Te Tarata, the White Terrace, was 'in nature what the Taj Mahal at Agra is in architecture—a thing indescribable'. A number of her sketches and paintings were exhibited in London at the Colonial and Indian Exhibition of 1886.

IT SEEMS THAT, at the instigation of a white man (who, for his own reasons, was anxious to curry favour with the Maoris), they have issued a printed notice, to the effect that no one shall take photographs in this district without paying them a tax of £5 for that privilege. From the first moment of my arrival at Wairoa, my sketching-blocks became a source of keen interest to the natives, who therein scented a possibility of extortion. From that moment they have returned to the attack again and again; and though, happily for me, they consider it useless to attack a stupid woman who cannot understand them, they have never ceased to annoy Mrs Way, whom they consider bound to take their part, and are very angry indeed because she tries to make them understand that water-colour painting and photography are distinct arts. They have decided that I ought, on the contrary, to pay them a larger sum, because the coloured drawings give a truer idea of the place, and must therefore be more valuable. It was quite in vain to suggest that the sight of these pictures would induce fresh visitors to come and spend their much-coveted gold in the district. This only added fresh fuel to the fire. They said it was certain I should make a fortune by showing those pictures in Auckland, perhaps even in Britain, while they, owners of the place, would have no share in the profits. Of course I was determined not to pay the money, both from a natural aversion to being done, and also

A female photographer in the thermal region, 1903. (F-111562-1/2, ATL)

because such a precedent would have settled the question, to the detriment of all future sketchers. But you can imagine the annoyance which these noisy talkers have caused us: happily they are all camped at the other side of the lake.

Now I am thoroughly tired, and am going to repeat the mud-bath of last night, and then turn in for a good night's rest.

OLD MISSION STATION, WAIROA, *April* 5.

We were aroused at 4 a.m. by Mr Way, who had ridden all the distance from Wairoa to bring us a loaf of bread, and to announce the unexpected arrival at his house of a party of friends, who purposed joining us in the course of the day. He had waded across the creek at the head of the lake; and having thus provided us with breakfast, he returned to rejoin his party at home.

Being now thoroughly awake, and dear old Mary being equally so, we stole quietly out of the tent and went off to bathe at the white terraces. It was a lovely sunrise; the water was delicious—temptations to linger manifold. Altogether it was a good deal later than we thought, when we returned along the shore, gracefully draped in our plaids and blankets, but by no means fully attired. To my dismay I perceived a large party of Maoris assembled round our cooking-spring, and another canoe lying beside ours. Mary recognised the party as being with two Scotch gentlemen, who had arrived on the other side of the lake the previous day, and with whom we had fraternised by small exchanges of fish and bread, matches, and pepper and salt. Fortunately they had gone off to the mud volcanoes; so having dressed with all speed, we were able on their return to invite them to share our breakfast, just taken out of the hot spring. Their arrival was most opportune; for the Maoris, having talked themselves into great excitement, just then came up *en masse* to inform Mrs Way that I must either at once pay them the coveted £5, or leave the place instantly. They were so very stormy and decided, that it would have been extremely unpleasant had we been alone. Happily the quiet determination of our new friends overawed them, and they fell back grumbling.

After this little episode we fell into home talk, and one of them asked me if I was any relation to Colonel G.C. of Auchintoul. On hearing I was his sister, he proceeded to tell me how, last year, he was fishing on the Deveron, and, much to his embarrassment, had hooked a seven-pound trout with a very light trout-line, when happily Colonel G.C. espied him, came to the rescue, and gaffed the fish. Strange, was it not, that Bill should have rescued a stranger from a wild fish in Banffshire, and that in the following season the fisher should come to the antipodes, just in time to rescue me from the wild Maoris! Thanks to this seasonable reinforcement, I was able to do a good deal of steady work for several hours.

In the course of the day, the other party of friends arrived, and included two ladies. Arthur Fisher also arrived. The day I left Tauranga he had been obliged to return to Kati Kati on business, which entailed a walk of forty miles. He walked back to Tauranga, which made forty more, before he was able to start on the actual trip to Rotomahana. Unfortunately he arrived so late that he had but a hurried glimpse of all the wonders.

Then we all started to row back here, and all the canoes raced down Lake Tarawara. It was very amusing, and the rowers became immensely excited. Arriving here, our kind hosts insisted on giving up their own room to the other two ladies and me, and we all had a very cheery evening. Early this morning, however, the Maoris returned to the charge with renewed vigour, determined to extort that wretched £5. They tell Mary that my pictures shall never leave the district; that they will seize my portfolios and destroy them all. Mary says it is only bluster, but Mrs Way is not so sure; and as I should have no redress if irreparable damage is done, we have packed the precious sketches securely in the middle of a huge bundle of plaids and pillows, so as to escape attention, and the faithful Hémé will carry it to the coach.

MRS WILSON'S HOTEL, OHINEMUTU, 10 P.M.

Victory! we have triumphed! By good luck a large party of Europeans happened to come up by coach, so we enlisted them, and formed altogether a party of fourteen whites, with the baggage in the middle. Then we marched through the village to the hotel, just as the coach-and-four was ready to start. The foe mustered strong, but apparently thought further attack undesirable, so we drove off in safety.

C.F. Gordon Cumming, *At Home in Fiji*, pp. 223–7.

Spending the night at Tahake (1877)

ALFRED MAUDSLAY

Maudslay, private secretary to Sir Arthur Gordon, the Governor of Fiji, came to New Zealand accompanying Lady Gordon, her children, and her companion, the travel writer Constance Gordon Cumming, in 1877. He left the Gordons at Kawau with Governor Grey and travelled through the King Country and Rotorua in the summer of 1877.

THE NEXT MORNING my guide returned with the horses to Tauranga, and I engaged fresh horses and a Maori, Tautere by name, to take me to Rotomahana. Tautere turned out to be an extremely good fellow, and we got on capitally. The following two days I spent on the borders of the two lakes Roto Rua and Roto Iti, sleeping at a little native village named Tahake. The country was not very interesting, much the same as I had already passed through. At Tahake there is a very fine large whare, covered with carvings beautifully executed, but horribly indecent. Tautere said the natives were 'very mean Maoris'. There was some difficulty in getting into this big house, as it was apparently unoccupied, and the old gentleman who had charge of the key was away, and had, as we were told, probably planted the key somewhere before starting. On the fence surrounding the house were the remains of part of a famous Maori war canoe, of which the side pieces were of great length and elaborately carved. From what was left of it, I should think that it must have been cut out of two huge trees pieced together in the middle, and would have held about 250 men. Tautere told me that a man to whom he acted as guide had offered £100 apiece for the side pieces, but the Maoris would not part with them. I did not think it was much good looking for the key, and began to try to get into the house through the single window. However, the whole village turned out on the hunt, and in about half an hour after searching all round the house, the key was found hidden away under an old bit of matting.

We took our saddles into the house and were just beginning to think about supper, and Tautere had pulled a packet of tea out of his pocket, when another Maori rushed at him and cried, 'Taboo', and then the mystery of the deserted appearance of the house was explained. A Chief of high rank had died, and his body was lying there to 'dry', previous to the bones being scraped and hidden away. As the house was full of rubbish and odds and ends of clothing, boxes, etc., I had not noticed a large box covered with black cloth, in which the chief was 'drying'. Now any food taken into a house where a dead body is lying is tabooed for ever, so I had all the tea to myself, as even my much Europeanized guide refused to touch it that night, although he did drink a little, freely diluted with milk, the next morning. Luckily for Tautere

E.W. Payton, 'Whatiwhatihoe Residence of the Maori King', c. 1880. (A-045-015, ATL)

the rest of the food had been left outside the house, so when some potatoes had been cooked (potatoes seem to be the principal food of the Maoris) we had our supper on the grass. The natives then asked me where I would like to sleep, and offered no objection to my sleeping in the big whare, and further mentioned that I could have it to myself, as no one else would dare to sleep there, and that the body was not 'high', and it seemed to me preferable to the dirty crowded huts of the villagers. After supper some of the people came into the whare to have a smoke, and we had a long talk. They were delighted to examine my knife and a few other things I had with me, and brought some of their baskets and carved work for me to look at in return. Altogether we had a very pleasant evening, and then they went off to their own huts to sleep.

I found I was not to be quite alone, as an old lady was left to watch the corpse. This watching is supposed to be a mark of great affection for the deceased chief, and usually falls to the lot of one of his near kindred, and the watcher becomes very much taboo indeed, and is not even allowed to feed herself; everything has to be put into her mouth by attendants, and this goes on for months and months, until the body is quite dry, and the bones ready for scraping. It is very seldom, I was told, that the body is kept in a large whare, usually a small house is built on purpose to hold it.

There was a large wooden bedstead in the house covered with a mat, on which I slept, and slept very soundly after my long ride, although I was dimly conscious of many fleas, and in the morning I found that I was bitten all over. Tautere told me it was lucky I had slept in the whare, for the hut to which he went was so full of fleas that he could get no sleep at all. After a bathe in the lake and a good breakfast of crayfish and potatoes and tabooed tea, we rode back to Ohinimotu, passing some curious hot springs and a small lake on the way, and a picturesque lake among the hills called Roto Kawau.

Alfred Maudslay, *Life in the Pacific Fifty Years Ago*, pp. 159–62.

Christmas Day amongst the Maoris (1876)

JAMES HINGSTON

The preface to The Australian Abroad *describes James Hingston as an 'Anglo-Australian' whose 'Notes of Travels' were first serially published in the Melbourne* Argus. *His journey begins at the wharf in San Francisco and moves from Japan to China and Indonesia before Hingston arrives in New Zealand in 1876. He continued a tradition of 'some very-out-of-the-common-way Christmas dinners' by taking himself uninvited to Arowainui, near Timaru, on a 'cruise for a Christmas dinner' from the local Maori.*

WE MUST GET ON TO DINNER, though that meal had lost much of its attractions since we had lost our hearts. What are dinners to the love-sick? Wandering down to the hall of the intended feast, we found all in preparation outside. We perceived then that our dinner was to be cold and our drink hot. We would have reversed that arrangement if we had our will in the matter. The drink was contained in ten large, wide-mouthed boiling pots, and was the very coarsest attempt at tea that we had ever tasted—and we have tasted some queer tea in our time. In '52, we had tea in Fryer's Creek, in Victoria, that was made with clayey water, that coloured it to the same extent that milk would have done, and in it there floated curious remains of vegetables that were called 'posts and rails.' We had tasted tea on ship-board also, that had been made with water from rusted tanks, and was of a strange reddish colour and we had tasted tea that had been made from tank water that had been too long preserved, and that smelt of anything but a rich pekoe bouquet. This Maori tea of Arowainui was, however, a thing by itself. It seemed to have been made long since, and to have got stale, and to have been warmed up again and again, and sweetened with treacle or some other nastiness. We have heard poor drink damned with the faint praise of being 'warm and wet'. This tea was all that, and was, in addition, sweet and nasty. Whenever we grumbled about anything in our school-days, we were told that it was to be hoped that we might never get worse. We echo that hope with regard to the Maori tea, with the full belief that we could never drink it if we did. Of course, with this Maori tea there was no milk, nor any substitute for it. We have had some substitutes for milk to tea in our days, and among them have been eggs, butter, and gin, but these were in centres of civilization—not in wharries.

Heads had been counted, and the dishes were being set apart for each of the little groups inside, and this seemed to be a troublesome business to settle. So much dried fish, so much of the dried mashed potato, cold, very high in flavour, and dreadfully hard, much like to stinking Portland cement; so much cake, made without leaven or eggs, and as tasteless and uneatable as an old door-mat; and so much cold mutton and a stuff intended to represent Christmas pud-ding, which was only the aforesaid cake in another shape, with plums here and there. We broke our nails in the first attempt to tear it, as the fingers do all duties—that of knives, forks and spoons—at Maori meals. That was a pudding of Christmas puddings! When masticated a little, it stuck to the mouth in a most provoking manner, and could neither be ejected nor swal-lowed. We brought a piece of it away as a souvenir, as also some of the dried fish and a piece of the cake and the cement-like potato. They are preserved in a native flax shoe, which we found in the wharry of Kiti's mother, and which we prize above all the viands it contains.

The groups inside the grand dining-hall had to be counted again and again, and the 'messes' for each to be arranged and rearranged. We got tired of lolloping about to see it done, and thought we could have set it right and square in a tithe of the time. We generally think that way of the difficulties of other people—'tis human nature. An old chief, Kohoo by name, a grandfather of Kiti's, we believe, and the middle-aged preacher at the morning service, seemed to have the arrangement of everything, and pottered and muddled over it just as men will do in these domestic matters. Women sat about—tailor-fashion—outside; some nursing their babies on their backs. Looking at the fashion attentively, there is much to be said in favour of back-nursing. It is easier altogether, and avoids compression of the lungs, and all the pains and weariness of constant bending of the head and shoulders. A swaying movement from side to side seemed to rock the child to sleep as easily as the backward and forward rocking of the white mother. Inside the building the utmost patience prevailed. Maories are not fidgety, and wait with the patience of people to whom it is not a usual matter to dine every day.

We found occupation for spare time with an intelligent Maori named Mohe Tehike. He knew a little English and was of a tractable nature. We got a bottle of beer and our tumbler, and getting him away to ourselves—behind a distant wharry—we drilled him into his intended duty of drinking our mother's health at the coming dinner. He got to perfection at last, and would have done for a Lord Mayor's toastmaster. That he did not know the meaning of the ceremony or of the words he uttered made it all the funnier and better. To see him grasping the glass in outstretched hand and roaring out, 'To te hent of Arar Hinkton!'—for that was as near as the fourteen letters in the Maori language would let him get—was a sublime sight to us, who had tutored the savage.

We went in to dinner at last, introduced by Mohe Tehike into his family party—two middle-aged women and an old man. We occupied a central position in the place, and counted twelve groups on each side, and four at one end. The other end was appropriated to a large fire-place, in which, on some dead ashes, part of the feast was piled up. We four whites got distributed somehow each into a different group. That arrangement was quite accidental, and was just as well as not, since we had more time for looking about us, instead of talking. Our Maori friends were quite useless to us, and we to them in the way of language, so that we could not communicate ideas, even supposing that either of us happened to have any. Squatting in tailor-fashion is very irksome to the novice, and we were beginning to tire of it when a walk round was called by the chief who stood fronting the fireplace. He chanted, or intoned something or other, on which every one started to their legs. Now the provisions had been spread on the ground down the middle avenue, a complete mess, kettle of tea and all, opposite to each group. We had to walk by the side of the fare, and all round the building several times, walking in single file, ourself being sandwiched between the two Maori women of our group. It was necessary to pick our steps carefully and yet it was an irresistible necessity to look up occasionally to see captain, driver, and squatter revolving around in this queer procession. Seats were then resumed, or, rather, we again squatted on the ground, and kept silence whilst the chief read something from a book, to which a chorus or something of the sort was responded at intervals by the company. There was then another chant and another procession, this time the reverse way to the previous one. We began to notice that the effect of these walkings around was to well dust the intended dinner spread at our feet. On this occasion it was five times go round and then another squatting, and another reading and more responses. It occurred to us now that all this was an imitation 'high church' service, and that, instead of standing up during the singing-part, we walked round instead—a very great improvement, and to be recommended for adoption by those who are bursting to make innovations in their church service arrangements. There were three more to come of these walks around, and it began to be a hard matter to keep from laughing at the looks of captain, driver, and squatter, as they, in turn, came opposite to us in this most monotonous 'breakdown'. As for the cake and fish, and potatoes and mutton and tea, they got nicely dusted, quite browned by the time that the order came to fall upon them. It came at last, and we tore away at the fish first, and then at the mutton, and then tried the pounded potatoes, the sawdust cake and the stickjaw pudding. We tried occasionally to suck our fingers, in order to be in the fashion, but we felt that we did not play our part well. What with love-sickness and the processions and other fakes, we had not appetite enough to do as others did. On looking round, we found that the three other guests, driver, captain, and squatter, had got together in the fireplace at the top, now that the provisions had been removed thence. They were comparing ideas, I could see, and taking stock of ourself in a very critical manner. Taking a partly-eaten chop in one hand, and a piece of cake in the other, we arose and joined them in the ashes. They were each gnawing away at something, and had got a kettle of the tea to themselves. They had to lift up this kettle and drink from out it, lip to rim. Somehow we seemed to get dirtier than the Maories did at this sort of business. We can easily understand why. We were not used to it. Every one has noticed how those unused to the pen will ink and smear their fingers in their efforts with it. All novices mess themselves in their attempts—so did we. We wanted well washing after that dinner, and well brushing too, and— oh, vanity!—we could not face Kiti Kohoota again in that plight.

We disappeared from the group to give the signal to Mohe Tehike, and then resumed squatting. He did his part well. Shifting himself to the end of the building, he arose, and holding out his tumbler, which, by the way, he stuck to afterwards, he shouted, 'To te hent of Arar Hinkton!' and then, emptying the glass, sat down. To say that we felt proud of our doings after that is but feebly to express our feelings. We distributed cigars all around, and ale to those that would drink it, and listened to many imitations of Mohe Tehike's toast. After that we gathered up some fragments of the feast as memorials of it, and shook hands with everybody.

When we were all seated in the buggy for our start, the natives came trooping out to see the departure, and we went on our way, waving hats and handkerchiefs, in a general and joyous manner, quite satisfied with our Christmas Day amongst the Maories.

James Hingston, *The Australian Abroad*, pp. 341–5.

The Duke of Berry at Akaroa (1877)

A GERMAN LADY

The author of Notes of a Tour *was identified by A.G. Bagnall from shipping information in the* New Zealand Herald *as Miss Muller. She arrived in New Zealand in March 1876 and published her notes of her tour in order to show 'how a lady may perfectly well travel by herself, provided she be healthy, strong, good-tempered and ready to put up with some hardships'. She became so fond of New Zealand in the two months she spent here that 'I knew I could never again live in Europe'. Miss Muller appears to have made her home in Sydney.*

My first coaching experience in New Zealand was gained from Christchurch to Akaroa, a small town beautifully situated on Banks Peninsula. The coach starts from the booking-office in Christchurch at 8 a.m. I had bespoken a box seat, but the granting of that lies solely with the driver who has the privilege of choosing those passengers that are to share the seat with him. The proprietor, Mr Cramond, drove up with the coach and a beautiful team of four brown horses. He was very pleasant and civil indeed (but then he comes from Timaru), so I felt sure I should enjoy my trip. At eight o'clock he relinquished the reins to the coachman, Joe Macfarlane, and off we started through the streets of warm-hearted Christchurch, leaving them soon far behind and rattling along a well made road that only becomes interesting after the half-way house in the Little Briar district is reached. Here the passengers stop for dinner and then we start again, this time with five horses for the road is very heavy in some parts.

In the meantime I was on the best of terms with the driver Mr Macfarlane, a good-looking Scotchman, who had only just returned from his wedding trip, and this was the first time he drove after his marriage. The joking along the road with his acquaintances reminded me strongly of Mr Weller and the coaching days in England, described by Dickens. It was capital fun to see Joe throwing kisses and waving his hand gracefully. He is much liked evidently and very obliging. His language too is superior for a man in his station, I did not hear one bad word, nor even slang expressions. To his horses he always speaks with evident affection such as, 'eh, my little beauties, get on!' and looks at them admiringly whenever they turn smartly round an abrupt curve in the road. We are now nearing the mountains on Banks Peninsula. Lake Ellesmere is seen but imperfectly from the coach road, and looks rather dreary with its flat shores. A number of water fowls may be shot there; we met several sportsmen, one of whom sold to the driver a pair of wild ducks for eighteenpence.

The next lake in view is Lake Forsyth, very prettily situated with a mountainous shore. The coach dashed on over a plain covered with tussocks, that look in the distance like short stubble, and as the five horses were dancing along it looked as if we were bearing down straight into the lake. The road that skirts it is very strong and rough; in winter it is often completely flooded when the lake rises through the increasing waters. When pretty Lake Forsyth is passed the roads become very hilly, and soon afterwards we are in the bush; beautiful high forest trees covered with creepers and ferns, charming gullies in which the tree fern grows luxuriantly and attains a great height. The birds sing here so loudly and joyously that the whole forest resounds with it; we had moreover a lovely day, and the ever varying scenes, seen to such advantage from the box seat, caused a thorough enjoyment. At a pretty little fountain that forms itself from a supply of water in the hills, and running through a delicious nook of ferns with the many tinted foliage over head, our horses had a drink and a few moments of rest. The poor animals stood panting and perspiring from their up hill journey. It was a lovely spot for a few moments delay, as the concert of the birds could now be heard in all its glory. To the left stretches a beautiful range of mountains, the highest point is 1800 feet, fine gorges and

Nicholas Chevalier, 'Wet or fine?', 1866. (A-102-034, ATL)

slopes intervene, dotted with groups of handsome cabbage trees. A secluded little cottage inhabited by some road-mender, stands in full view of all this loveliness, and the wife appearing in the door to have a look at the coach, Joe called out to her, 'I daresay you won't fall out with your neighbours!' The roads were heavy and rough in many places, so that it required skill and care to get over them safely. When the coach dashed down the precipitate parts, it became necessary to hold on somewhere, and as I sat between Joe and a dark-haired solicitor, I had to slip a hand under an arm of each of these gentlemen; in this way alone was it possible to escape being hurled off the seat.

It is surprising how soon one becomes accustomed to the bad roads, the lovely scenery as we are nearing Akaroa soon engages all attention. An inn on the hill top, where the horses are changed for the last time, looks down upon the harbour of Akaroa; surrounded by high hills as it lies there so silent in the clear afternoon sunshine, quite landlocked, it resembles a Swiss lake. I repeat that the picture as seen from the hill top, is so lovely that this view alone will repay the visitor to Akaroa. As yet, no photographs are to be had, neither of this nor any other part of the lovely peninsula, which seems all the more strange as the beautiful and varied views cannot fail to find ready purchasers.

Our last team of horses, five again, was a shapely and comely one altogether, the three leaders especially, and it was a pleasure to see them draw together gracefully and promptly at the sudden curves in the road which occurred very frequently indeed. Though the end of the journey seemed quite near, yet in reality it was still fifteen miles off. For the first time in my life I was taught to hold the reins by Joe, who pretended that it was amazing how well I did it in so short a time; but somehow Joe's hands were very near the ribbands, and I do believe he held the important part of them. As we are nearing Akaroa, the beauties of scenery by no way diminish; we stop at pretty little bays with foreign names, here the driver delivers letters, newspapers, or parcels, and chaffs the respective persons who stand waiting for them. One exceedingly steep and rather dangerous hill has to be descended, and then we are in Akaroa, a quiet village-like place, at the foot of the harbour, with mountains on the background. I believe that representatives of almost all nations live here peaceably together. The few original French settlers to begin with, who went there thirty-five years ago and have remained ever since. Then there are Danes, Scandinavians, Germans, one Portuguese, a Swiss and a Greek. The hotel kept by Mr Wagstaff is a very superior establishment; it lies in beautiful grounds near the harbour, from the verandah the view is superior indeed. Those who disdain mixing with their fellow creatures, can have private rooms engaged by telegram at Mr Wagstaff's, and exclude themselves in cosy quarters to their heart's content. Those who wish to study human nature and manners can have a pretty bedroom, and take their meals at the table where kind Mrs Wagstaff presides over good cheer, and afterwards a comfortable sitting-room, with a lamp that sheds the mildest light is at their disposal.

On my arrival there were but two guests, the bicicle hero and his follower, who had lately completed the journey from Christchurch to Hokitika and back, and who had come to Akaroa by the same mode of conveyance. A promenade after tea through the hotel grounds and then through the town by moonlight was exceedingly agreeable. The whole place was so quiet, the little houses contrasted so well against the dark mountains, and in front of it all the beautiful lake-like harbour so silent and grand in the moonlight. It was exceedingly pleasant to hear a friendly 'Good evening,' from everyone who passed, a habit so different from that of large towns, and peculiarly grateful to the ear of a stranger. The next day being Sunday I went to the little English Church, but the service having a strong *high* flavour I returned disappointed. Then the mountains began to weep as the Maoris say, it rained and continued to do so for two days. I was weather-bound, and could make no excursions into the neighbourhood, but I made the acquaintance of a little Irishman, the Duke of Berry, and who lived in a whare not very far away where he made cheese and roughed it thoroughly. The Duke, a little man of small dimensions and insignificant appearance, being prematurely bald though only 26 years old, gained decidedly upon closer acquaintance. He is thoroughly good-natured, and every inch a gentleman in heart, feelings, and also in manners, though he would occasionally wrest his little body, clad in a dismal suit of grey, in the most extraordinary positions, his arms stretched high over his head like telegraph posts, and wriggling about whilst telling some funny Irish stories. One significant look from me at the arms or the wriggling extremities would make him start up with the excuse, 'Oh, I beg your pardon, but really I am not accustomed to talk with ladies, I am always among cows and ploughboys, I really beg your pardon!' And then he would look so pleading and so beseeching, poor little Duke, one could not be angry with him.

It was arranged that the Duke should take me about the country sight-seeing the next day if fine, and we started accordingly at 10 o'clock, with provisions to spend the greater part of the day out among the mountains. As I abhor the smoking of short pipes and the Duke knew this, I met him near the kitchen, puffing away with all his might and with such a queer dismal expression of countenance when he espied me. 'I am smoking now, you see my last pipe as I may not indulge in it when I am out with you.' Now this complaisance touched me. 'Well,' said I, 'perhaps I am not so dreadfully particular as all that, considering that we shall be in the open air.' Nevertheless, he had no other pipe that day. It was our intention to ascend Brazenose, the highest mountain near Akaroa. Immediately after setting out the road was exceedingly rough and always up hill. The Duke in a pair of bush boots and slouching bandit's hat trudged in front, carrying a small kit with provisions and enlivening the walk with merry talk, and imitations of foreigners' queer pronunciation of English. When we had walked for about a mile, Brazenose was yet as far off as ever, so I proposed to draw straws whether we should go to the Brazenose or to the Captain's, a partner of the Duke in the cheese making, who lived a good distance off. The longest straw meant 'the Captain', and I drew it. This operation of straw drawing in which the Duke had not indulged since his boyhood, evidently touched a soft chord. We sat down on the grass and attacked the lunch, looking at the beautiful scenery and views of Akaroa at our feet, when the Duke suddenly began to make a clean breast of it by accusing himself of being quite a disreputable character, fond of 'nips', and all that sort of thing ending with, 'Oh, yes, you may believe me, I am very bad indeed, it is no use hiding it, if I didn't tell you all the people of Akaroa would.' What was it, little Duke, that made you so loveable in spite of all your confession of unworthiness! By degrees the sky had assumed a threatening look, and Brazenose was enveloped in clouds; as we were not far from the Duke's whare we went down to it at the foot of a hill and I found it not at all the miserable place that he depicted it. The bush all around was lovely, and had it not been for the ever threatening sky, a walk in his domain would have been very pleasant indeed. We proposed remaining in the whare till the sky should clear, and meanwhile the Duke made active preparations for a cup of tea. The cow-boy on seeing a lady approach the hut had fled. He could with difficulty be coaxed to come within gun shot to be asked whether he had any cream in the dairy, and then the Duke had to fetch it himself. It having cleared up in the afternoon, we turned homewards, visiting on our way the cemetery which is prettily situated, but not very carefully kept. On a small grave, evidently recently made, stood a wineglass filled with water, intended for holding flowers. I am sorry to say that the Duke took it to be put there as an offering to a 'thirsty soul'.

That evening at tea, we had two additional guests at the table, travellers from foreign parts, but Englishmen who had come on foot from Pigeon Bay and were thoroughly drenched. One was an old gentleman, very corpulent, with a rubicund face and loud voice, bearing the appropriate name of Captain Hornblower. His companion was quite a young man, rough and ready, his name was Ostryd. Old Hornblower was in ecstatics with the lake country in the North Island, 'Bless my soul,' cried he, 'it is wonderful, there is nothing like it in the world and a visit there should on no account be a hurried one.' Young Ostryd said nothing, he pegged away at the cold beef, and looked profoundly wise. After tea I saw no more of these two, but I *heard* them, for at ten o'clock there arose a dreadfully alarming noise, and on coming out of my bedroom and inquiring for the cause of this disturbance, I was told that it was 'only the Captain sneezing'. Sneezing, indeed! surely the noise did not sound like that, and having been informed by the Duke in the course of the evening that it was alarming to see of what capacious tonnage the Captain was, and that he could stow away a marvellous amount of spirits without showing bad results, I began to doubt that sneezing had anything to do with the Captain's unearthly noises. What bad company for the Duke, both the Hornblower and the Ostryd! However, the next morning, both were down to breakfast in time, the Captain looking as robust as possible, rolling his large innocent eyes in all directions, and young Ostryd looked thirsty.

A German Lady [Miss Muller], *Notes of a Tour through Various Parts of New Zealand*, pp. 12–14.

Maori at Tauranga (late 1870s)

WILLIAM SENIOR

An Englishman who emigrated to Queensland, William Senior was a well-known angler who wrote under the name 'Red Spinner'. Senior visited New Zealand in the late 1870s to try out the fishing.

TAURANGA GAVE ME my first practical acquaintance with the Maoris. There were a few walking about the streets of Auckland, but they were only analogous to the Australian aboriginals. At Tauranga we had almost the genuine article; that is to say, the modernized Maoris as they appear to the eye of civilization, though not as you find them in their own country villages. It happened that a Government land court was being held in the town, and thither, in consequence, had flocked the natives from every part of the district. They overran the hotels, peeping into your bedroom with childlike confidence; they deafened you with their chatter and clamour; but I would not have missed the sight for the world. Their errand naturally induced excitement, for the land titles of the Maoris are troublesome problems for the

Tauranga looking towards Monmouth Redoubt, c. 1880s. (F-22639-1/2, ATL)

officials, and the Maoris themselves are remarkably shrewd in managing their own affairs. Some acquired land by conquest, some by occupation, some by right of fishing in river and sea; some under the old customs by which the chief, and after him his first and second son, had a right to the lion's share; while all free natives were proprietors of the soil, some by fair means and some by unfair. These are complicated matters, as New Zealand Governments still find; suffice to say the Maoris are very tenacious of their rights, and very bitter are some of the colonists because the Maori sticks to his inheritance and refuses to part with it to the white coveter. The Maoris have learnt the use of a legal title; and it was to settle disputes, and confirm or reject titles, that this land court was being held at Tauranga.

These Maoris were a motley crew; and most of them played the jew's-harp. Sitting on the pavement, lying about on the beach and the grassy borders of it, or in the hotels, they still keep the jew's-harp twanging. Not only was this taste for classical music displayed by the youthful; it was no uncommon thing to meet an aged man talking along the pavement, solemnly twiddling his jew's-harp as he went. Some of the Maoris around Tauranga are quite wealthy, and drive their buggies. Their dress, as I saw it worn at Tauranga, the occasion having probably somewhat of a holiday character, was remarkably mixed. Many, especially the young men, who have never disfigured themselves by tattooing, wore orthodox European costume, and in good taste too, but these were possibly swell members of a swell tribe. The general costume, however, was to put on a belltopper hat, Garibaldi shirt, paper collar, and necktie, a pilot jacket, a plaid shawl or blanket twisted round the waist, after the style of the Malay sarong, and descending to the knee, below which the bare bronzed leg was shown, with, at the lower end, socks and side-spring boots. They seemed to be particular about the kilt—it is a venerable kilt, and it will be for me evermore a moot question whether the Highlanders got it from the Maoris, or the Maoris from the Highlanders—and the elastic-side boots.

There was no absolute uniformity in hats. The chimney-pot was *de rigeur*, apparently; but French caps, deerstalkers, and wide-awakes were to be seen, together with nondescript *chapeaux* that must have been the cast-off property of strolling nigger minstrels. There were some Maoris who scorned the use of anything more than an honest shawl or blanket; but they knew how to use it both for covering and adornment. The colours were decidedly loud, and a man appeared to be not properly attired without something, greenstone or metal chiefly, hanging from his ear. The most distinguished Maori I saw at this time was an old grey-haired chief. He wore a belltopper that was evidently made for a small boy, an antique swallow-tail coat, a Rob Roy kilt, blue socks, and patent leather shoes; he was elaborately tattooed, and from his right ear was dangling a black bird about the size of a starling, with a curved slender beak quite three inches long. The beak was thrust through a hole in the ear, and held fast.

Many of the Maori ladies of the upper ten wore neat European dresses complete, but the humbler orders were innocent of stockings and shoes, and were conveniently draped in a shawl which did duty also as a covering for the head. But they are not, as a rule, good look-ing, particularly those who are tattooed. They have fine eyes and teeth, incline to stoutness towards middle age, have graceful carriage, and have good black hair, if they would only keep it in order. And they all smoke. In a well-horsed buggy, approaching the hotel door, sat a young Maori lady, dressed in fashionably cut sky-blue silk costume, with duchess hat and feather, and parasol to match. Her gipsy eyes and hair were black as the night; her features handsome as a gipsy's are handsome; her comportment modest and even pensive; I dare say her white handkerchief was duly perfumed. She surveyed the bustle of the street with an intel-ligent smile; then turned to a male Maori sitting on the back seat. She had asked him for something, perhaps a prayer-book or a fan. He fumbled in his pocket, and at length handed her a short, black, stinking pipe, which she stuck between her ivory teeth, and smoked like a chimney. I have in my time seen elegantly dressed women smoking delicate cigarettes, but never before saw a short clay pipe puffed by a young lady in sky-blue silk dress. The Maori women have a most musical way of talking, and you might back them for making play with their big liquid eyes—when they choose—against the beauties of Seville. This may be pleas-ant when the performer is a good-looking half-caste, whose broken English is sweetly fasci-nating; but not so when the lady is an unadulterated, fully matured Maori, with broad nose, cavernous mouth, and frizzy unkempt hair, whose underlip, thanks to the national tattoo, is blue as a dew-worm, who carries a baby bundle at her back under her shawl, and who smokes her perpetual pipe, with the smutty bowl downwards.

Some Europeans say that the Maoris are lazy. Why not? They work enough to live, and mankind must go to school and church before it finds out that work is dignified and noble. I met colonists who could not use objurgations too strong against the Maoris—'niggers' as, John Bull fashion, they term them; but there was generally room for suspicion that the secret of this hatred was that the Maoris were too acute for them. My first impression of them was that, bodily and mentally (considering what they are), they were a fine and very interesting race, and nothing that I subsequently saw—and I saw a good deal of them—corrected the impression. We may call them savages, of course. It is our nature to; and they may be savages still. In many things, nevertheless, they can show some claims to be considered civilized; they can boast of wars as bloody and skilful—of alliances and quarrels between men and men as ruthless—of keeping the weak in subjection to the strong as rigorously—of their poets and orators as famous in their way—of religious beliefs and ceremonies as mysterious—as any nation in Christendom.

William Senior, *Travel and Trout in the Antipodes*, pp. 195–9.

Mr Jones at Rotomahana (1877)

A GERMAN LADY

Miss Muller's account of her trip to Rotomahana illustrates some of the difficulties of a woman travelling alone: undesirable companions and the sheer hard work of making arrangements. Miss Muller's personality and the liveliness of her observations are strikingly clear in her description of the unattractive Mr Jones, who soon loses part of his title and becomes simply 'Jones'.

THE CELEBRATED LAKE ROTOMAHANA, about 12 miles distant from Lake Rotorua, had next to be visited, but there happened to be no one at the hotel to make up a party with me. Mr Glowworm had joined his brother at Ohinemutu[.] [H]e was a colossal creature, clad in a bandit's costume, and they both explored the neighbourhood together. I therefore determined to go alone and to profit by the fine weather. A coach was expected that evening from Tauranga, which might bring probably some tourists for Rotomahana, and as I strolled out among the springs later on, I saw a tall stout individual, in a suit of grey, poking with his walking stick into a fiercely boiling hole, and leaning forward to peep down into it. The old man looked in that posture so much like a Kiwi (a native bird without a tail, but has a very long pointed bill which it thrusts into the earth for insects), that I laughed, and hearing the sound, the stranger turned round and said to me in a thick, slow utterance, 'A wonderful country this!' Then we got into conversation, and he told me that he had come from Tauranga, where he had business transactions, when finding he was so close to the Rotomahana he had come on to see it. When I said that I was ready to go there, and would be glad of company, he thought that we might share the expense, but did not bind himself ultimately, saying that he would let me know on the morrow. I then guided him about the various springs, and after having told him my name and the hotel I lived in, we parted.

The only person who has a conveyance and horses for hire wanted £3 to take me to Wairoa, a small Maori settlement with one accommodation house, where travellers to Rotomahana generally pass the night. I did not choose to pay this enormous sum, but determined on walking to Wairoa, as it is only 10 miles distance, and starting early in the morning I would have all day to get there comfortably. I engaged a native guide, Hone Wallace, at ten shillings a day and board, who was to carry my luggage. He is a very reliable young man who can speak English very well. The next morning about nine o'clock, when I was ready to start, my acquaintance of the previous night came, with indecision on his countenance, to enquire whether I was going to Rotomahana. I told him of the arrangement I had made, and the cost of the trip, leaving it to him to join me or not. After a great deal of inward struggle and repeating twice in his heavy way, 'It would be a pity to be so near Rotomahana and not to see it,' he said, 'if you have no objection I should like to join you.' He then went for his coat, and the guide having just come up, we started at once. On the road I asked my companion his name, he told me it was 'Jones'. I found him to be a well educated man and pleasant enough. The first part of the road was hilly, and the sun made exercise rather fatiguing; but soon we reached a beautiful piece of bush where the high native trees met together overhead, and the supple Jack, a strong, rape-like creeper that interlaces the branches of trees and creeps up to the very top hanging down to the ground, makes it appear like a primeval forest, which can but be traversed with difficulty. It was beautifully cool here, and lovely ferns grow in abundance.

Mr Jones and Hone had arranged a seat for me, and we partook of some pork and porter. As I had only a pint bottle of porter and no glass to drink it out of, I took some myself from the bottle, and gave the rest to the guide, who was not accustomed to walking and must be thirsty. I regretted that I could not offer any to Mr Jones who was very thirsty, and went in quest of some water.

Whilst Hone took his dinner at a respectful distance from me, I tried to press as many ferns as it was possible to put among blotting paper. The forest looked lovely, here and there a strong sunbeam upon the branches and across beautiful fern nooks, and perfect stillness everywhere. At last, the tall figure of Mr Jones was seen stalking up among the trees, he had not been able to find any water, and from that moment his temper was no more the same. He walked along grumbling at the expense of the trip, saying what a pity it was that I had engaged a guide, he could have carried my luggage and so on. Then he declared that he must be back at Ohinemutu the next night to catch the coach for Tauranga the following day, and when I told him there was nothing to prevent him from doing so, he yet continued finding fault, and to crown all, I detected him in sniffing his nose with his fingers. I think after this the term of Mr may go to the winds and he be called simply Jones.

When we had traversed the forest and emerged again into sunlight we soon came to a lovely lake, Tikitapu, surrounded by wooded hills. The water is deep blue, and we descended through high fern to the pretty beach, where Jones declared he should like to build a house, that is, if he had a fixed salary of £300 a year. Whether the lake would be embellished by Jones' residence on its shores I know not, but at present lying there in its stillness it cannot be more beautiful. Quite close to it is another lake Rotokakahi (still lake), with a small island in the middle, and likewise surrounded by hills. Some wild ducks were swimming in the water, and the sinking sun cast its rays across the lake. We tried the echo by calling 'Pakeha' (stranger, European), Hone and ho! I answered back very powerfully. At the last named lake we had overtaken a Maori family proceeding to Wairoa. They shouted something to our guide, and when I asked him to translate to me what they were saying, he told me that they wanted to know why we were on foot, and why the wahine who was so stout could walk so well.

At last we arrived in Wairoa where a number of natives were assembled before the hotel where they had lately been having a Tangi (lamentation for the dead). Some of their relatives had come from the Waikato fever stricken, and died.

Mr Wakeham has called his accommodation house the Cascade Hotel, it is a humble dwelling, but I had a comfortable bedroom assigned to me, and both the landlord and the wife did all they could to make us comfortable. Here again the fatal mistake was made of taking Jones to be my husband, and then he was heard worrying me about the expense of the trip, and that explains their error. Indeed Jones now launched forth in incessant grumblings, asking whether the guide was to have any food, and if so would we have to pay for it? Assuredly we would have to pay exactly the same amount for him as for ourselves, but we would divide the cost. 'Surely,' said he, 'that Maori ought to be content with a piece of bread!' But the Maori had an appetite as well as ourselves, and would be hungry enough after the unaccustomed long walk. The verandah of the hotel was crowded with natives in all sorts of costumes, they looked in at us as we were waiting for tea getting ready. Some old chief came forward to shake hands, and when they came to Jones he growled, 'Oh, take care of my hat! What is the use of all this gushing,' and looked so cross at the kind faces that I felt ashamed of such manners. Mr Glowworm and his brother were expected that night from Rotomahana, but as they did not make an appearance when the usual tea hour had come, we sat down without them. After tea, a Frenchman, Pierre de Fangerrand, who acts as guide to travellers, and used formerly to accommodate them in his whare, when there existed no hotel, spoke to me in his native tongue, and seemed ill-pleased that I had not secured his services instead of those of a native. However, after he had given vent to his displeasure on that head, he bore us no further malice, but seeing that Jones and I suffered from the cold, there being no fireplace at the hotel, he invited us very kindly to his whare, where he had lighted a fire. The evening was very cold and damp, and the natives were carousing in the bar when we went to the Frenchman's residence, where everything was beautifully neat. A small garden in front, well cultivated, provided him amply with vegetables of all kinds. He kills plenty of wild fowl at the neighbouring lakes, and is said to be an excellent cook. In the middle of the floor on entering the whare, a kind of hearth has been made, on which a merry wood fire was burning. The smoke escaped through an opening in the roof, after being first turned to account by smoking wild ducks. Mr Fangerrand then told us reminiscences of his life, especially his adventures during the Maori war, when he acted as scout, and that drew Jones out who spoke about Samoa a great deal. I also saw the list of visitors who had been staying under Mr Fangerrand's roof, and seen Rotomahana under his guidance. Then we partook of some fine apples and went back to the hotel. Here, everything had become quiet; the natives were all in their homes, and we enjoyed in consequence a good night's rest. At six o'clock, while it was yet dark, we got up, and whilst breakfast was getting ready, Jones began growling and doubting whether we should be back in time that night for him to start for Ohinemutu.

The landlord whispered to me, 'Get rid of that man ma'am, or he will be a perfect pest to you.' Indeed that had been my conviction long before, so I stepped boldly forward addressing Jones in these words: 'We are going to see great beauties of nature, the poetry of which we cannot enjoy if you go there in such a grumbling spirit. If you regret the arrangement made with me, I release you from it, and will bear all the expense myself; now, say no more, for I am not accustomed to be bothered in this way, and do not at all like it.' Then he began making excuses, but declared that he would engage a canoe for himself, saying that he ought to give me some money towards the expense of the guide. But I would not have his money, and begged not to have the matter mentioned again. Then Jones departed with two natives, and soon after I started with my guide Hone and four natives. It was a little after seven o'clock a dense fog enveloped everything around, we had to descend a steep hill full of ruts and broken ground. It was hard work to get down, but the guide helped me very kindly, and at last we reached the bottom quite warm with the exertion. A small creek had to be crossed before Lake Tarawera is reached, the natives being barefoot, did this very nimbly, the guide and myself were carried respectively on the back of a native. This was very new indeed to me, for the first time in my life had I been carried over water in this manner. I truly regret that I cannot furnish a sketch of the proceeding, for I should really like to see myself how it looked. I must leave it to the imagination of anyone who may read this, reserving to myself all description of the position I occupied on the native's back.

A nice, strong-looking canoe, about 26 feet in length, called Ngarararua (the lizard with two tails), lay ready to receive us. Dry fern had been placed in the bottom and a seat arranged for me to sit on a rug. The natives then used their paddles, and we moved on. Together with us started a wretched, unseaworthy looking canoe, with Jones seated in the middle, and two mischievous looking young natives at each end, calling Jones Pakeha, and laughing and winking over at my natives. Certainly Pakeha Jones did look funny, a heavy crouching mass covered with a grey cloak on his head, a white helmet hat under which the discontented face and turn-up nose provoked a smile.

The thick fog prevented us from seeing the beautiful shores of Lake Tarawera, and hindered the natives from rowing quickly, as they could not see their way. Four whole hours we spent on this lake before reaching the creek Ariki, which connects Lake Tarawera with Rotomahana. My natives behaved admirably, was it because I had a native guide with me, or was it the case bottle of rum that I discovered lying in the coat, and which I took to be belonging to the Maoris. In reality it was Mr Wakeham who had put it there without my knowledge, in order to secure for me a proper behaviour from the natives. I learned that afterwards, when the bill was presented, and felt disappointed, for I fondly believed that the much maligned natives had been so respectful on my own account.

When we passed a large projecting rock the native nearest me thrust some dry fern into my hand, took some himself, threw it on the stone, and motioned to me to do likewise. My guide explained that it is a peace offering to the Taipo (evil spirit), who dwells there, and raises a contrary wind on our return if he is not pacified by some gift. It appears that Pakeha Jones was also urged by his crew to throw something to the Taipo, and as he did not understand what they meant he threw a lighted match that he happened to have in his hand on the stone. This caused great dissatisfaction. The narrow creek Ariki that connects Lake Tarawera with Rotomahana is one seamile long, and has a very swift current. Luxuriant vegetation on each side droops over the banks, and make it very hard work to push the canoe along. Indeed the natives earn their money well, five shillings each and five shillings for the canoe for the whole day. As the creek is shallow, the Maoris one after the other stripped partly and jumped into the water pushing the canoe along. In and out like lightning they jumped, arranging themselves so decently and dexterously that the most timid person need feel no alarm. I admired their grace when, with uplifted arms they moved a long pole by way of a rudder in the water, their beautifully shaped limbs coming out in full strength, and their good-humoured ways and combined efforts in pushing the canoe along were pleasant to watch. When a party of tourists is in such a canoe, they have to alight at the creek and walk along the shore to the Terraces, but as only myself and guide were in the canoe, we remained sitting quietly. Every now and then I dipped my hand into the water and felt it to be quite warm, mahana, the native opposite would say, nodding very good-humouredly.

On a small projecting peninsula in the creek stood a native whare and the family had all gathered on the shore to see us pass. A lively conversation then began with the crew of the two canoes, my guide translated part of it to me. These good people wanted to know why the

Josiah Martin, 'White Terrace cups', a view of the White Terraces at Rotomahana, c. 1880 (F-103404-1/2, ATL)

wahine and the Pakeha had two separate canoes, why the wahine was alone and where she came from? My crew asked the guide to enquire of me why I had come so far to see the hot lakes, surely the world was full of Rotomahanas and Terraces everywhere?

The natives look upon all these wonderful natural curiosities with the greatest indifference, not only because the sight is familiar to them, but they lack admiration of nature altogether. When the creek had been traversed I was told to get out now and very glad was I to hear it, for the prolonged sitting in the flat bottomed canoe for four hours had become very tedious. For a short distance I walked along accompanied by the guide and one of the crew, when all of a sudden the white Terrace came in view with the water flowing down its marble like steps, and a fierce steam breaking out of the top basin. The weather was rather gloomy, everything was quiet round about, Lake Rotomahana looked rather insignificant, but what did it all matter compared to the majesty of this white Terrace, the first aspect of which was to me overpowering. I wanted to stop and look but we had not over much time to spare, so we ascended the steps at once, wading all the time through warm water, and going as near the crater as the sulphurous smoke would let us. The lovely shaped basins with delicate designs, looking like frosted tracings on stone with the water flowing down incessantly, are quite beyond description, they must be seen. Unfortunately the wind blew the steam from the top crater so strongly into our faces that we could not approach and look down into it. But there are days when the top basin is quite empty, and then one may go round it and also ascend the island in the middle. When the white Terrace has got all the attention that may be bestowed on it during the short space of time, the guide turns to the right side into some ti-tree scrub, and here are more marvels to behold. A beautiful dark green substance boils up from the side of the hill covering all the way down with it, and hot drops jump out of the top. Then there are numerous boiling mud pools, a huge hole out of which steam booms with such noise that one cannot hear one's own words, several geysers inactive for the moment and boiling wells in every direction. It looks very awful and wonderful. Plenty of sulphur is everywhere, in the atmosphere, and crystallised. My guide constructed a little mountain of boiling mud sulphur on the top, the whole fastened to a flat stone, we called it mount Tarawera, and it caused much amusement among the natives.

In order to reach the Pink Terrace, Lake Rotomahana has to be crossed. Before doing that, my guide proposed to have lunch first. The natives had been busy boiling their potatoes, in one of the hot wells close to the shore of the lake. They sat down to this frugal meal, while my guide prepared a seat for me apart and opened a tin of preserved meat. There was besides bread and beer, and the Maoris stook looking on like children. After having served my guide and myself I gave them all the rest.

They do not say 'thank you', but looked exceedingly pleased and proceeded forthwith to warm the meat by suspending the tin from a string into the hot spring. This is a great improvement to the meat I am told. When I cast my eyes into the direction where the Maoris were sitting busily engaged eating their food, I had to withdraw them very quickly, for their fingers were dabbling in the tin and they sucked the meat off them. I said kapai (good). Kapai was the unanimous rejoinder, coupled with a most expressive pantomime.

During this time Pakeha Jones and his two natives had nothing at all to eat, the Pakeha would not incur the expense of taking provisions for himself, and he never troubled about the two Maoris. Crossing the lake towards the Pink Terrace lasts but a few minutes. This Terrace looked lovely, for the sun appeared now and then showing off the delicate pink hue of the basins in all its delicacy. In some parts the beauty of the steps is quite overwhelming. Steam also issues from the crater here, and the water that fills the basins is of an indescribable blue tint, beautiful in the extreme. When bathing in it, the limbs look like pure marble. I did bathe in the middle basin of beautiful shape and deep enough to let the water reach up to the shoulders.

In the ti-tree scrub I undressed, and the bath was reached from there very quickly. The water was so exquisitely soft and agreeably warm that I could hardly persuade myself to leave it. A rather cold wind was blowing in the back, but it has no bad effects while one is in the bath. Behind me the steam was ascending from the crater, and I looked down from the middle basin upon the lake and the opposite shore. I was apparently quite alone, for the guide and the natives had retired, and let me say this for their discretion that they not once attempted to look back at me; they are so accustomed to see each other scantily dressed that it never enters their heads to be curious on this subject. Besides, why should they wish to see European live statues when they themselves are so far superior in shape?

When my guide had joined me again, he pointed out a place where to write my name, but I now regret having written it, for seeing the beautiful steps of the Pink Terrace defiled with these written names, is really a disgrace. It is desecration felt all the more, because the writings will remain indelible thereon. The first names that caught my notice were those of Mr Glowworm and his brother, the bandit, written with a blue pencil, and occupying a large space. I met Pakeha Jones sauntering leisurely about the steps of the Terrace, with his arms under his coat tails, and his nose was turned up more than ever. I said: 'What do you think of these marvellous beauties, are they not splendid?' 'Yes', drawled he, with pursed up mouth. I afterwards knew that he had been disappointed in both Terraces. I then took a last comprehensive view of the whole Terrace, just when the sun was shining full upon it. Impossible to imagine the glorious beauty of it! Then my natives cried, 'hokitata' (we will go home), and I entered the canoe again to turn my back for ever on Rotomahana.

A German Lady [Miss Muller], *Notes of a Tour through Various Parts of New Zealand*, pp. 23–7.

With the Maoris (1880)

W. TOWERS BROWN

William Towers Brown visited New Zealand during a world tour in 1880 when he was 21. Notes of Travel *was compiled from letters sent home to his parents and published in memoriam after he and his wife drowned in a shipwreck off Dieppe in 1887, less than three months after their wedding.*

AT WHATOO THEY are accustomed to see Europeans, because overland to the Waikato from the south travellers generally come this way. One of the 'wharrys' or native huts is therefore a sort of accommodation house, and you can get a bed (a luxury unknown to the Maoris of course) and a meal. We made for this 'wharry', and were received by the household. Shall I describe how they were dressed? Well, there was a middle-aged man with shirt, waistcoat and blanket, an old gentleman ditto, with the exception of the waistcoat. Then, there were several boys with trousers instead of blanket, and some girls. I shall come to the latter's costume directly. After a wash, we went down in the village. On a green in front of three of the principal 'wharries' were a lot of men, squatting down and talking. Others were playing cards, or looking after horses, &c., and there was a constant stream of new arrivals. Some wore shirt, trousers, and blanket; some shirt, trousers, and no blanket; some shirt, blanket, no trousers; others blanket, no shirt or trousers. Some also wore coats, but these, I suspect, were the swells. My guide could understand a little Maori, so we sat down with the company I first mentioned, shaking hands all round. They are *very* fond of shaking hands. I went in for this more yesterday, at least with a greater number of people, than during the last six months almost. They knew my guide, but did not go in for the hand-shaking with him to the same extent. One was reading a letter to the others, and when a listener thought something in it rather silly, he made a noise in his mouth somewhat as if he was gargling, in the same way that we should say Tut, tut, tut. As I could not understand anything that was being said, I found it rather dull, so I went to the entrance of the 'pah', the name given to the fence or high paling, that runs all round the principal 'wharry'. Here were a lot of the women and girls and children. I soon had a great crowd round me, and a vigorous hand-shaking followed. I know the Maori for 'Good day,' so I repeated this to each, and each repeated it to me; then they would say a few words, and I would shake my head, whereupon they would laugh, and then I would laugh; and so we were very friendly. At last one old lady came with an empty pipe, and showed me that it was so. This was a fairly broad hint; so I brought out my pouch, and gave her a little tobacco. In a minute I had at least a dozen women and girls all with outstretched hands clamouring for some. I gave away a good deal, but as the numbers only increased, I had to stop, and tried to show them I had only enough for myself. You would like to know how the female part of the population dressed. I do not feel competent to tell you. They all had petticoats of various colours, and shirts, blouses, and so on, but their dresses looked such bunches of gaudy rags, it was impossible to make out exactly what was what. Taking them altogether, they were a very ugly lot: there was only one girl who could be called at all pretty, and I do not suppose she was more than thirteen. Many of the old dames were simply frightful, and I do not think the tattooing adds as much to their charms as they no doubt themselves consider it to do.

The tobacco excitement having calmed down, I saw what really was a very curious and very interesting sight. A man, with two women, two boys, and two small children came into the village. A number of the inhabitants stood in front of one of the wharries, facing the new arrivals who stood about fifty yards off. Then, when they had thus arranged themselves, each party simultaneously began a long, low, wailing cry. It seemed the cry of bitterest anguish, rising gradually to a high note, and then dying away. Some words, I fancy, were used, but generally it seemed an inarticulate cry. One old woman, holding a green bough in her hand, came forward from the rest of the home party, seeming to be sometimes perfectly overcome with emotion, and breaking into sobs. The man newly arrived seemed also much affected. They kept this up with great vigour for over ten minutes, and then all shut up, and went on with their ordinary duties.

'The Zulu War, Battle of Ulundi, Final rush of the Zulus against the British', from the *Illustrated London News*, 1879. (C-23598-1/2, ATL)

The full explanation of this scene was given me in the evening. I then went to another 'pah', and introduced myself to the company there. I shook hands with all the men. The women were busy preparing supper. The former were kind enough to ask me to join, which I gladly did, having had nothing since breakfast, and it was then 6. There were no mahogany tables or chairs, but we sat down on the ground round a big tin dish, into which we put our fingers and pulled out a smoking hot potato and a little bit of very fat bacon. The gravy was poured into a pannakin (which is the Colonial name for a little tin drinking cup) and each one had a drink. This formed the only drinkable. One of them was kind enough to give me a plate with knife and fork, and the tit-bits of meat were got out and put on it. All the men and boys fed first. When their wants had been seen to, the women looked after their own. The meal was surprisingly soon over. The food perhaps was not the daintiest, and the native way of eating it certainly a little piggy, but still it was very acceptable to my hungry stomach. One of this party who spoke English suggested I should become a 'pakeha' Maori, that is, an Englishman who lives entirely with the natives, and adopts all their customs and habits. I then went back to the 'wharry' where we were being put up. My guide had got back before. We had tea and some more pork and potatoes, served in civilised fashion, in the house, on a table. This 'wharry' was much larger than the generality, and had three rooms. In the first the family lived, the second and third were given up to visitors. On the wall of the second was that large picture that appeared in the *Illustrated London News* some months ago: 'Battle of Ulundi—Final Rush of the Zulus upon the British.' Below was written in Maori the interpretation of this heading. Just to think of its finding its way to a Maori hut in the wilds of New Zealand. The illustration must come home to the war-loving hearts of the Maoris. I wonder with which side they feel most sympathy. They are friendly enough with us, but still the Zulus are more a people after themselves.

After tea, we saw to the horses, and then walked down again into the village. I was asked to join a party of men, where there was one who could, knowing a little English, interpret what I said to the others, and interpret what the others said, to me. So I sat down with them on the grass, and we began to talk. The idea was most successful, and we got on swimmingly. They asked such questions as, How long had I been away from England? How far did I live from the Queen? How much money was required to go to England? Whether there were hot springs in England? whether any bush? whether such fine trees? Whether I had seen any Maoris there? I answered all these as well as I could, and asked several in return. The man who acted as amateur interpreter explained the curious performance in the afternoon.

The man who had just arrived had been away ten years. Those with him were his belongings. The old lady who displayed the extra amount of sorrow was the widow of this man's brother. You will think, now you have got the explanation, that the people were wailing because the death of their friend was brought back to their minds by the presence of his brother, and that the latter was overcome at hearing the news. Nothing of the kind. There would have been just the same scene, barring the exhibition of the old woman, had no one died. The interpreter said: 'If my brother go away for two months and come back, I cry to him and he cry to me, as those people. We must cry before we speak. We stand far off from each other like those.' I asked, 'Is it always done?' 'Yes, always when any one returns from a journey of any length.' I asked why they should cry at being home again? He said he did not know; it was Maori fashion. I asked then about the old woman, and he told me what I have told you: but he said the death of her husband was not in any way the cause of the demonstration. Close by us were a lot of boys and young men, having what with Maoris is called a *dance*, but the performance, if given the name, would not convey at all a correct idea of what it was. They stood round a blazing fire in a semicircle, and using arms, legs and heads, kept up a series of exercises. It really was a ludicrous sight, and the way they all enjoyed it was delightful. All through the dance they sang; stopping short now and then most unexpectedly. The effect of the whole was wonderful. If they could be brought to Wokingham and do it at an entertainment, they would 'bring the house down.' And how much more worth seeing when they were doing it for their own pleasure round the blazing logs in their own native wilds! Rain put a stop to our talk, and also to the dance. All went in to their respective wharries, and my guide and I groped our way in the dark up the hill to our 'hotel'. The party here were all playing cards. We got to bed at once. Rather rough beds of course, but still *beds*. I did not fall asleep for some time, thinking of the strange evening I had spent; and besides, the card-players were very noisy.

W. Towers Brown, *Notes of Travel*, pp. 80–5.

Food and fire at Kumara (1881)

JAMES EDGE PARTINGTON

James Edge Partington's journal of his three-year tour of the world, which began in 1879, formed the basis for his book Random Rot. *Edge Partington spent three months in New Zealand at the beginning of 1881. He subsequently published articles on Maori artefacts in the British press.*

THE SCENERY BETWEEN Waimea and Kumara was very pretty, bold cliffs standing out in strong contrast to the rich green of the bush, rolling mountains, thickly timbered, backed up by the snow-clad Alps. Kumara is an ordinary bush township, showing evident signs of its late origin—stumps on all sides. It is, in fact, hardly six years old, and possesses, at the very least, thirty public-houses. At one of these we stopped to dine, and then went for a stroll as far as Dillman's Town, about two miles away. Here there are tremendous sluicing works. The water is carried in races and then led down by pipes, either of tin or canvas, terminating in a large nozzle, to where they are working. The height from which the water comes causes it to be forced out with great violence. This they direct upon the side of some hill, which, by degrees, is washed away through a tail race, at the bottom of which are round slabs to prevent the gold being washed down. The number of races is something extraordinary. How intricate, indeed, must be all the water rights. The whole country round seems undergoing the process of being slowly washed away. Huge piles of stones lay about in all directions. After we had seen all the works we returned to Kumara in time to catch the tram for Greymouth, which is drawn by one horse over wooden rails. The line passes through the thickest bush; huge forest trees were on either side, the space cleared being only just broad enough for the single line of rails. It reminded me very much of the old convict tramway on Tasman's Peninsula, in Tasmania. Arrived at the Teremakau river, we had to cross in a cage running on two strong wire ropes. The distance across is 750 feet, and the weight of the cage with the runners about nine cwt. On the near bank is a saw-mill, used for cutting rails for the line. The same engine draws the cage backwards and forwards. The wires are fastened by strong anchors, let some distance into the ground, and pass over uprights. Going over is a pleasant sensation, more so for me on this occasion, as we had an evidently newly-married couple in the cage, as well as two men, and the bride, getting frightened, suddenly threw her arms round my neck. In crossing we did a very foolish thing. Four of us sat on one side and only one on the other, throwing the whole weight on to the one wire. On the other side was a fresh tram, waiting to carry us on. It was curious how the character of the bush differs on either side of the river. Up to the Teremakau it had been entirely of red pine, and on the other side of it there was nothing but black birch. From this into Greymouth the line ran along the beach. The sea has encroached, as for miles the beach was sluiced away, and much gold found. This must be a curious road in winter; with a westerly gale blowing it becomes sometimes almost impassable, on account of the foam. The driver told us that about six months ago the foam was fourteen feet deep, and entirely stopped him. Men had to go on with shovels and beat it down. Some horses get so accustomed to it that they will actually go through it. We reached Greymouth at six o'clock, and found some difficulty in finding rooms, as yesterday and to-day have been their annual race days, and consequently the town is very full. We got a room, however, at the Albion, and there found a most loquacious landlord, quite a character. The town is built at the mouth of the Grey river, and along its southerly bank the main street faces to the river, with the railway running alongside. Here, too, there is a bad bar.

23rd March.—We started by the mid-day train for Brunnerton, about nine miles away, to visit the coal pits. The line up is particularly pretty, following along the bank of the Grey river. At Brunnerton there are three mines, two worked by shafts and one by a level cutting; it was for the latter that we had an order. In the managing engineer Tim discovered a man who had for many years worked at some of the large pits in Yorkshire, and many were the mutual friends they discovered. In conversation Tim and I discovered that we both knew J.B. S—, and he told me some rather amusing anecdotes about him. In this mine they turn out about 30,000 tons a year, working on an average three days a week. The other two mines turn out only about 20,000 tons. The coal is about the best in the colonies for gas-making purposes. A large quantity of it goes to Ballaarat, where it fetches 4s. per ton more than any other coal. Had they only a decent harbour within reach this would be a most thriving place, turning out any quantity of coal. The seam varies from ten feet to sixteen feet in thickness. There is coal all over this district, and at Westport it is worked also. They are at present trying very hard to overcome the bar difficulty by throwing out a tremendous breakwater. They have already spent on this over £150,000. To-day at high water there was only four feet of water on the bar. The 'Charlie Edward' is in. Supposing we had gone by her! When should we have got away? We talked to several of the miners, and they all of them regretted having ever left home. One man had been earning as much as 50s. a week, with house and food, and as much beer as he could drink, fire, education for his children, and one of his boys was earning besides 10s. a week for taking the newspapers round at night. This was at Nelson, and all this he had thrown up because he had heard there were large wages on the West Coast. The wages here average about 10s a day. He ended up by exclaiming, 'Old England, with all thy faults I love thee still.' That was too much for me, so I invited my friend to come with me to the nearest public-house, to discuss the matter over a pint of beer. Their great grievance is the price of beer, and its badness; a small glass for sixpence for a thirsty man soon runs away with money. After leaving the mine we went down to the river side, and helped a man wash for gold. All

DIETARY.

This has always been a special feature on board the Company's vessels, the cuisine being unsurpassed by that of any line in the world. The **Saloon** table is of the most ample and elaborate kind, and will be found to satisfy the most fastidious tastes. By means of the refrigerating chambers fitted in all the Company's steamers, fresh meat, poultry, game, fish, butter, milk, ice, &c., are available throughout the voyage, and the other provisions are also kept cool and fresh. **Second Class** passengers also get a free and excellent table, the dishes supplied to them, although not so numerous as at the saloon table, being of similar quality. **Third Class** passengers have a full supply of the best provisions, and a very liberal allowance of fresh meat.

The **Hours for Meals** are, as a rule :—

1st SALOON ...	Tea and Coffee ...	...	6.0 a.m.
„ ...	Breakfast ...	...	9.0 „
„ ...	Luncheon ...	...	1.0 p.m.
„ ...	Afternoon Tea ...	...	4.0 „
„ ...	Dinner ...	...	6.0 „

Tea and Coffee in the evening and Ices occasionally.

2nd SALOON...	Tea and Coffee ...	...	6.0 a.m.
„ ...	Breakfast ...	...	8.30 „
„ ...	Dinner ...	...	1.30 p.m.
„ ...	Meat Tea ...	...	6.0 „

3rd CLASS passengers have their meals at the same hours as the Second Class, and the following is a fair sample of a week's bill of fare :—

	BREAKFAST.	DINNER.	TEA.
SUNDAY ...	Coffee, Irish Stew, and Bread and Butter.	Soup, Fresh Meat, Potatoes, Bread and Plum Pudding.	Fresh Bread and Butter (Jam or Marmalade if preferred) and Tea.
MONDAY ...	Porridge, Coffee, Bread and Butter, and Sugar or Syrup.	Preserved Meat, Potatoes, Curry and Rice, and Bread.	do.
TUESDAY ...	Coffee, Bread, and Hashed Meat.	Pea Soup, Salt Pork, Potatoes, Pickles, and Bread.	do.
WEDNESDAY.	Coffee, Bread and Butter, Porridge, and Sugar or Syrup.	Fresh Meat, Bread and Potatoes.	do.
THURSDAY ...	Coffee, Irish Stew, Bread and Butter.	Corned Beef, Potatoes, Pickles, Carrots, Bread and Plum Pudding.	do.
FRIDAY... ...	Coffee, Bread and Butter, Porridge, and Sugar or Syrup.	Soup, Salt Fish, and Sauce, Potatoes, Bread and Meat Pies.	do.
SATURDAY ...	Coffee, Bread and Hashed Meat.	Fresh Meat, Potatoes, Curry and Rice and Bread.	do.

The provisions for all classes of passengers are cooked by the ship's cooks and served by stewards.

ENTERTAINMENTS. — Concerts, Athletic Sports, &c., are organised during the course of the voyage for the amusement of passengers, and everything is done on board to render the passage a thoroughly enjoyable one.

'Dietary' from Shaw Savill & Albion Co., *Handbook of Information for Passengers*, c. 1890. (C-23284-1/2, ATL)

this country has, of course, been worked before, but there is still plenty of gold. We reached Greymouth again in time for dinner, and in the evening went to a theatrical performance. 'Aurora Floyd' and 'H.M.S. Pinbehind' were the two pieces performed. In the town we discovered a most amusing barber, a German, who has been in many parts of the world. He likens the life here to worse than being in prison. Nothing to do but eat, sleep and work, and no enjoyment, besides every luxury being so fearfully expensive. He longed for his café, where he could sit and listen to singing and drink his coffee.

24th March.—We returned by the early train, stopping again at Kumara for dinner. It is astonishing how clean these out-of-the-way hotels are, and how well they feed you. Imagine a town at home, only five years old, giving you the following *Menu:*—Kidney soup. Salmon. *Roast:* Lamb and mint sauce; beef. *Boiled:* Loin of mutton and caper sauce. Pickled pork. Stewed steak and olives. *Vegetables:* Cabbage, potatoes, carrots, peas. Marmalade roley-poley, apple pie, baked custard, black currant tarts, stewed apples, and custard. Cheese. And all for half-a-crown! We reached Hokitika at about four o'clock, and went in to see Mr C——. Before we left for Greymouth he had offered us £5 for our saddles and bridles on the chance of finding them. He had since heard by telegram that they had turned up all right, and that it was the livery stable keeper who had forgotten to put them into the horse box along with the horses. He gave us the £5, and made us each a present of a small nugget of gold, worth, I should say, about £2 each. They will make good scarf pins. In the evening, we went to see a Christy Minstrel performance, which was announced in the streets by the bellman, 'Now, ladies and gentlemen, hurry up, &c.'

25th March.—At two o'clock this morning we were awakened by the fire-bell, and at once turned out. It was one of the large stores in the main street, and great was the excitement in the town, as you can well imagine, as in a wooden town, if there is a strong wind blowing, there is no telling where it may stop. When we arrived at the scene of the fire no engine had begun, but there were two in attendance. They were busy pulling the blazing house to pieces with a huge grapnel at the end of a pole with a rope attached, so that the crowd could assist. It was most exciting: the houses on either side were dragging their belongings out wholesale. I saw an old lady dancing wildly amongst a lot of glass globes, and when spoken to by the owner replied that she was too excited to know what she was doing. Some of the costumes were amusing, they, too, evidently having been too excited to wait and adorn themselves. Fortunately, there was no wind, and they confined the fire to the one store. At five o'clock we started on our return journey to Christchurch, with every prospect of lovely weather. Besides ourselves there was only one other passenger—rather different to the coach K— and H— went by, as they were crammed full both inside and out. The rivers and falls were marvellously low. In some, which had been roaring torrents, there was now hardly a pannikin full of water. We noticed this particularly yesterday at the Kapitea Creek, where the bridge was washed away. We had a most lovely drive now. We could see all the hill tops and the wooded slopes, down which were plainly marked the course of this year's avalanches. We crossed the Taipo, and even now it was a nasty ford. Going some distance up stream, the ford is right down the very centre of the river. We reached the Bealey once more at about five o'clock. On the hills above there was a large bush fire raging. In the dark the burning fences looked exactly like streams of lava. We were a goodly number at tea, as three coaches meet here.

James Edge Partington, *Random Rot*, pp. 336–9.

Brown bread (1882)

THORPE TALBOT

Thorpe Talbot was the pseudonym of Frances Ellen Talbot, who was born in Yorkshire and lived part of her life in Victoria and in Dunedin. Little is known about Talbot, but she is identified on the title page of The New Guide to the Lakes and Hot Springs *as the author of three novels. She was said to have been the mistress of Judge C.D. Ward, whom she married in 1902. She published travel articles in the Otago* Witness *in 1887.*

OUR FELLOW PASSENGERS were two: a thin little man, with meek eyes and gentle expression of countenance; and a rusty complexioned individual, nearly six feet high, and bulky in proportion. We were not five minutes on our road before the latter began to grumble about the difficulty he always had in getting brown bread anywhere outside of big towns. He hadn't had brown bread that morning for breakfast, he said, and he spoke of his misfortune in a tone that seemed to imply that we were to blame for it. The little man shifted nervously in his seat, and made some consolatory remarks in the smallest and softest of voices. But this seemed only to increase the big man's exasperation. He abused the country, the coach, the weather, the road, the people; and all in that same tone of aggressive personal reproach that had already irritated us into wishing the gods had loved him so that he had died young. We felt that such blossoms as he should be nipped in the bud, and that scarlatina and measles were doubtless wise dispensations when they carried to a brighter and a better world infants that might otherwise grow up and be men like unto this man. As we approached the site of the Gate Pa, Robertson, our driver, began to relate the story of the great skirmish of 1864. He repeats that story to every tourist, of course; it is part of his bounden duty, and how sick he must be of the repetition! He told us how the 43rd regiment fired ruthlessly on the 68th in the dark, firmly believing that it was Maori foes they were slaughtering; and how—here he was interrupted by our rusty traveller, who said, excuse him, but it was the 68th who fired on the 43rd. Robertson said it was not. Rusty said it was. Reference was made to me, but I distinctly declined giving an opinion. I had already heard four entirely contradictory accounts of that massacre and read several others, so I begged to stand out.

The meek little man, raising his voice a bit, took sides with our driver. Rusty, pitching his to a thunderous shout, wanted to know how anybody dared to contradict him. He had heard all about that fight, a hundred and fifty times at least, from eye-witnesses, and he knew perfectly well he was right. Robertson was just getting ready something to say, when, all of a sudden, the little man made a lunge at the big one, that, taking him by surprise, actually overset him into the bottom of the coach.

'Can it be possible,' I said, 'that there is going to be a fight?' 'Not in the coach, certainly,' replied Robertson. 'Catch hold a minute,' giving me the reins. I caught hold, and he leaned over into the interior just as Rusty was plunging up out of the depths of his astonishment and the little man—standing erect, with feet well planted apart, fists clenched, and head bulging out the leathern roof of the coach—was making ready for a collision. Just as the collision took place, Robertson reached over, laid his shoulder against the two, and out they went. Rusty seemed dumbfounded. The little man scrambled up, and played round him like forked lightning.

'Brown bread,' he shrieked, in a voice as ferocious as the pipe of an insulted canary or the squeak of an indignant mouse. 'Brown bread! Pitching into me about your brown bread— ach! Get up, till I knock manners into you; get up, till I teach you who licked at Gate Pa; get up, before I make another sanguinary massacre to lie about. Get up, I say—ach!'

Then he began to swear in Welsh, and Rusty, leaning upon his elbow, tried to figure out the exact position of affairs; and then Robertson remarked that time was up, but he didn't want to hurry anybody. He would pull up at Oropi for a few minutes and they might catch up the coach there. If not quite through by then, they might come on to the stables at Mangorewa, where we should lunch and change horses. But all this was wasted, for the little man was encircling the big one like a halo, and the big one was busy turning his head round, as if it were fixed on a revolving screw, in order to watch the little one, so that neither of them heard a word. Robertson lashed up our fiery chargers, and we ambled on at the usual number of knots per hour. Before we reached Oropi the little man, hot and panting with his run, caught up to us.

'What's come o' the other warrior?' enquired Robertson, calmly pulling up.

'Left him wiping the blood off with fern-leaves,' was the laconic response, and the little man clambered in. After that there was dead silence until some time after we entered the bush, and then the little man began to sing hymns in a sweet, thin tenor, and he quoted descriptive passages from the poets, and raved like an aesthetic about the loveliness of the scenery. Robertson said to me, 'This is an entirely new experience.' I said, 'I shouldn't wonder.'

Somewhere amidst that loveliest of forests we stopped to lunch and change horses. The rain was still falling, only a little heavier, if possible, than before. It seemed to come down in condensed streams between the high wooded ranges that shut in the road. We went into a whare, inhabited by a Maori roadmaker, named Nikora, and his wife, to eat lunch; and Mrs Nikora, a fine buxom specimen of brown womanhood, made us some tea. Just as we were remounting our coach, that of the opposition line came tearing up, and, behold, in it was Rusty. Instantly our little man became demoniacal again. 'Brown bread!' he screamed. 'Hi! Stop, you there! Brown bread—ach!' But the opposition flew on, and a curve in the road hid it quickly from view. The little man said that if Robertson would race that coach and lick it, he would pay double fare. Robertson said he wasn't ambitious about racing, and, besides, he couldn't spare time to attend any inquests, anyhow. So the little man smiled and grew meek and humble again, and sang and quoted poetry; and such a singular combination of pugnacity and amiability it was never my lot to come in contact with before or since. He told us some good stories too, and gave us advice that would likely be useful in travelling anywhere. And that reminds me of similar advice I heard elsewhere the other day. A gentleman was speaking of the nuisance of having to carry much luggage; he said the best way was only to have an empty waterproof bag. Someone asked what for, and he replied that then in case of rain you could take off your clothes and put them in the bag, thus ensuring a dry suit when the shower should be over. 'But what would you wear in the meantime?' 'Oh, you could wear a smile, you know; a smile is always becoming', was the response.

Thorpe Talbot, 'A Month in Hot Water', *The New Guide to the Lakes and Hot Springs*, pp. 6–8.

Fire at Te Ore Ore (1883)

HUGH STANLEY HEAD

Hugh Stanley Head left England in 1883 on a voyage for his health as a boy of 18. His letters and journals were kept by his mother and published by her after his death from consumption in 1890. He spent most of 1883 in New Zealand.

MASTERTON,
July 5th, 1883.

My Dear Mother,

I have just received your letter and the photographs, which were luckily a week late as you will see by the sequel. I am afraid you will never see the photographs I had taken in Wellington; however, they were not very good. Your letter is delightful, and cheered me up a good deal. Now I must tell my story, but you must excuse the writing, &c., as I am still rather shaky. You must know that Hood and Tom had gone over to a meeting at Carterton (some ten miles distant) on Friday, intending to return on Saturday. However the society of the Tancreds was too much for them, and they did not return till Monday. I had arranged to go up to Glendonald with Hood for a few days on Sunday afternoon. In the meantime I had been amusing myself one way and another, and had been particularly interested in reading again that remarkable book of Lytton's 'A Strange Story,' and had got all sorts of curious thoughts in my head. On

Sunday night I was determined to get rid of them, and so rode over to Masterton, where I spent a very lazy evening with Mrs Hosking. (I must mention that in the afternoon I had intended unpacking my box, which I had not done since I returned from Wellington, and putting my room in order. It only contained my dress suit and one other suit of clothes, one or two shirts, a few collars, ties, &c., but, as it was left in the hall, it struck me that in case of any emergency I should be able to save it.) But to return. When I got home I was still thinking over all the curious things in the story, and my thoughts did not leave off with sleep for my dreams were remarkable. I had some vague idea of some mysterious creature drawing blood from my face and telling me that this was only a preparation for something more that was to follow. I woke and put my hand to my face where I found blood, at the same time a large rat ran across my body and disappeared, he had been gnawing my mouth and chin. I got up and lit my candle to keep him off, but could not go to sleep with my candle in my basin, so I got up and put it in my bath full of water, but even that did not satisfy me, for after some time I blew it out and lumped the rats. I had a vague feeling of fire, and thought to myself that I could never sleep in that room again and be devoured by rats. The next morning I got up as usual, and put all my dreams and fears down to 'The Strange Story' and the rats. However, I wrote them all down in my diary, as I usually do anything that strikes me as curious. I rode into Masterton in the afternoon and cashed a cheque, as I wanted to pay a small debt, but not finding the man, I returned with all the money in my pocket. Tom turned up in a bad temper, as he said he was certain everything was going wrong, but after he had ridden round the run he seemed cheerful enough as things were very satisfactory. In the evening Tom received a business telegram from Wellington, which caused him to take out all his business papers from my box. He was very sleepy and lay on the sofa the whole evening. I read, but several times got up to look round as I thought I heard fire, but discovered it was only the crackling of our own logs. We went to bed at eleven. I felt a curious inclination to put out my better clothes for the morrow, but as it was too much trouble I laid my old suit with a flannel shirt by my bed. They were things of no value, and the clothes were spoiled by rough work. Tom took his book to bed as he was not sleepy. I soon fell into a very heavy sleep, but at about 2. 30 I was awakened by Tom, who called out 'The house is on fire!' I did not feel at all frightened, and said I had expected it. I snatched up the first things in my way—my old clothes, and rushed out to call the man who slept behind the kitchen. I took some time to open all the doors between my room and his. He is very deaf, and sleeps soundly, so I had some difficulty in rousing him. After this, I rushed back and down the passage to help Tom save his things. By this time the fire was issuing from the door of his room. In the chiffoniere outside there was a case of gunpowder and lots of cartridges. The drawing room was next door. We got in through a window and saved a table, four books, a work box, a blue vase, also our two greatcoats, both very burnt, two saddles that were in the veranda, and I just managed to pull out my box, which was close to the powder. Then I remembered my papers, and thinking the back of the house would be all right, and as we could save nothing more out of the front, I dashed through the flames, getting my hair all burnt off with the falling ceiling, and by the time I got through the flames, I saw at once it was impossible to reach my room or to return, as the whole place was full of smoke, which was fast choking me. I could not see, and had to close my eyes. At last I found the kitchen door, but could not find the handle. The fumes were suffocating, and I began to despair of ever getting through. A thing struck me then which must have made an impression on me at the time. I suppose I must have been only four or five years old, when a small house was burnt down at Stoke Newington, and a girl in trying to save her watch was suffocated. I remembered seeing the hearse. At last I found the handle and staggered through into the kitchen. I could hardly stand, and did not know where to find the door. I heard the powder explode, and at last by a lucky fluke found the door, and fell out into the open air. I felt more dead than alive, but the fresh air soon revived me. By the time I returned to Tom, in the front of the house, the whole place was one big blaze, and my room must have been alight when I passed it, as the current of air blowing down the passage spread the flames in that direction. The house was level with the ground in half an hour. Tom had saved nothing but his night shirt, greatcoat and a pair of boots, so he was very cold. Luckily the wind was not blowing in the direction of the outhouses and stable. It appears that Tom could not sleep, and after reading till about one, blew out his candle and went to sleep. In an hour and a half he woke up with all one side of his bed and room alight. The door was locked, and he only just escaped with his life. The fire must have been caused either by a spark from the candle, falling into some old picture frames covered with gauze that were standing by his bed, or by a piece of burning wood from his fire.

At about 5.30 we both rode into Masterton; by that time the reaction had begun and we both felt utterly homeless. Poor Tom looked inclined to cry at the slightest thought of it; he was quite unnerved. We managed to get some tea made at the hotel, and then tried to sleep, but found it was impossible. I felt very wretched during the morning, but a visit to Mrs Hosking made me feel much better. I was more lucky than Tom, having saved a few things and having a good many at the wash, but all my linen and most of my clothes were of course burnt, both our watches, all my jewellery, but what I valued most were my books, papers, and letters, all my little presents from home, things I can never replace, books I had had for years, that Tennyson Uncle Blomfield gave me, a book that was Charlie's, two volumes of my journal, besides nearly thirty pages of other writing. It is a record of nearly six months gone! Lots of things I wanted to tell you about when I came home, all my sketches (I had made a good many), in fact every bit of my large outfit completely destroyed. I did not even save a pair of boots. My poor seals were all melted, my studs and pins likewise, my introductions and photographs burnt. The only present I saved was that little book of Mrs Fox's, I am glad it was not burnt. Don't let anyone think it was Tom's fault, it was pure accident, and I owe my life to him, as I should have been burnt in my bed if he had not been in the house.

H.S. Head, *The Journals and Letters of Hugh Stanley Head*, pp. 37–40.

The haka, Sophia, and the White Terrace (1883)

B.H. BARTON

Bertram Hugh Barton wrote his journal while on a twenty-one-month tour of the world and sent it home as letters. He travelled with his brother and two cousins, leaving Ireland in 1881. They spent September and October 1883 in New Zealand. Barton records that he wrote his journal in 'one of Wedgewood's copying books with an agate pen'.

HALF-A-MILE FURTHER and we are in Wairoa, and surrounded by a young crowd of chattering Maoris. We are told we must go and see the waterfall before it is dark, so select a couple of bright-eyed urchins (they will only hunt in couples) to guide us to the spot. They are jolly little fellows, one especially. Ten years old he tells us he is, and goes on to give a complete history of his family, his schooling, &c., all in capital English, and with a very pure accent. At times he comes out with some delightful expressions, slang and otherwise, but in such a grave way and with such a deep voice, that it is impossible to help laughing; at the same time he has brass and cheek enough for twenty. The waterfall is pretty, but nothing very wonderful, and it is really almost too dark to see much, so we make for the hotel, a very decent little place under the same management as the 'Lake House'. As we were going in we were asked whether we would like to see the 'Hakka' danced. We had heard of this Maori revel, and after a short consultation determined to see what it was like. Accordingly, after dinner, we repaired to the building which is used for such entertainments, as well as for some religious services, legal courts, and other miscellaneous uses. It is not a large room, but it was packed as tight as ever it could hold with an audience of rather *lofty* ideas, all seated on the ground. We found our way into some 'reserved seats,' and saw the performance very well. It began soon after our entrance. It is a mistake perhaps to call it a dance, as the artists do not move out of their double row of fifteen, women in front, men behind. Neither of the sexes are remarkable for personal beauty, though some of their men are finely made fellows. One and all throw themselves heart and soul into the business of the evening, and it is certainly a very quaint and characteristic performance. It consists of all sorts of gesticulations, of their arms for the most part, and turning their bodies about, accompanied by various shrieks, groans, and wonderful snorting and roaring sounds through the throat; but the great feature is the wonderful unison with which

Sophia Hinerangi on the Terraces at Rotomahana. (F-43274-1/2, ATL)

they all act. There is but one motion all along the line, and the head, arms, and voices move like a machine. They are directed by a man standing at the end of the line in front, who guides their actions by some cabalistic signs of his own. There is not a great deal of variety about it, and after ten minutes you have really seen it all. (We had it for over an hour.) The only change is when the men come to the front, and then the gesticulations and shouting reach a tremendous pitch, and are extremely effective. I astonished the house slightly in the middle of the proceedings by lighting a piece of magnesian wire which I happened to have put in my pocket at the Fish River Caves. The 'Oh's!' the amazed silence, and then the shouts of applause, were highly amusing and of course they were not content till I had allowed one or two of them to light a piece for themselves. Equally of course, they burnt their fingers over it.

September 20*th*.—We got under weigh for the Terraces at 6. 30 on a lovely bright morning. A quarter of an hour's walk brought us down to the Lake (Tarawera) on which we were to embark, but we had to wait some time for our very deliberate crew, and then it required a good deal of chattering and settling to get them fairly started. There were five of them, very fair specimens of their tribe, and one or two of them really fine-looking men. The rowing was, to say the least, erratic, and frequent 'easies' were the order of the day—indeed, there were seldom more than four oars going at once. Their tongues, however, went incessantly and simultaneously, and apparently they were of an extremely facetious disposition, for they were in perpetual 'guffaws,' and then they would pull frantically for a dozen strokes or so, but as this was followed by an extra long easy we did not really get on much faster. The quantity of water too that they poured down their throats! literally *poured* down—I thought the glass would follow once or twice—was astonishing. Luckily we were in no hurry, and the Lake was most enjoyable, so we did not mind dawdling. It is a good-sized piece of water, with mountains rising up out of it all round, and running out into rocky peninsulas in places, or retiring into little bays and coves. At the helm was our guide and commandress-in-chief, the celebrated 'Sophia', a half-caste lady of middle age, and the proud mother of fifteen children. She is one of the two regular guides to the Terraces. Her dress was rather a curious combination; externally she revolved herself into an old ulster, and a cotton frock appearing at intervals, a frock that had seen better and cleaner days, and on her feet a pair of canvas shoes. She chatted away merrily in first-rate English with us, and now and again 'swore at' the crew, as she sat perched up in the stern of the boat, a short black pipe in her mouth, and a white handkerchief tied over her black curly thatch of hair. At one point on the shores of the wood we easied by a large rock, where one of the men got out and made a long speech or incantation to the Water Nymph of the place, afterwards coming round to beg an alms for the deity, which he was by way of hiding in a hole in the rock, in which we were solemnly assured a large sum lay amassed, presented by all passing boats to ensure a safe and prosperous voyage; such was the old belief of the natives. Now I need hardly say who takes charge of the deity's deposit account. About two hours' row brought us to land, and about a couple of miles' walk to Lake Rotomahana and the foot of the 'White Terraces'. These are a series of perfect terraces, irregular in height and form, and rising to a height of near 200 feet above the Lake. They are covered by a crest of mineral deposit from the water which trickles down all over them, the outflow of the several springs which rise to the surface all the way up. The colour of the Terraces is not exactly pure white, but resembles delicate tinted porcelain rather in appearance, while the water in all the pools and little cups is of pure opal, and seen from the top the effect of the contrast and the general view is striking and beautiful, as you look down this strange watercourse, with the blue lakes lying all about, and the staircase descending in broad platforms or narrow frosted steps. These are all quite clearly marked, except just at the bottom, where there is more of a gradual slope, and the edges are of a bold massive fringe of porcelain-like stalactites, looking as if suddenly petrified before falling quite over. The terraces all curve out in long sweeping curve, the lower one being, I should think, 200 yards in length, the ones above gradually narrowing up until reaching the top. The water varies as to the depth of the cascade. Now it was trickling down just over the soles of our boots, quite cold as it flows into the Lake, but getting warmer by degrees the higher you go, until arriving at the top you reach the main source, a huge boiling cauldron, about 100 feet across, and almost a perfect circle in shape. This is quite the best view of the terraces, and very beautiful it is, the different shelves of almost pure white or delicate rose tint opening out one after another underneath, and the lovely shell-like basins holding the water, bright sky-blue in colour, and looking so delightfully soft and inviting. We had to wait some minutes on the edge of the spring, as the steam

H.G. Robley, native games at Te Papa Camp, Tauranga, New Zealand, 1865: 'War dance of the Ngaiterangi'. (F-38108-1/2, ATL)

was so dense we could see nothing, until a gust of wind came and blew it away sufficiently for us to catch a flying glimpse of deep clear blue water, a much deeper shade than the water lower down, boiling and bubbling and occasionally spurting up a jet several feet into the air. At times this jet spouts up an immense height; at others, again, after a continuance of southerly winds, the crater, 90 feet deep, is left quite dry, and you can go down to the bottom of it. Its normal condition, however, is pretty much as we saw it. Round the edge of this enormous basin are encrustations of purest white all filigreed out, and forming a lovely contrast to the dark blue of the water. Right above and surrounding the crater on three sides rises a perpendicular cliff, all seared and burnt, and pierced with jets of steam. It looks very weird as you gaze upwards, the dense clouds of steam as they ascend adding to this effect, and making the cliffs seem higher than they really are. All this we saw only by dint of patience and waiting for the intervals for the steam to clear off. It was hot work, as the vapours had rather a suffocating effect, though not objectionally strong, and our feet felt rather as if we were standing on an oven; but it was well worth what little inconvenience we suffered. Sophia was most attentive and careful of our safety, and had lots of stories for our benefit of unfortunate individuals who had slipped into some of these scalding baths. She looked like business too, did the good lady, having discarded her ulster, her shoes, and stockings, and tucked up her dress so as to bring to view a short red flannel petticoat down to her knees and a fine pair of legs below them.

B.H. Barton, *Far from the Old Folks at Home*, pp. 334–7.

Te Tarata (1883)

J. KERRY NICHOLLS

Adventurer, scholar, and explorer James Kerry Nicholls explored the hostile King Country in 1883, having been given a letter of introduction from Sir George Grey to King Tawhiao. He also spent time in the 'Wonderland of New Zealand' and bathed at Te Tarata, the White Terrace.

WHEN WE HAD WALKED about a mile through the scrub, guided by the stately strides of Sophia, we ascended the summit of a low hill which looked down upon Lake Rotomahana, whose green-tinted waters, surrounded by clouds of steam, shone with an emerald-like brightness in the sunlight, while immediately in front of us the White Terrace, or famed Te Tarata, burst upon the view like a glittering heap of frozen snow just fresh from heaven. We were still some hundreds of yards from it, with the Kaiwaka flowing below, and although at first glance fair Te Tarata looked chaste and beautiful enough beneath the golden light, it appeared as if her proportions were somewhat cramped and stunted, and I began mentally to question the wisdom of Nature in not placing the wondrous monument of her handiwork higher up on the slope of the mountain which decked the delicate outline of the terrace in a variegated fringe of green. To my eye, the crystallized structure of pure white silica as it fell in congealed waves, as it were, from the steaming cauldron above, appeared too flat, and required height to add more effect to its grandeur, while the rugged mountain, which formed its background, as it rose above a vapoury cloud of steam, looked dwarfed and insignificant in comparison with the giant form of Mount Tarawera, which frowned in silent majesty from beneath its spiked crown, as if eager to annihilate everything that failed to come up to its own idea of ponderous beauty. Presently we descended the hill on which we stood, and crossed Kaiwaka by the canoe which had brought up the ladies, and, after picking our way through a small scrub, we suddenly came into the open, when, as if by the magic touch of an enchanter's wand, the whole scene changed, and Te Tarata, gleaming still white in the sun, rose in grand, yet delicate proportions high above our heads. The white ethereal vapour wreathed its summit, like a graceful summer cloud, the rugged hill which held Te Tarata, as it were, in its arms, stood out in bold relief against the clear blue sky, and nature, true to the inspired genius of her marvellous creative power, stood revealed in all her pristine loveliness.

I had seen the Himalayas and the Alps, the Blue Mountains of Tartary, the Rocky Mountains, and the Sierra Nevadas—all of these were ponderously grand and awe-inspiring. I had sailed over the principal lakes of Europe and America, floated down the Nile, the

Ganges, the Yangtze Kiang, the Missouri, and the Mississippi, through the thousand innumerable other rivers, all fair and beautiful. I had beheld the giant marvels of the Yosemite, and stood by the thrilling waters of Niagara; but for delicate, unique beauty, for chaste design, and sublime detail of constructions never had I gazed upon so wonderful a sight as Te Tarata. It seemed as if Nature had created the wonders of the lakes and mountains of this fair region with all the marvels of fire and water after the most enchanting design of earthly beauty, and had then gone into the realms of fable and romance, and thrown in a piece of Fairyland to complete the picture; or as if the gods, when they called these sublime works into being, had fashioned Te Tarata as a throne to recline upon whilst they gazed in admiration upon the beauties of their wondrous creations.

As we looked upwards the whole outline of the terrace assumed a semicircular form, which spread out at its base in a graceful curve of many hundreds of feet, as it sloped gently down to the margin of the lake. Then broad, flat, rounded steps of pure white silica rose tier above tier, white and smooth as Parian marble, and above them terrace after terrace mounted upward, rounded and semicircular in form, as if designed by the hand of man, guided by the inspiration of the Divine Architect. All were formed out of a delicate tracery of silica which appeared like lacework congealed into alabaster of the purest hue. Each lamination, or fold, of this beautiful design was clearly and marvellously defined, and as the glittering warm water came rippling over them in a continuous flow, Te Tarata sparkled beneath the sun as if bedecked with diamonds and myriads of other precious gems. Crystal pools, shaped as if to resemble the form of shells and leaves, and filled to their brims with water, blue and shining as liquid turquoise, charmed the eye as we mounted to every step, while around the edges the bright crystals of silica had formed encrustations which made them appear as if set in a margin of miniature pearls. Every successive terrace seemed to spring up in grander proportions from the one immediately below it as we approached the summit, not in formal angular-shaped steps, but in flat-topped elevations, with rounded edges and sweeping curves, from which the wet, glittering silica hung in the shape of sparkling stalactites, which, interlacing themselves and mingling together, formed a delicate and almost transparent fringe which looked like a fantastic network of icicles, so exquisitely beautiful in appearance and so delicately formed as to appear as if fashioned by the magic touch of a fairy hand. Mounting upward and upward where it seemed sacrilege for the booted foot of man to tread, and where the snowy, crisp, silicious crystal formed a carpet-like covering beneath the feet, we reached the summit, and sat down upon a cluster of rocks which rose in fantastic shape upon the very margin of the cup-shaped crater.

J. Kerry Nicholls, *The King Country*, pp. 94–7.

Graffiti on the Terraces (1885)

C . E . R . S C H W A R T Z E

C.E.R. Schwartze had probably just finished his BA at Oxford, referred to on the title page of his book, when he set out on a world tour in 1884. He had to return home before the end owing to a 'sad domestic calamity', but published his journal at the insistence of friends the following year.

AT NIGHT WE WITNESSED a *Haka*, or native dance, one of the most peculiar sights, I should think, in the world. Imagine the Maori meeting house, with its carved figures and representations all around the walls. In the centre are placed five or six sticks with a candle tied to each. Then fifteen men and fifteen women draw up in line, and at a signal from the leader of the dance, commence swaying their bodies to and fro, clapping their hands, shouting, groaning, and sniffing the air in the most alarming way, sufficient to strike terror into the hearts of their foes. I shall never forget the scene; the dark forms moving wildly to and fro, the distorted features of the dancers, the wild unearthly yells which rent the air, and the fearful sounds which the male dancers produced towards the close of each figure. The candles, giving but a dim light, made the whole thing more weird and ghostly in appearance, and the carved figures on the wall seemed to be grinning approval of the antics which were being performed.

On the following morning we started for the celebrated Terraces of Rotomahana. Our guide was a Maori woman, named Sophia, a most intelligent and cheery old lady, who did all she could to make our trip pleasant and profitable. Proceeding on foot to Lake Tarawera, we embarked on a large boat manned by six Maoris, and rowed across the lake. On disembarking we proceeded at once to the White Terrace, one of the most marvellous sights in the world. On all sides steam is rising from the fissures in the rocks; a strong smell of sulphur pervades the air, and in every direction you come across pools and small lakes of boiling water. This water is generally of a magnificent blue colour, and looks perfectly beautiful in amongst the white-coated rock. Some of the pools are not boiling hot, but only pleasantly warm, and in one of these we took a most delicious bath. After our dip we inspected the most noisy and wonderful geysers, and then sat down to lunch, consisting of crayfish and potatoes, which we cooked ourselves in the boiling waters of Rotomahana.

Lunch over, we proceeded to the Pink Terrace, chiefly remarkable for the lake of clear blue water at the summit, which beats the Blue Grotto at Capri into nothing, and is a grand and glorious sight. Unfortunately, however, even this beautiful spot has been invaded by Vandals, and the Pink Terrace is covered with interesting pencil inscriptions, informing all whom it

'A visit to the hot lakes of New Zealand' from the *Graphic*, 1880 (B-K 404-92, ATL)

may concern that Harry Snooks visited this place last October; or that Jane Brown came here in December with her lover, Bill Jones, and they were pleased with the scene. These hideous inscriptions can never be erased, for the mineral water as it flows over the terrace has the effect of hardening all marks on the rocks, and there is absolutely no means of removing this blot on a surpassingly fair scene.

C.E.R. Schwartze, *Travels in Greater Britain*, pp. 124–7.

A Maori school at the Terraces (1885)

FRANK HENLEY

Frank Henley, a deeply religious young man, set out on a voyage round the world in 1884, after several haemorrhages the year before had caused a crisis in his health. His letters home were printed after his death in Victoria at the end of 1885. His account of New Zealand is interesting as he was a guest of the Hazard family, most of whom were killed in the Tarawera eruption in June 1886.

The Schoolhouse, Te Wairoa, Lake Terawera
April 9th, 1885.

HERE I AM, RIGHT AMONGST THE MAORIS! Whilst I write, a woman walks into the room with her baby on her back—they come for medicine. During my first meal here a man came right into the room with nothing but a shirt and blanket on, with a baby who was ill, and sat down on the floor. The natives all have such splendid eyes, and many of them good black hair, although often 'à la shock-headed Peter.' Our regard is mutual, for the Maoris have taken a fancy to me and I to them. They say they are not going to let me leave this place, so if I don't come back again you'll know where I am! Of course one has to be very careful how one deals with the Maoris, but if they like anybody they are easily managed, otherwise no pigs can be more contrary … I spoke at one of their Temperance meetings last night, Miss Hazard translating; they listened most attentively. I do not find that speaking one sentence at a time is at all conducive to anything like oratory, and sometimes when I had to give the next sentence I had almost forgotten what my last idea had been! Still, I managed somehow to make my meaning understood. An American gentleman named Snow lived here for some little while, and did a great deal of good; the Maoris loved him and would do anything for him; many of them became abstainers for his sake. He is dead now, and his mother and widow have come here for a few months to visit the places Mr Snow went to, and to try to keep up the good he did.

I went to the Maori service on Sunday morning, and helped with the singing. In the school-house there is an American organ, and I have played at all the meetings since I have been here, besides taking a class in the day-school. The children have to be taught to read in both languages, yet they are almost as forward as English children of the same age. They read, spell, and cypher capitally. Mr Hazard says if I will apply for a Maori school, he will give me a recommendation! I have learnt to read Maori, but cannot understand much yet, of course. They have only fourteen or fifteen letters—vowels pronounced as in French; *k*, *m*, *n*, *r*, *t*, *ng*, are the most frequent consonants; *à* and *e* come into almost every word, and the language is crammed full of idioms. My being at Mr Hazard's is very nice, for anyone staying here is allowed to go where they like and do as they like, whilst people at the hotel get watched about and have to pay for a guide. Mr H. has been here eight years, and this is the only Maori school which is really successful. The chief and the committee work well with Mr H., and are very severe on the parents who do not send their children to school. They have to come and ask Mr Hazard's leave before they go anywhere else during school hours; but when they ask, he never refuses them.

Carakia (church) is held every morning and evening in one of the *whares* (houses); prayer is offered, a chapter read, and one or two hymns sung. The service lasts from twenty minutes to half-an-hour; I have been several times. They give the *pakehas* (lit. strangers) seats, but the rest all squat on the floor. At church on Sunday we had forms (awfully uncomfortable), the Maories squatting all round the room on the floor. They sing very heartily, though without much taste, and are very fond of it. When I am playing the organ they crowd around me, and when I sing they watch my mouth with surprise. Some of them would quite echo the remark of that young hopeful at Victoria Park 'cathedral'—'An't he got a vice!' only Maori children always speak (Maori) correctly!

Last night after the Temperance meeting I was asked to sing, so I gave them 'I have read of a beautiful city'—of course in English—but I can read well enough to sing in Maori with the others.

ROTOMAHANA (WARM LAKE) AND THE TERRACES

April 10th, 1885.

It would be useless to expect to give any adequate idea of what the Terraces are really like, but I will do my best, that you may enjoy it as much as you can till you come to see for yourselves.

Called at six—a magnificent sunrise through a gap in the hills at the further side of Lake Tarawera—very foggy, yet just a bright space for the red glowing rays of king Sol to shine through—'twas splendid.

A party of two ladies (one a friend of Mr Viccars, whom I first met on board the steamer *Tarawera*, coming from Dunedin to Auckland, and then found lodging at Mr Hazard's at Lake Tarawera when I got there) and four gentlemen, started soon after eight in a big boat across

Lake Tarawera, rowed by six Maories, with 'Sophie,' the Blue Ribbon guide. From the landing place we had to walk about 1¹/₂ miles, as the river connecting the two lakes is too rapid to take passengers up it.

The first sight of Rotomahana and the White Terrace is very disappointing—a lime kiln turning out lime down a pretty steep hill into the lake would look as pretty—and the lake itself, compared with Tarawera, looked like a reedy slimy pool with steam-holes all round it. But patience, good friends—here comes the empty canoe which is to ferry you across the river, as there is no bridge; and don't growl till you come back. A few yards brings you to the outer edge of the bottom of the terraces, and you walk into the warm water about two inches deep. (N.B.—Old boots or shoes should be worn here, as hot water doesn't agree with the complexion of leather.) And now, a little further on, you come to the wonderland. A big basin, irregular in shape—probably ovate—of lovely white limestone or marble, contains water of the most exquisite pale blue, but the water is only warm. Then you step up on the edge of this pool, and you see a series of others higher up, some larger, some smaller, some deep, some shallow—in fact, ladies and gentlemen, you can 'pay your money and take your choice'. Then up you go two or three 'terraces' more, and the further you go the more change you get: the water becomes hot, the basins are larger and deeper, the water darker blue, and the terraces to be surmounted higher. Your feet begin to get queer but comfortable, and when, near the top, you put your hand to the water you find it hotter than you bargained for. Now just look back the way you have come, and spread before you, tier below tier, are white marble fountains, terraces, baths, in succession: here a tiny waterfall; there a dripping of water down over what might be graceful draperies fossilized, and looking like a silver fringe on the edges as it falls into the pool beneath. But still we have to go up—so don't waste breath—still the water is hotter, till you are picking out the dry spots to walk in. Now at the top—hark! what's that noise? Oh, it's only the furnace boiling up! the water comes up in a great heap, and then falling back finds its level again and is quiet for a few minutes; then a roar and a volley, and the water is on a level with your head in a great heap, after which it tumbles back. To see this you stand on the edge of a big pit, and look down on this quiet blue steaming water, and try to realise what 'twould be like to tumble in and get boiled; and meanwhile the water has come up again, and you instinctively draw back lest you should get a small scald as it falls. A few more steps bring us to the top, where the chief cause of these terraces lies. Standing on the brink, you look down on a pool of blue water steaming away and almost hidden by steam, in a hollow about 70 feet wide which it seems to have washed out for itself on the bosom of the hill, not at the top. The wind lifts the steam for a moment, and you see the lovely blue water contrasted with the white, red, and yellow clay, and earths of all shades, red predominating, of which the basin is formed. Pick up a piece of it and you'll be glad to put it down again; the very ground is hot to your feet, though ferns and many plants grow in it. Sometimes this pool gets dried up—all the water goes—and venturesome people may walk down into the hollow, and over

C. Spencer, 'A party of tourists on the White Terraces', c. 1880. (F-51250-1/2, ATL)

at one side may look down the funnel-shaped opening through which the water may come up at any moment; or speculative people may push their sticks into the ground and try to discover the thickness of the earth's crust at that particular spot; or nervous people may draw back in alarm and fright, and the thoughtful man may think—

'How wondrous are thy works, O Lord!'

and then—

'This awful God is ours,
Our Father and our friend!'

From the top of the White Terrace we are led to 'Geyser Pool', 'Steam-hammer' Hole, and pools, mud geysers, 'Stomach-ache' Hole (supposed to make the noise of a giant with that sad complaint), 'Giants' Hole' (where a giant is said to have thrown himself down and has been screeching ever since), 'Steam Whistle Hole,' 'Porridge Pot' (where a tiny mud volcano makes porridge which Maoris say is very nourishing! It tastes very much like grit pounded very fine and warmed in oil or milk—not bad.) Then a cave was shown us, amongst other wonders, where a whole line of chiefs with unpronounceable names and unrememberable histories were born; it is *tapu*, that is, sacred. I put my head in and intended going in, but as 'twas about the size of a small kitchen table, and about three feet from roof to floor, I thought better, and didn't. Then across 'Mud Flat,' a veritable wilderness of tiny mud volcanoes, to the 'Soda-water Pool,' which it is supposed to be like; but except salt I could taste nothing special, and it looked like a green slime pond. In this flat we had to walk very circumspectly in the footsteps of our guide, for a single slip might have found us in boiling mud or water.

Next we had lunch on the shores of the lake, with small boiling springs all round us. We had tea (boiled in a tin can called a 'billy' in one of the springs), and potatoes and kouras also cooked *au naturel*. Kouras are small cray-fish caught in the lake, very much like prawns, only larger, and very nice. We gave our meat to the Maoris, and ate kouras and potatoes till we were tired! Then we had all to bundle into the canoe—a real Maori canoe, made of a dead tree hollowed out; there are no seats, so you sit on the fern spread out, with the knowledge that if you lift the fern you will find water, which a small boy had to be baling out all the time. You feel queer at first, for the water comes up to within two inches of the top. So all you have to do is to 'part your hair in the middle, and sit still!' It is a most lovely sensation! a Maori at either end paddles his canoe, and you glide along splendidly, with sundry misgivings about the water under you and the water outside, and as to whether you will get turned over or not. Still, there was one comfort—'twas in warm water, and that would be much better than drowning in cold! But by this time the Pink Terrace ought to be in sight. Now, be careful how you step out of that canoe, or you'll get a wetting! This terrace is smaller than the white, but the colour is exceedingly pretty, and the terraces rather more regular. As, however, the formations are much the same, we'll just say ditto to the description of the other, only put in pink instead of white. Whilst the ladies go to the top to have a bath, we male folks stay below and examine the names of Browns, Joneses, Smiths, &c, &c, who have chosen to spoil a matchless piece of God's nature by writing their vile names, &c, all over some of the loveliest spots on the Terrace—some in letters big enough to teach an elephant to read! Idiots!—RI (not 'RIP,' but 'righteous indignation'.) I have cooled down a bit—and now for a warm bath as the ladies are returning. Undressing in the 'ti tree' scrub isn't pleasant, but the bath is worth the bother: first, into an almost cold one big enough to swim in, then into a warm one, next into a warmer one (but didn't the cold wind catch me as I was migrating!) then into a real hot one, which was just grand! This pool was deeper, but not wide, so one could just lie back on the edge of the basin and dream of—well, anything comfortable! You can go into the next bath higher up if you like, but as I didn't relish being boiled, and as Maoris are not cannibals now, it would be a sheer waste of good flesh and life, for that pool is just boiling hot; still, if you wish it, go on! Then I began to go down again, finishing off with the cold bath, and pulling on my clothes as fast as possible; and then down we go to the ladies, who 'thought we had been an awful long time!' Into the canoe, across the lake, down the rapid rolling river of hot water, down a few rapids, now round a sharp turn, then gliding on splendidly, another rapid, and we go down like fury, another bend (by this time you feel quite comfie, and don't fear being drowned), then away again, and we land, get into our own boat, then nine miles across Roto Tarawera by sail, a steep walk up to the house—and I am sure you would have been quite ready for tea if you had been there too.

Frank Henley, *Bright Memories*, pp. 87–93.

Small miseries (1885)

JAMES ANTHONY FROUDE

James Anthony Froude was a renowned Victorian historian and author of Oceana, *the most widely read travel book of the late 1880s. He visited New Zealand and Australia, accompanied by his son and Lord Elphinstone, in 1885.* Oceana *was criticised by Edward Wakefield in the journal* Nineteenth Century *in 1886 for 'almost incredible inaccuracy', but the book is an opinionated and entertaining read.*

THE ROADS IN NEW COUNTRIES are not macadamised; they are mere tracks smoothed with a spade, and in wet weather and in soft soil, hoof and wheel cut considerable holes in them. Travelling therefore has its difficulties. We had bespoken a light carriage and four horses; the distance which we had to go was but sixty miles, and the charge was twelve pounds. But the price, of all things, is what people are willing to pay; and Australians with long purses and easy temper spoil the market for strangers less amply provided. We found, too, afterwards that the regular coach would have taken us for a third of the cost. Knowledge, like other things, has to be paid for. We went early to bed: I to be bitten by mosquitoes again and spend a night of misery. Breakfast next morning might have been a compensation could we have seen clearly what we were eating; but tablecloth, plates and dishes were black with house-flies. The sugar-basin swarmed with them, and the milk was only saved by a cover over the jugs. They followed the forks into our mouths; they plunged into our teacups and were boiled. I should have said that I never anywhere saw so many of these detestable vermin, had we not found even more at the place to which we were bound.

Small miseries which do no harm we execrate and forget the next minute. By nine o'clock we were off, the coach-proprietor condescending to conduct us and explain the wonders of the road. The scene was utterly new; something fresh and unexpected met us at every turn. On the whole it was the most interesting drive which I remember in the course of my life.

James Anthony Froude, *Oceana*, pp. 262–3.

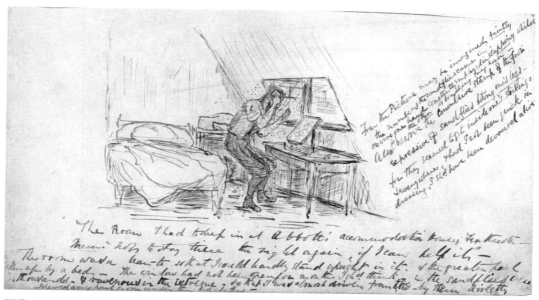

William Hawkins, from 'My Expedition up the Wairarapa' (1867): 'The room I had to sleep in at Abbott's Accommodation House, Featherston. Memo—Not to stay there again if I can help it'. (E-370-006-2, ATL)

Kate or Sophia (1885)

JAMES ANTHONY FROUDE

Kate and Sophia were the two guides most frequently used by tourists when visiting the Terraces. They became very well known through tourist accounts and guidebooks, and there are many photographs of them. Kate was credited with saving the life of a tourist who fell out of a canoe, and Sophia was one of the survivors of the Tarawera eruption (June 1886). Her whare was one of the few buildings left intact, and a number of people who sheltered in it were saved.

THE NEXT DAY'S ARRANGEMENTS had now to be completed. We dined first, and were then called on to choose our guide, a crowd outside the inn door waiting to learn which it was to be—Kate or Sophia. Neither of them had as yet presented herself. But Sophia had been with the party whom we had seen in the boat. It seemed to be Kate's turn. Kate would save our lives if they needed saving, and besides we learnt that she was stone-deaf. She would show us

Kate Middlemass, one of the guides at Rotomahana, c. 1880. (PA2-2581, ATL)

all that was to be seen, and we should escape conversation, so we determined on Kate. A loud howl rose from the mob, it seemed as of satisfaction. 'Kate! Kate!' a hundred voices cried, and presently there appeared a big, half-caste, bony woman of forty, with a form like an Amazon's, features like a prize-fighter's, and an arm that would fell an ox. She had a blue petticoat on, a brown jacket, and a red handkerchief about her hair. Deaf she might be, but her war-whoop might be heard for a mile. I inquired whether this virago (for such she appeared) had a husband. I was told that she had had eight husbands, and on my asking what had become of them, I got for answer that they had died away somehow. Poor Kate! I don't know that she had ever had so much as one. There were lying tongues at Wairoa as well as in other places. She was a little elated, I believe, when we first saw her. She was quiet and womanly enough next day. Her strength she had done good service with, and she herself was probably better, and not worse, than many of her neighbours. But I was a little alarmed, and regretted that I had been so precipitate, especially after I saw Sophia. Sir George's old chief called on us in the evening, and Sophia was invited in as interpreter. The chief was in plain European clothes, but had an air of dignity. He had given orders, he said, that we should be well attended to. He was sorry that he could not himself go with us to the Terraces, but we should want nothing. Sophia was as pretty as her picture represented her—slight, graceful, delicate, and with a quiet, interesting manner. We were committed, however, and could not change, and our Kate, after all, did very well for us.

It was getting late when the chief went. We were about to go to bed, when a further message was brought in to us. The tribe were anxious to show us some of their native dances by torchlight. We asked for particulars. We learnt that we might have a brief ordinary dance on moderate terms. If we wished for a performance complete—complete with its indecencies, which they said gentlemen usually preferred—they would expect 3*l*. 10*s*. Tourists, it seems, do encourage these things, and the miserable people are paid to disgrace themselves, that they may have a drunken orgie afterwards, for that is the way in which the money is invariably spent. The tourists, I presume, wish to teach the poor savage 'the blessings of civilisation.' We declined any performance, mutilated or entire.

In the morning we had to start early, for we had a long day's work cut out for us. We were on foot at seven. The weather was fine, with a faint cool breeze, a few clouds, but no sign of rain. Five Maori boatmen were in attendance, to carry coats and luncheon basket. Kate presented herself with a subdued demeanour, as agreeable as it was unexpected. She looked picturesque, with a grey, tight-fitting, woollen bodice, a scarlet skirt, a light scarf about her neck, and a grey billicock hat with pink riband. She had a headache, she said, but was mild and gentle. I disbelieved entirely in the story of the eight husbands.

We descended to the lake head by the path up which we had seen the party returning the previous evening. The boat was a long, light gig, unfit for storms, but Tarawara lay unruffled in the sunshine, tree and mountain peacefully mirrored on the surface.

The colour was again green, as of a shallow sea. Heavy bushes fringed the shore. High, wooded mountains rose on all sides of us as we left the creek and came out upon the open water. The men rowed well, laughing and talking among themselves, and carried us in little more than an hour to a point eight miles distant. Little life of any kind showed on the way; no boat was visible but our own; there were a few cormorants, a few ducks, a coot or two, three or four seagulls, come from the ocean to catch sprats, and that was all. Kate said that the lake held enormous eels as big round as a man's leg, which were caught occasionally with night lines; but we saw nothing of them and did not entirely believe. At the point, or behind it, we came on a Maori farm on the water's edge. There were boats, and nets hung up to dry, a maize-field, an orchard, and a cabin. We stopped, and they offered us cray-fish, which we declined, but bought a basket of apples for the crew.

James Anthony Froude, *Oceana*, pp. 282–4.

En plein pays des Maoris (1885)

EMILE WENZ

*Wenz, a native of Reims, decided to travel to New Zealand and
Australia before beginning his chosen career, in the belief that knowing something about other countries would help him serve his own. He
arrived in New Zealand four months before Froude and, like Froude,
reviled the food on offer across the Tasman. Wenz followed the usual
tourist route to the Terraces. His opinions about Maori and the facilities in New Zealand are very similar to those of British tourists.*

FRIDAY 21 NOVEMBER.—At seven in the morning, after a splendid voyage, we disembarked at
Tauranga. The coach didn't usually leave until the next day, but because there were enough of
us, we were able to leave the same day, at nine o'clock. My friend and I had to confirm our
places on the box seat. The journey took eight hours with no hope of a hotel or restaurant, so
we had to bring provisions with us. The empty space under the seats was filled with packets
of *sandwiches*, bread, meat, and a customary bottle of *whisky*; the hotelkeeper had also gener-
ously added a beautiful pineapple and some bananas. The *coach* was a light carriage with eight
seats, pulled by five vigorous horses. Our coachman we were told, was the best in the colony,
sensitive to people unused to the bad New Zealand roads. We left at the appointed hour, and,
having crossed the village, found ourselves in the open country. We drove by Gate Pah where
the English sustained a big defeat twenty years ago in their fight against the Maoris. The general aspect of the country is broken, but the low hills are devoid of trees and entirely covered
with fern. Here and there you see solitary *cabbage trees* rising up or clumps of *phormium tenax*
(New Zealand flax) whose leaves supply a fibre both very fine and strong, an important export
trade; but immense areas have been devastated by fire and mark the landscape like great black
stains.

   After two hours we entered a thick forest which we had to travel through for 18 miles. It
would be unwise to break through the line of trees bordering the road and venture into the
thick bush! We contented ourselves admiring the two walls of magnificent vegetation. Several
of the gigantic trees were dead; but they stayed upright: innumerable plants enveloped them
in leaves to their tops; and ferns of all sorts had seeded themselves in the holes in the trunks.
Other giants were still full of life, spreading out their thick foliage; interlaced with creepers,
branches of thousands of different leaves, with a thousand tiny differences; it is a jungle
impenetrable to the sun's rays. Our road, primitive and filled with obstacles, would be impassable by any other coachman than ours. On the box seat we could see all his difficulties; those

View of the Pink Terraces from the shore of Lake Rotomahana. (F-139876-1/2, ATL)

in the interior of the coach could only feel the jolts. We had never seen such a bad road, and more than twenty times thought we were sure to overturn. Nothing, for example, could be worse than the descent to the bottom of the wonderful gorge of Mangarewa, squeezed between immense rocks, between walls of trees, of ferns, seeming hardly to hold on without falling to the bottom of the abyss. The road zigzagged down steep slopes, and often, to prevent slips after rain, it had been paved with tree trunks, that were laid across the road. And the coach, with its travellers, drove over it with a series of sharp and disagreeable jolts.

After four hours we arrived at a little house where the passengers and the horses had an hour to rest and refresh themselves: a duty we carried out well on our part thanks to our provisions and the fresh water we mixed with *whisky*.

However the weather, which had been magnificent all day, started to deteriorate, and we left in pouring rain, which didn't stop till five pm, when we arrived in Ohinemutu where we were planning to spend several days. This village is on the banks of a great lake, Roto Rua, in the middle of which is the island of Mokoia. We were truly in Maori country.

Emile Wenz, *Mon Journal*, pp. 135–7 (trans. Lydia Wevers).

My lodging is on the cold ground (1885)

GEORGE AUGUSTUS SALA

The flamboyant and celebrated Victorian journalist George Augustus Sala came to New Zealand and Australia on a lecture tour in September 1885. He arrived in Wellington, to find all the hotels booked out by visitors to the Colonial Exhibition. During his tour he corresponded with British and local papers. He opened the Blue Bath in Rotorua and spent a day at the Terraces.

' 'TWAS A VERY FINE THING', again, to have passed so quiet a night in a comfortable state-room on shipboard in Wellington Harbour; but when Monday morning came it brought with it no better prospect of hotel accommodation than we had had on the previous evening. 'No one to love me!'; that would be a trite complaint at this time of day. It would be unreasonable to expect anybody to love you when you are old, and broken, and growing stupid. 'Nothing to wear!' That lamentation has been repeated, with or without justification, *ad nauseam*. But nowhere to sleep! To have come all these thousands of miles to be houseless, at last! To be presented with the key of the street at Wellington, New Zealand. There was horror in the thought. Leaving my luggage on deck, and in a state of extreme dejection, I landed at Waterloo Wharf, and fell into the hands of a tall young man with a blue worsted comforter round his neck, who drove a hackney carriage and pair. Charge—four shillings an hour, and a shilling for wharfage. The pair of horses weedy, but swift of foot. The tall young driver has a companion on the box—a companion shorter and slighter than he, but in degree as lanky. As they went, this twain on the box, they both whistled—not, I should say, for want of thought, but the rather, I should say, from the soothing reflection that something exceptionally remunerative in the way of cab-hire was about to be made out of me. The carriage itself was a pleasing example of the survival of the fittest. It was a barouche that closed. It had survived, I should say, several seasons at Brighton or St Leonards and one or two at Melbourne, and for the time it made one feel quite at home. The homelike feeling, however, vanished as we continued to rumble 'half a league, half a league, half a league onward'—and, to my thinking, considerably more than half a league—vainly searching for an hotel of which the landlord or landlady would be so charitable as to take me in. Again, to my distraction, had I reckoned without my host. Not only had the circumstance of Parliament being in session to be taken into account, but the *trôp plein* of the Wellington Industrial and Artistic Exhibition was approaching its culmination, and the congress in question had brought to the legislative capital crowds of visitors from every province in the colony; in spite, too, of the universal business depression which I am told, on authority I dare not question, is existent. A fearful depression. An awful depression. New Zealand, I learn, is thirty millions in debt to the public creditor alone. Every child that comes into the world in this beautiful land is handicapped from his first entrance into life with indebtedness to the extent of fifty-five pounds sterling—imagine such a load of pecuniary embarrassment on the baby's head before even the sutures in its tender young cranium are knit together. A million and a half of pounds sterling must go out of the country every year to pay the implacable home creditor's tale of interest; and, while he justifiably insists on his pound of flesh, the prices of wool and grain continue to rule desperately low, and the meat-preserving companies of New Zealand find that they cannot deliver their frozen mutton at a lower rate than threepence per pound, and that at home their profits are, to a disastrous extent, eaten up by the middlemen and distributors. Truly a shocking state of things. Yet I am told that the attendance at the Wellington Exhibition averages twelve hundred a day, and families continue to flock in from the provinces to see the show, and cram the hotels to suffocation.

As for the twain on the box, the depression apparently had not reached *them*. They ceased not to whistle, and, as the American humourist put it, 'to drive me round, promiscuously'. To no avail. There are many—well, so called 'hotels' in Wellington; but not even the proprietor of the lowliest 'pub' would have anything to say to us. They were all full—'chock-a-block', as one of the Bonifaces phrased it to whom I made unsuccessful suit. The worst of it was that, throughout our quest, we were pursued by a shaggy man of ferocious aspect, but actuated by the friendliest intentions towards us, who was, indeed, the driver of an express wagon, and who had made up his mind that he was destined to convey our luggage from the steamer to the place where eventually we were to find shelter for our unhappy heads. I will not pretend to enumerate either consecutively or accurately the hostelries at which we vainly knocked; but I fancy that there was a Royal and an Empire, a Masonic and a Metropolitan, a Victoria, a Princess's, a Melbourne, a Panama, a Te Aro, a Star, an Albert, and a Bank. There should have been a Tattersall's. Mr Edmund Tattersall would feel highly flattered were he aware of the many scores, not only of horse auction yards, but of hotels, to which his esteemed name is attached in the Southern Hemisphere. Similarly is it with the Criterion. I am not quite certain as to whether there be an hotel with that particular cognisance at Wellington; but I am certain that I have stayed at at least half a dozen Criterion hotels, and have been aware of at least half a hundred more, while travelling up and down the Australian continent; and in Maoriland the Criterion is almost as popular a sign as in Australia.

When we had exhausted the hotels, and I was beginning—the shades of mental gloom continuing to thicken around me—to think of adding a fresh stanza to the mournful ditty of 'My Lodging is on the Cold Ground', the friendly express wagoner with the ferocious aspect

The Occidental Hotel, Wellington, on the corner of Lambton Quay and Johnston Street, 1890s.
(G-3938-1/2, Tyree Collection, ATL)

suggested that we should make a tour among the boarding and lodging houses. 'Board and Residence' are prominent among the institutions of the Southern Hemisphere. You may 'board and reside' all over the Australasian colonies, in the great cities as in the smallest bush towns, on terms varying between ten or fifteen shillings a day and eighteen shillings a week. The best hotels are only boarding-houses of a somewhat superior class. In very few establishments where the Australian traveller is 'taken in and done for' is his right to breakfast, dine, or sup when he pleases, and not when the landlord or landlady pleases, fully and cheerfully recognised. The traveller is reminded—sometimes with slightly offensive iteration—that this is 'a young country' and he has to submit with as good a grace as he may to the young country's ways. He is the periodical slave of the bell or the gong. He is rung or 'gonged' in to all his meals. On Sundays he is bound to dine at one o'clock in the afternoon. After that he will only have a 'high tea' at six p.m. Analogous rules, as you are aware, prevail in the hotels and boarding-houses of the United States—only there you will find a plenitude of servants to wait upon you. In Australasia the major portion of the waiting must be done by yourself if you wish it done at all.

Failure was the result of the earlier stages of our excursion among the boarding-houses. The apparently comfortable ones were all full. The as evidently uncomfortable ones offered equivocal accommodation at an inflated tariff. The great difficulty was to procure a private sitting-room with the promise of having our meals served therein. At length we obtained all that we required, at very moderate rates, and with a great deal of cordial kindness and attention into—or rather outside—the bargain, at an establishment styled Heavitree House, in Molesworth Street, a pretty, rural road, hard by the gardens of Government House, which Viceregal residence is situated on Lambton Quay, close to the harbour. From our verandah at Heavitree House we had a splendid view of the beautiful mountain scenery which surrounds Wellington. Along Molesworth Street itself—so named, I apprehend, after the learned and genial English baronet and statesman who edited Hobbes—there was a continuous and cheerful stream of carriages full of sightseers, bound, I suppose, to Mr McNab's garden, famous for its strawberries, for which, with cream, there is the briskest of demands among visitors at the pleasant little village of the Hutt, on the western side of the bay. The Houses of Parliament, the Museum, the Treasury, and Exhibition buildings are all within a few minutes' walk of Heavitree House, to which we were glad to return on two subsequent visits to Wellington; for we found an appreciable amount of comfort and attention there at the hands of a very worthy couple who, with their buxom, cheery, and neat-handed little sixteen-year-old daughter 'Cammy'—short, if you please, for Cameron—did all they possibly could to meet and even to anticipate our wishes. They were, in truth, as kind as Mr and Mrs Cairns, of the Star Hotel, Auckland, had been, which is saying a great deal. The good folks who ministered to our wants at Heavitree House had seen better days. They had been, not so very long before, burnt out of house and home at Nelson, where they were not sufficiently insured; but worse had gone before, as they had lost a whole fortune in a sugar and cotton plantation at Fiji. The cheery and smiling little lass, 'Cammy', spoke with a sigh of Fiji as the home of her childhood, and of the days when her papa and mamma's pigs were fed with peaches and bananas, and pineapples, oranges, and citrons were to be had for the picking. There was nothing rude or awkward in her manner; nothing archaic or rough in her accent; she looked and moved and talked like a little lady; and her earliest recollections were of Fiji—the cane brake, the cotton grounds, and the naked savages. Well, 'Cammy' had been evidently carefully brought up by prudent and cultured parents—her mamma prided herself on having heard Charles Dickens read and Thackeray lecture, and, as the twig is bent—you know the rest. These good people were very anxious that I should make it known to all whom it might concern—members of the Legislature and their families for example, seeking accommodation during the session—that they had had nothing to do with Heavitree House at the period of its tenancy by a lady presumably of Milesian descent, and whose ideas of housekeeping appeared to be slightly susceptible of improvement, inasmuch as in her time the cocks and hens which should have been disporting themselves in the back yard were suffered to penetrate to the interior of the mansion, and to wander up and down stairs. The Honourable the Speaker had, I was told, at one time occupied apartments at Heavitree House, and had complained of the presence of the domestic poultry in the upper chambers.

George Augustus Sala, *The Land of the Golden Fleece*, pp. 121–4.

Steaming to Kinlock (1885)

J. HERBERT ROBERTS

After finishing his course at Cambridge in 1884, J. Herbert Roberts travelled abroad for twelve months with two friends before he began his business life. During his trip he kept a diary, which he forwarded to his family and on his return printed for private circulation. He arrived in New Zealand in the autumn of 1885, and was one of many tourists to bathe at the Pink Terrace.

THURSDAY, APRIL 2.—The outlook from my window in the morning reminded me of Geneva, the lake being a lovely dark blue in colour, and surrounded by grand mountain ranges, covered with rich foliage two-thirds of the way up, the rest snow-tinted. We sat down to an early breakfast, and were somewhat surprised to find a large number of the last evening's passengers also sitting at the table, evidently having the same intention as ourselves of rushing away to the head of the lake to avoid the volunteers. This discovery rather alarmed us. We heard the steamer's whistle, and went on board the *Antrim*, an old hulk, with two immense paddle-boxes fixed on each side. Taking on board a supply of butcher's meat and other such necessaries for the hotels at the head of the lake, we steamed out of Queenstown and were very soon being tossed about in a regular sea; a strong wind was also blowing against us, the waves continually watered our decks. The passengers stowed themselves away under canvas, inside boats, behind the paddle-boxes—anywhere out of reach of the spray. The breeze was, however, most invigorating, and the scenery very fine. Lake Wakatipu is decidedly peculiar in shape, being a perfect zig-zag; its length is fifty-two miles, with a breadth of a mile to a mile and a half, and it has a tremendous depth, ranging from 1,100 to 1,200 feet. We had about thirty-five miles to traverse, and, with such a strong wind against us, it took five hours to gain the head. The northern end of the lake is shut in by the Mount Earnslaw Range. The mountain which gave this range its name is 10,000 feet high and the finest peak in the neighbourhood. There are two hotels at the head of the lake, situated within a few miles of each other; one is called Glenorchy and the other Kinlock. We decided to stay at the latter, and as we neared the shore, we could see three small wooden houses, with neat verandahs and encircled by trim gardens. Of course, all depended, as there were so many passengers wishing to obtain accommodation, on getting out quickly and securing rooms. I was this time deputed to make a rush for it, and I managed to get on to the jetty first, and to my joy found one of the houses empty. This had four single bedrooms and a sitting-room, which just suited us. The poor landlord was in a great way, not being prepared for such an inroad of passengers, and at once ordered a sheep to be slaughtered and a few geese to be hung up. We were extremely comfortable in our bachelor quarters, having a log fire in our sitting-room, where we made merry. The dining-room was in another house, and there all the guests met and discussed their several plans. We had decided to start next morning to a mountain tarn known as Lake Harris, an expedition of two days. The weather was bleak and cloudy, very unsuitable for such an excursion, but we had sufficient enthusiasm to order our horses and provisions, and to make the necessary arrangements on the chance of its clearing up.

J. Herbert Roberts, *A World Tour*, pp. 466–7.

Soup on board the Zealandia *(1885)*

RUSSELL J. COLMAN

Russell Colman's letters were written home during his trip around the world in 1885–86 and published by his mother. Colman was accompanied by two friends. His visit to the Pink and White Terraces caused him to resort to quoting the guidebook. He also went to Glenorchy.

THE ONLY THING one feels inclined to do is to write about the rolling of the ship, which today is as bad as ever, if not worse. She is without exception the greatest roller it has been my lot to travel in, but at the same time she is a very seaworthy vessel. At meal times we amuse ourselves occasionally by races across the table, with such things as will slide or roll. This passes the time. The most entertaining thing to take is *soup*: it always forms a little sort of 'puddle' (if I may so express it) at the *side* of the plate, and when your spoon gets down into it there is shoal water, or rather shoal soup, on that side, and a fathom or two of soup on the other. You move your spoon to the other side of the plate, but not being quick enough the soup dodges underneath, and you 'get left' again. At last you get a spoon full, and are congratulating yourself, when a bigger roll than usual comes along. You let go the spoon and catch up the plate, at the same time twining your leg round the leg of the table or the leg of your neighbour, as the case may be, and keeping the other hand ready to catch hold of anything that looks like missing your neighbour's and coming into your own lap. Taking everything into consideration, I think soup is about the most interesting pastime we have yet struck.

Russell J. Colman, *Trifles from a Tourist*, pp. 61–2.

iv

HOW TO PREVENT SEA-SICKNESS.

COCAINE LOZENGES. (Lorimer's).

In Tin Boxes for the Pocket .. .. 1s. 1½d. each.

We confidently recommend them as being an absolute cure for, and preventative of SEA SICKNESS; there is no reason now why the most timid should not thoroughly enjoy the tossing of the billows like true Britons.

These Lozenges were first prepared by Mr. Lorimer, the author, for his own experiment during a voyage to and from America, in June, 1886. He had never previously been afloat without being sick, even on the Thames.

The result of the experiment was that he was afloat 22 days in all weathers, and was never sick once or missed a single meal. Every time the premonitory symptoms presented themselves, he took from one to six Lozenges, according to the state of the weather, and they were in every case perfectly efficacious, and without any unpleasant after effect: they have since been used with equally good results in many other cases; therefore Mr. Lorimer advises all timid sailors to take his Cocaine Lozenges. If they do not act as represented, money will be refunded on application.

COCAINE LOZENGES will probably cure every other form of sickness, but we have not yet had opportunities of testing them, and shall be grateful for reports from those who may try them.

The following Letter is representative of those reaching us daily :—

22nd April, 1887.

" A lady friend of mine has had occasion to cross the Irish Sea several times, and has always been ill; I urged her to give your Lozenges a fair trial, and her voyage across, last week, was for the first time thoroughly enjoyed—a result which she attributes solely to their use. " GEORGE STABLES,

" 3, Dale Villas, Harrowgate, 2, Albion Place, Leeds."

Mr. R. M. SUMNER (*Pharmaceutical Journal*, 1886, p. 713), at a Meeting of the Liverpool Chemists' Association, gave his own experience of Cocaine in various forms, none of which were quite satisfactory, but FOUND THE LOZENGES EVERYTHING THAT COULD BE DESIRED.

" So far then, as my opportunities have permitted, I have tested—and severely tested—the powers of Cocaine over *Mal-de-Mer*; I have nothing but good to report; of the best of nostrums and prescriptions it can only be said that if the patient lies down and is fortunate, he may not be ill, but Cocaine will put him on his feet. Therefore I say, try Cocaine. "J. L."

Lancet, November, 1885, p. 451, records several cases, in all of which it was successful—one in particular—a girl of 18 had been sea-sick 24 hours, and tried Cocaine, with " a truly magical effect."

COCA JELLY (Hoffman's Patent).

IN BOTTLES, 1/- & 2/- EACH.

FOR SICKNESS AND NERVOUS EXHAUSTION.

This is a pure Calves' Feet Jelly, containing all the properties of the Coca leaf. It is most pleasant and palatable, and for Invalids, Convalescents, Singers, Public Speakers, and especially its food replacing power, it is equal to "Coca Wine."

Many cases have been reported to the Proprietors in which it has been most successful in at once allaying the distressing symptoms of above affections, and the undermentioned quotations will demonstrate its usefulness in supplying the place of food, in any cases where it is impossible to take it, from sea sickness or any other causes.

Dr. AUSTIN, in the *Practitioner*, of October, 1869, says that in Coca Erythroxylon, it is evident that we possess an uncommonly powerful nervous stimulant, and if it is established as a fact, as appears likely, that arterial tension is very considerably heightened by it, together with the singular power of the drug to enable the subject of it to dispense with sleep for a long period without feeling any after fatigue, it is plain that we shall have a remedy of real and high value.

Dr. ARCHIBALD SMITH—"PERU AS IT IS"—states that "Coca" increases energy, removes drowsiness, enlivens the spirits, and makes the consumer to bear cold, wet, great bodily exertion, and even want of food, to a surprising degree, with ease and impunity.

Lorimer's Coca Wine is a powerful Muscular and Nerve Tonic, giving unusual powers of endurance in both mental and physical labour; it is also remarkable for its food replacing power, and has become almost as well known as "Port" or "Sherry"—for either of which it is a most wholesome substitute. Bottles 4/- each.

Sold by all respectable Chemists, or sent direct by the Sole Proprietors and Makers:

LORIMER & Co., Britannia Row, London, N.

'How to prevent sea-sickness', an advertisement from the *Orient Line Guide*, 1889. (B-K 402-IV, ATL)

Unhomelike (1886)

ANNIE BUTLER

Annie Butler wrote a number of works for the Religious Tract Society, mostly for children. She came to New Zealand, a place in which she had never had the 'faintest' interest, to help look after her ill brother-in-law. While in the country she and her party travelled extensively, observing mission work.

HALF WAY UP THESE HILLS, after a somewhat tiresome search, we found a temporary resting-place, a rough but pleasant boarding-house.

At first nothing seemed pleasant. Though even now we scarcely realized that we were at the antipodes, and repeatedly asked, 'Is the world really no larger than this? Can we have come to the end of it already?' yet we were undoubtedly strangers in a strange land, and we felt like it too.

The house was made of wooden planks placed horizontally, as indeed all the houses and public edifices here are built, in order to withstand earthquakes. Shaw and Savill's great range of shipping offices is the exception to prove the rule, and stands out red and conspicuous. Fire insurance, as may be imagined, is made a great point of, and great labels, 'New Zealand,' 'Colonial,' meet one's eye at every turn, indicating the names of offices in which policies have been effected.

My room that night was certainly very unhomelike. It was one of several under a great sky-light which covered the whole of my wing of the house. I had no other window; and as the lath partition walls were run up only part of the way, everything said in one of the compartments could be distinctly heard in the next. I had a hay bed, a washhand-stand and a little table—both without a drawer—a chair, and a tiny bit of carpet. (My brother-in-law had found much the same accommodation at a 'first-class hotel' where he had spent the previous day.) Nothing was unpacked; and indeed there was no place to put anything in if I did unpack. Altogether the place looked rather a desolation to English eyes. One ray of light, however, had shone on the dreariness of that first day on land. For a whole hour, after our three months' fast from such luxuries, we had been able to sit and warm ourselves through at a blazing fire!

Things did not, as is usually the case, look better in the morning. My sister and her husband were feeling the reaction from the fatigues and excitements of the last few days, and I went down alone to the great breakfast-room, off which a kitchen opened. It was, I should think, about forty feet long; a plain table ran down its centre, and round the walls were ranged tables, presses, and hooks, on or under which books, boxes, and coats appeared in a somewhat promiscuous fashion. The table looked bare. Breakfast was brought in only as the boarders required it, and very few of them were as yet down; and, with the exception of one or two, I did not care for the look of those whom I did see. In a word—truth must out—my heart was on board our beloved 'Eporem.' I was what our captain's wife would have called 'fairly ship-sick.'

Annie Butler, *Glimpses of Maori-land*, pp. 68–70.

Oysters at Bluff (1886)

MATURIN M. BALLOU

A well-known American travel writer, Maturin Ballou visited New Zealand not long after the Tarawera eruption of June 1886. He arrived at Bluff and travelled north. Under the Southern Cross *is a descriptive account of the landscape, history, and society of New Zealand more than an account of Ballou's experiences.*

JUST AS THE SUN SET like a blazing fire-ball in the sea upon the western horizon, the ship rounded the bold promontory known as 'the Bluff,' and winding up the narrow channel into the harbor was soon moored to the one pier of the place. This was none too promptly done, for no sooner was the ship made fast than the darkness of night enshrouded both land and water.

A woman who had anticipated the arrival of the 'Mararoa' had set up a temporary oyster-stand on the pier, by placing a couple of boards across two barrels, beside which she had raised a powerful blazing flambeau. Here she opened and dispensed fresh bivalves. And *such* oysters we have rarely seen; they were in their prime, large, full, and perfect in flavor. Blue Points could not excel them. It seems that oysters are a specialty here, whence they are shipped in large quantities to Tasmania and Australia. It was a weird and curious picture presented by the group on the pier,—the blazing, flickering flambeau casting flashes upon the many faces, and all surrounded by deep shadows and darkness. Among the spectators of the ship's arrival who had come to the pier were a score of half-breeds,—Maori girls and men, laughing and chattering like monkeys. A night's sleep, a quiet night in harbor and on board ship, was a needful process of recuperation after the experience of the previous one on a raging sea, and we rose wonderfully refreshed the next morning. At breakfast we were regaled with New Zealand oysters and fresh fish.

The Bluff—also known as Campbelltown—is located in the very track of storms, and is open to the entire sweep of the great Antarctic Ocean. Its shelving side, sloping toward the harbor, forms a sort of lee,—a sheltered position which is occupied by a pretty little fishing village of some sixty houses, with a population of less than a thousand. These people gain their living mostly from the neighboring sea, and from such labor as is consequent upon the occasional arrival of steamships on their way to the north. Here we took refreshment at the Golden Age Hotel,—a primitive little inn, quaint to the last degree, its reception-room ornamented with many species of stuffed birds, mostly sea-fowls, among which was a preserved specimen of the albatross even larger than the one whose dimensions we have already given. There was a well-preserved seal hanging from a hook in the wall; also a sword-fish, and a young shark of the man-eating species. On one side of this room was a glass case of curious shells, large and small; and on the opposite side was an open bar presided over by a ruby-nosed Bardolph.

The Golden Age is noticeable as being the most *southerly* public house of entertainment in the world. Twelve months previous, being exactly one year to a day, we had partaken, at Hammerfest, in Norway, of the hospitality of the most *northerly* hotel on the globe. When this coincidence was casually mentioned to the host of the Golden Age, he would have immolated us on the altar of his hospitality had we not discreetly retreated to the ship.

Maturin M. Ballou, *Under the Southern Cross*, pp. 286–8.

After the eruption (1887)

J.L. LAMBE

Like so many others, J.L. Lambe was a young Englishman on a world tour when he came to New Zealand in 1887, and Twelve Months of Travel *is his diary. With several other Cambridge friends he toured north from Bluff, amusing himself by cutting down large forest trees. He also took a week's horse trek down the West Coast. An acquaintance of Edwin Bainbridge, who was killed in the Tarawera eruption, he made a trip to Wairoa after it was buried.*

October 1st, Saturday.
At 7.30 a.m. we started on horseback for Rotomahana, the scene of the late Tarawera eruption (10th June, 1886). We cantered round the southern end of Lake Rotorua, over flat and sulphurous country, covered with ti-tree scrub and bracken fern, for three or four miles, until forced to walk up the steep hill which lay between us and Tarawera Lake. As soon as we

commenced this ascent, we noticed the first evidence of the late eruption in the thin layer of mud on the neighbouring hill sides. Every step further, this deposit increased in thickness, and before us on the summit stood bare and leafless forests, scathed with the terrible rain of boiling mud. Nor did the road escape, for the hideous torrent carried it away entirely in many places, and left great ravines all the way along, which called for some care in riding. A few more miles brought us to the forest, through which we passed, and were pleased to note that the undergrowth is again springing up, and many of the large trees budding, despite the loss of their more tender twigs. Here the road was entirely destroyed, and we were compelled to dismount, leaving our horses to pick their own way over tree trunks and fallen branches. Then remounting, we descended the hill to the shores of a lake known as the Blue Lake, tho' alas! no longer blue, but a dirty yellow-brown since the awful night, which colour it is likely to keep for years, as it is continually fed with mud from the hill sides. Here the road had entirely gone, and we were forced to ride through the lake, keeping as close to the brink as overhanging vegetation would permit. We were unable to ride very much farther, for, from the high sides on the left, several enormous outbursts had taken place, bringing down thousands of tons of rock, and rendering the road quite impassable for our horses. As soon as we had crossed these newly-formed gulleys, we came upon our Maori boatmen, who were to row us across the Tarawera Lake, and were waiting for us here, as they were afraid to proceed alone towards the dreaded mountain. No words can describe the scene of desolation which now opened on our view, for on every side as far as the eye could see there was nothing but mud and ashes, with forests of blighted trees.

In front of us lay the ruined village of Wairoa, overwhelmed by that fatal shower in little more than an hour's time, a ghastly sight. From a sea of mud here and there stands out the top of a Maori *whare*, and the two hotels remain—'The Terrace,' with the sign still on the wall, and that other where poor Bainbridge was killed, crushed under the falling balcony. The drawing-room floor of the latter now comes nearly to the top of the fireplace, and just outside on the fatal verandah I found a book, which has apparently but recently come to the surface, washed out by the rain. I picked it up. It was Adam Smith's 'Wealth of Nations,' probably Bainbridge's property; but though I thought of taking a page for a memento, I could not for the life of me, and I replaced the book in the mud where I had found it. A short distance off was the Chief's *whare*, now broken down, and almost completely covered. His buggy stands outside with just the tops of the wheels and the back of the seat above the surface. In another place is Sophia's *whare*, larger and stronger than the others, which withstood the weight on its roof, and was the means of saving all but one who outlived that dreadful night. In one corner there is a hole in the roof made by a fireball from Tarawera, eight miles off, which luckily did not injure any of the terrified refugees. Up the hill is the schoolmaster's house, where he met his death, together with several of his children, his wife and two daughters alone escaping. How many poor people lie buried beneath that hideous mud? We turned

The Old Mill at Te Wairoa, which was buried during the eruption of Mount Tarawera, c. 1886.
(F-2923-1/4, Burton Bros Collection, ATL)

away, and continued our journey, descending towards the shores of Lake Tarawera, which now lay before us, some 400 feet below. On the way down we were shown the spot where an old *Tahunga*, or soothsayer, 102 years old, had been dug out from the ruins of the *whare* in which he had taken refuge. He was four days buried in the mud before he was rescued, much against the wishes of the Maoris, who attributed the disaster to him, and would have left him to die. But the old man only lived for a fortnight after his release. The Maoris say that a few days before the eruption, a phantom canoe filled with men was seen making away from the fated mountain across the still waters of the lake, their chieftains standing up amongst them urging them on with violent gesticulations, and beckoning to those on shore. Lake Tarawera is very much altered. The water has risen twelve feet, and instead of the clear blue expanse that it was a few months ago, girt by ferny banks and green slopes, there is now a great, sullen, dirty pool, lying in a desert of mud. The forest shows not a spark of life, the mighty trees for the most part lying felled by the fearful hurricane which swept up the valley. The pull across the lake was a very long and tedious one, taking us two hours. The distance was about nine miles, and the energy displayed by the Maoris by no means excessive. Tarawera drew nearer and nearer, and at length we landed a little to the south-east of the volcano, which was smoking peacefully. We walked along a newly-formed delta up a newly-formed creek. Below our feet lay the buried village of Ariki. (On the southern shore we had passed the site of another buried village, namely, Kariri.)

We continued for about a mile up this creek, beneath which, eighteen feet down, is supposed to lie the bed of the old stream that flowed from Rotomahana. The whole country is undergoing very rapid disintegration, the soft volcanic deposits being traversed throughout by countless deep-cutting streams, perfect miniatures of the great *cañon* systems of North America.

We had now reached a slight eminence from which we could gaze upon the site of the lost terraces. Behind us rose the volcano, blackened with its recent cinder shower, the whole of one side blown away and forming the commencement of the huge rent that runs from here through Rotomahana, for a distance of nine miles. The sides and hollows of this rent alone enrich the dismal landscape, for the rock free from mud and ashes, is in many places a rich crimson, very beautiful. We were standing on the spot where the White Terrace is supposed to lie buried, and looking towards the site of the Pink Terrace. The rent passes right through the latter, so it is evident that the Pink Terrace at any rate was entirely destroyed. Nothing now remains but domes of mud and scars of bare rock, between which, from every crevice, issue volumes of steam, here curling slowly up in gentle wreaths, there rushing out with a terrific roar.

The original lake of Rotomohana is gone entirely, but a new sulphurous lake is forming in a depression of one part of the rent. The scene is really extraordinary; such a chaotic desolation it would be difficult to imagine.

J.L. Lambe, Twelve Months of Travel, pp. 120–4.

PART 4
Globetrotting

Winnie Northwood, wife of the photographer, c. 1900.

A picnic at Hunua (1888)

E. W. PAYTON

*Edward Payton's account of his three years wandering in the antipodes
is illustrated with his sketches. He visited Rotomahana before and after
the eruption, and is an important source for the pictorial record of
the Terraces. Intensely interested in scenery, Payton both describes and
illustrates the landscape.*

ONE OF THE MOST FAVOURED neighbourhoods for picnics is Hunua. It is a quiet and charming spot within twenty miles of Auckland, on the Waikato line of railway. Now twenty miles is a considerable distance for a New Zealand railway to accomplish all at once, so they give themselves one hour by the time-bills, and sometimes take one and a half hours in reality. Having some knowledge of colonial railways, I thought of going prepared to spend a night on the way before reaching it, but ascertained that this was not necessary.

8.25 a.m. is an early hour to start for a picnic even in this early-rising country, especially when one has to get breakfast before starting. But at that time I was at Auckland station, much to my credit be it said; and off I went down to Hunua.

Don't think, reader dear, that I had the picnic all to myself. No; at another station I was joined by a bevy of ladies and gentlemen and children, and on we went whirling down into the Waikato at the fearful pace, of say fifteen miles an hour. No accident happened. Even this speed did not cause us to run off the rails, or run into any trains ahead that had started on the previous evening. It appeared that Hunua was only a 'flag-station', that is, it wasn't a station at all. There is a platform and a sort of dog-kennel to wait in, but the trains don't stop unless the guard is informed beforehand. We informed the guard, and consequently the train stopped.

At the station a large brake met us, and conveyed us some three miles into the bush, close to our destination. Everything unloaded, with the assistance of two matrons from a neighbouring *wharé*, off we went to a spot that some of the party had visited before, led by a mountain-maid who seemed, somehow, more familiar with the slippery hill-side than we were. First we traversed a winding path through some burnt *manuka*, and then down, down, down, we went into a deep fern-clad, bush-covered gully, till the pleasing sound of falling water broke on our ears. Still a little further and deeper, and then we saw the cause of the noise. A pretty over-grown creek, wandering gently between steep banks of rich fern and trees, came suddenly out of the greenwood into an open space, bounded by a wall of rock, over which it fell dashing, splashing, and hissing into a deep pool some sixty or seventy feet below. Still on we went, by circuitous windings, having first crossed the creek by stepping-stones, in which process one or two of our party put their feet in by accident; then one more steep descent, and we emerged from the bush at the bottom of the fall. What a delightful scene was now before us! In front, a most picturesque waterfall, tumbling down the rocks in charming streamlets and clouds of spray, into the deep dark pool at our feet; while at the other side the creek wandered rippling away into the recesses of a dense bush, among which ferns and fern-trees were to be seen in endless number; on each side were steep banks covered with ferns and small, graceful forest trees. It was a charming spot to be in on a hot day, and beautiful even in the New Zealand bush, where such places are not uncommon. Of course we set to work to sketch this, at least some of us did, and of course we did not do it justice—*cela va sans dire*. For I have come to the conclusion, long ago, that picnics and sketching excursions don't go well together. Flake white and linseed oil lose all their interest beside potted chicken and cream; after emptying the luncheon-basket one doesn't feel inclined for serious work. But we did try to be serious, and sketched away merrily; while the non-artistic portion of the party devoted themselves to fern gathering, and the children to fishing. In the creek are numerous eels, some of good size; and among these was an old patriarch, who had enjoyed many picnics. He had partaken of the contents of many a luncheon-basket, and was said to be bristling with hooks, which he always succeeded in breaking when anglers tried to catch him. Our young friends were soon at work after him, and very soon lost all their hooks; when a girl who had brought us cream, &c., said she had a hook at home, and set off to fetch it. In a short time our sketching was interrupted by a terrific yell, and looking up to the top of the fall, where they were fishing, we saw the boys dancing a regular *haka* round the wriggling form of a big eel. He was caught at last, this old patriarch, and died game. By the aid of the various picnics at which he had assisted, he had managed to get fat, and weighed five and a half pounds.

Not far away is another waterfall, much higher than the first one, being some 200 feet high, but not so picturesquely situated. Some of our party started for it, but the climbing up and down hill, through bush and creeks, was rather severe, and one or two of the explorers gave it up, and quietly went to sleep in the fern till the others came back. They were well punished for their laziness, for the sand-flies and mosquitoes got at them and attacked them valiantly.

It would be worth any one's while, who is interested in ferns, to pay a visit to Hunua to see the luxuriance of some of the rare ferns in the neighbourhood. They seem to disdain growing in small single roots, but cover whole banks with their beautiful leaves. Kidney ferns (Lycopodium) and the small 'Prince of Wales' feather' fern (a most delicate and graceful leaf) are here growing in large masses, with dozens of other kinds, whose names I will not attempt, for fear of my printer getting uproarious. A finer array of beautiful ferns I never saw. Besides the small ferns, of course the usual large graceful ones peculiar to the New Zealand bush are here; and the tall tree-fern is everywhere to be seen.

E.W. Payton, 'Tree Ferns, Wellington', 1880s. (ATL)

When we had finished our sketching, and got as many specimens of ferns as we could carry, we set off back to the only habitation in the neighbourhood; and the cooks of the party set to work again to prepare another meal. Supplemented by rich cream and milk from the cottage, the tea was most satisfactory; and the day's excursion was unanimously voted a success. On leaving our good friends at the *wharé*, they pressed specimens of *kauri* gum, &c., upon us, and seemed quite happy to have seen any one from the busy world, of which they see so little. Loading our traps on to the brake, we set out for a walk to the station, as we had plenty of time before the arrival of the train. The real reason of our walk, however, was the downright refusal of one or two of the ladies to be driven up and down some of the hills on the way. They certainly were steep, almost dangerously so, but we had good horses. On coming down some of the hills on our way to the Falls, the ladies who were sitting at the back of the vehicle complained that they could not see the horses at all, so steep was the road; and this seemed rather to disturb their peace of mind; so we walked back, and the brake followed us solemnly with our spoils.

Arrived at the station, the next thing was to prepare to stop the train. Trains do not stop at these flag-stations unless requested to do so, or signalled. The mode of procedure at night is to construct a torch of paper, and light it when the train approaches as a signal. So we collected all the paper and wood we could find, determined not to be left behind even if we had to set fire to the station-shed as a signal, as there was no other train after this one. Of course, as soon as the train was nearing (it was now quite dark) the torch, carefully constructed on a new and improved principle, would not light—that was only natural in the ordinary course of perversities of human nature—but by dint of making 'fireworks' with a glowing stick, we managed to stop the train, and got safely back to our homes after a jolly day.

E.W. Payton, *Round about New Zealand*, pp. 77–83.

Life on board a first-class liner (1889)

M . E . M .

M.E.M.'s ingenuous but vivid diary of her first voyage around the world in 1889 was published by her father on her return.

LIFE ON BOARD these first-class liners is always much the same; at seven o'clock the steward or stewardess brings a cup of tea or coffee to your cabin, then, on with your dressing gown, to the bath rooms, where a black man is waiting to mix your sea-bath the required temperature. On your way thither, you are apt to meet gentlemen strolling along in their pyjamas to the barber's shop, or to their baths, but it is a point of etiquette on board not to recognise anyone before 8 o'clock in the morning. Breakfast at 8.30, or 9, and then, morning promenades round the deck, first with one, then with another, exchanging a few words of friendly greeting with everyone you meet; then study the chart freshly put up, and inquire the 'run' of the last twenty-four hours; then a lounge chair, an interesting book, or a quiet study of your own particular part in the theatricals now on the 'tapis;' and before you realise that the morning has flown, the luncheon bell is ringing; and after lunch comes choir practice (for we have quite a large choir), rehearsals, a game of cricket for the ladies, sports for the gentlemen, and then the great institution, 'afternoon tea'. Nearly every lady goes provided with a special service of

The promenade deck of a liner, from the *Orient Line Guide*, 1889. (B-K 402-10, ATL)

her own, and at each port we buy cakes and biscuits and sweetmeats for this favourite meal, to which we invite our special friends; and have many a hearty laugh and pleasant chat during the half-hour or so every day that it lasts. Another promenade on deck, and the dressing bell rings, and all disappear below—the girls put fresh curl into their hair, which the sea air and wind have decidedly straightened, and don pretty evening dresses; while, if it is very hot, the men put on clean white suits, and all wear different coloured silk sashes round their waists, so that the effect at the dinner tables in the well-filled dining saloon is very pleasing. The food is splendid—we could not have wished for better, and every want is attended to: the captain has impressed his own order and regularity on all his officers and crew, with the result that everything goes like clockwork. Then comes either a dance on deck or a concert, a walk round to the watch, the moonlight flashing on the water, and the phosphorescence on the waves, as they lap against the side of the ship, and then to our cabins to sleep soundly till daylight the next morning.

M.E.M., *My First Voyage Around the World*, pp. 11–12.

Wirth's Wild West Show (1890)

PHILIP WIRTH

Wirth's World Famous Circus was founded by Philip Wirth's father in the 1870s and has been a frequent visitor to New Zealand. The 1890 visit featured an American Wild West show and received a lot of publicity and large audiences.

TO RETURN TO OUR SEASON OF 1890. For three months we played in Auckland, in the large hall which was variously known as the drill hall, skating rink, market, and agricultural hall, while awaiting the return of my brother Harry, who had made a hurried trip to the United States of America to engage a Wild West Show for our Australian and New Zealand tours. When he returned he was still spellbound by the size of Barnum & Bailey's Three-Ring Circus Hippodrome and Wild West Show. Their tent had five poles and held over 20,000 people. As this huge affair was packed twice daily he insisted that we should adopt the system of performing three acts simultaneously in as many rings. Consequently we hired a piece of waste land in Auckland on which to practise hippodrome riding with two and four horses, in chariots and bare-back, until our Wild West Show arrived on the 'Zealandia' on September 13th, 1890. This was the first time a show of this description had visited Australasia and crowds lined the pier to watch the arrival of the steamer. It was the fashion in Auckland at this time for the men to wear cowboy hats, and when our friends on the steamer saw so many of the people on the wharf wearing them, they remarked that there seemed to be more cowboys in Auckland than in Texas. All the cowboys were splendidly built, tall, handsome fellows, and with the exception of two were straight from ranches in America. The other two, Broncho [*sic*] George and Captain Sutton were the only two showmen in the troupe. Captain Sutton had the misfortune to lose his wife on the voyage out, and she was buried at sea. She had been known as 'Prairie Pearl,' and was a sharp-shooter and helped in the Wild West Programme in 'The Chase for a Bride.' In this she had to cut with a bullet a rope with which a horse thief was being hung. My sister, Marizles, undertook to play this part and had to start learning straight away to shoot and lasso, but knowing how dangerous it was to discharge a loaded rifle in a crowded tent, we allowed the rifles to be loaded with blank only, and faked the rope for this particular act, with a dog slip. We now had a five-pole tent, three rings and a hippodrome track for the chariot races and the Wild West Show.

Rain fell heavily on the day set for the opening, but to our great delight the huge tent was packed, and all went well until after the Grand Parade. Each ring was then occupied by a stallion. I had 'John Bull' in the first; the centre was occupied by Harry with 'General Gordon',

Poster for Wirth Bros' Wild West Show, 1890. (Eph-D-CIRCUS-1890, ATL)

and in the third were George and 'Sultan'. Each horse had been galloped around its respective ring once or twice when 'John Bull' and 'Sultan', both of whom hated 'General Gordon', saw him performing in the centre ring. They both tackled him simultaneously and for about 10 minutes there was a terrific fight with George, Harry and myself trying to quieten them. Eventually we calmed them and led them away leaving the stage to the bucking horses which were brought on by Captain Sutton, Cowboy George and the Arkansas Kid. As soon as they mounted they bucked so very efficiently that they kicked their way out of the rings on to the seats where the audience was sitting. His Worship the Mayor, who was sitting with his party in the front row, was knocked over, but by some miracle escaped unhurt from the flurry of flying hooves. By this time the rain had increased to such an extent that water was beginning to run under the tent into the ring, so I had the band play the National Anthem and the audience went home very wet but most amused.

Philip Wirth, *The Life of Philip Wirth*, pp. 49–51.

A *pleasant party in the West Coast sounds (1890)*

C.R. SAIL

C.R. Sail, who is described in his book's subtitle as an 'Anglo-Indian Globe-trotter', published Farthest East, and South and West, *an account of his journey home from India on two years' furlough. He spent three months in New Zealand in 1890, travelling from south to north and visiting most of the renowned beauty spots, including the Wanganui River, looking for 'unwesternized Maori'.*

THE ONLY MEANS AT PRESENT available for visiting the West Coast Sounds is to join one of the three excursions made thither by the Union Company's s.s. *Tarawera* in the months of January and February. The probabilities of your having fine weather increase in direct ratio with the lateness of the trip, but exigencies of time compelled me to go by the first. The ship is given up wholly to this excursion business, so long as it lasts; and the Company's advertisements assert that it assumes the form of an extended picnic. Not a picnic at all in the proper sense of the term, but as to its extension there is no doubt—the ten days devoted to it might be cut down by half, or to a week at most. Of course, among a troop of over one hundred excursionists, parties form themselves, that hang together, holding more or less aloof from the rest; and equally of course, among the rest there are sure to be a certain number that you would be likely to keep aloof from in any place. The plan of the trip is to make one of the Sounds and there remain all day, sending off the excursionists in boats to fish or botanize, or scramble about on shore and picnic amongst the sandflies. We were a very pleasant party on No. 4 boat. There was Our Enthusiast, up early and late, not to miss any possible 'bit' of scenery, and rapturizing over it all under the most adverse circumstances of weather and temperature; and as a counterpoise Our General, or opposite pole, who enthused not at all, and showered cynicisms, tempered with much genial laughter, on the whole arrangement. He was abetted therein by Our Ceylon Benedict, one of the best of fellows, in whose train came wife and sister and brother-in-law. Then there was Our Warrior Bold, and his wife the Authoress— (I have not read any of her books and do not know whether they are Hentyresting)—dear good people—he tottery of step, poor martyr to gout; and Our Humorist and his wife, let us say Mrs H. Lastly, a youth, a scion of a noble house, and Our Stanley (so designated from his fondness for forcing his way through pathless jungles), or Indian Exotic (being particularly

A group at the top of the Falls, George Sound, c. 1900. (F-97333-1/2, ATL)

touchy to the cold). Perhaps I need hardly say that I mention myself last. Well, this was the boat that, after we had reached Preservation Inlet and duly proceeded up to the end of the fjord and returned to Cuttle Cove and anchored there all night, proceeded to the shore in spite of the half gale of wind that blew and the squalls of rain that at times descended upon them.

The day's proceedings were very much the same at each place of halt: to go ashore to lunch or afternoon tea or both and spend the afternoon or the day in rambling about in the forest or catching fish in the sea. Here, then, is the journal. First and Second days as already stated. Third day: To Dusky Sound and Wet Jacket Arm by 11 a.m. Fourth day: Doubtful and Smith Sounds, Hall's Arm, Thompson's Sound; George Sound; anchored at 2 p.m. Fifth day: At George Sound. Sixth day: Milford Sound by 8 a.m. Seventh day: At Milford. Eighth day: Left Milford at 3 p.m. Remaining two days getting back via Bluff to Dunedin. Now of all these days there was only one wholly fine day—the third. Yet we enjoyed ourselves for all the wet. There is no denying that the scenery is fine; and it is so kind as to get better and better as you go on. Cuttle Cove is pretty when you see it first, but, after you have been through the rest up to the climax of Milford Sound, it is quite a poor thing to look back upon. All the little adventures that befall you—how one boat catches a shark, another a thirty-eight pound fish of ugly shape and uglier name, how one gets bogged and another deprived by a carelessly dropped match of the inexpensive gingham, what splendours of ferns have been found here, the fine waterfall or lovely lake successfully scrambled to there, how the sandflies have lunched on you—all these form the amusement of the day; and at night concert or dance or entertainment (for me the social rubber) make the time pass as gaily as may be. Our cynics declared the whole thing to be too much of the " 'Arry hout for a 'oliday' style of thing. And to my mind it would certainly be far pleasanter if one could do the Sounds with a small nice party of one's own friends rather than in the company of a mixed crowd, to most of whom you are no more interesting, I presume, than they, I am sure, are to you. How can one delight in the society of the Honourable?—(the 'Orrible Our Humorist aptly called him)—a life peer of some Australian colony, and oh, so colonial! To see him and Our Hereditary legislator play 'bull' together was a sight 'to shake the midriff of despair with laughter.' Then the young man got up regardless of expense, 'Calico' he was named; and the detachment of undisguised cads, and of cads disguised (as far as dress goes) as decent fellows—their room had been better than their company. Therefore our 'push' (this I understand is Australian for a party of people) left the ship, wet or fine, at each anchoring-place; preferring forest solitudes and a wetting to the deck of the *Tarawera*. The bush is different from anything I have ever seen. It is always wet here; for though its rainfall is not so heavy as at (say) Akyab, I think the rain is more constant; the intervals of pallid sunshine are so brief that nothing has time to get dry. Then there are no men nor any quadruped in these jungles; 'no birds are flying overhead—there are no birds to fly,' or at least very few; so that the Vegetable Kingdom has it all to itself, and evidently has had for many a long age past. Accordingly the soil is hidden beneath mass upon mass of decaying vegetation, clothed over with a wonderful wealth of moss and fern. You tread on a mossy knoll, and sink knee-deep into the rotting trunk of a fallen tree. You simply cannot walk on the ground, you walk or scramble on dead wood in all stages of decay, on wide banks of moss of varied kinds, lovely to look upon, through thickets of splendid ferns. The *Todea superba*, most exquisitely frilled, shaped like the Prince of Wales's feathers; the Kidney fern, most curious and delicate of tree-ferns (I mean ferns that grow on trees): here it is in seed—note the spores sticking out round the edge like a line of spikes; fern-trees (I mean ferns that grow to the size of a tree) many and large and handsome. There are few flowers; here the crimson blossom of the rata, there the thick-clustering small white flowers of the manuka. And never a thorn nor a briar; the 'bush lawyer' is absent; nor do creepers annoy you, except here and there a 'supple Jack,' a kind of cane. And the whole of this wild land is covered with bush; no break nor clearing. Except only that one hermit lives in Dusky Sound, and that there are two huts in Milford City, there is no settlement, no station, no human soul in all the long deep-indented coast-line. I have not seen the fjords of Norway, with which, as I read, these challenge comparison; but in their utter solitude and silence—undisturbed for who shall say how many ages?—I imagine these Sounds of the Farthest South must offer strong contrast with their cousins of the Remote North.

C.R. Sail, *Farthest East, and South and West*, pp. 178–82.

Eating kiwi (1891)

RUDYARD KIPLING

Kipling's visit to Australia and New Zealand, described in his auto-biography Something of Myself, *took place after a bout of illness that left him feeling he needed to get 'clean away and re-sort' himself. His vivid terse notes on New Zealand are an accompaniment to the famous line of poetry he wrote about Auckland: 'Last, loneliest, loveliest, exquisite, apart' (from 'The Song of the Cities'), often quoted by other travellers.*

THEN CAME NEW ZEALAND by steamer (one was always taking small and rickety coast-wise craft across those big seas), and at Wellington I was met, precisely where warned to expect him, by 'Pelorus Jack,' the big, white-marked shark, who held it his duty to escort shipping up the harbour. He enjoyed a special protection of the Legislature proclaiming him sacred, but, years later, some animal shot and wounded him and he was no more seen. Wellington opened another world of kindly people, more homogeneous, it struck me, than the Australian, large, long-eyelashed, and extraordinarily good-looking. Maybe I was prejudiced, because no less than ten beautiful maidens took me for a row in a big canoe by moonlight on the still waters of Wellington Harbour, and every one generally put aside everything for my behoof, instruction, amusement, and comfort. So, indeed, it has always been. For which reason I deserve no credit when my work happens to be accurate in detail. A friend long ago taxed me with having enjoyed the 'income of a Prince and the treatment of an Ambassador,' and with not appreciating it. He even called me, among other things, 'an ungrateful hound.' But what, I ask you, could I have done except go on with my work and try to add to the pleasure of those that had found it pleasant? One cannot repay the unrepayable by grins and handshakes.

From Wellington I went north towards Auckland in a buggy with a small grey mare, and a most taciturn driver. It was bush country after rain. We crossed a rising river twenty-three times in one day, and came out on great plains where wild horses stared at us, and caught their feet in long blown manes as they stamped and snorted. At one of our halts I was given for dinner a roast bird with a skin like pork crackling, but it had no wings nor trace of any. It was a kiwi—an apteryx. I ought to have saved its skeleton, for few men have eaten apteryx. Hereabouts my driver—I had seen the like happen in lonely places before—exploded, as sometimes solitaries will. We passed a horse's skull beside the track, at which he began to swear horribly but without passion. He had, he said, driven and ridden past that skull for a very long time. To him it meant the lock on the chain of his bondage to circumstance, and why the hell

'A chat with Rudyard Kipling [right] in New Zealand', c. 1891. (F-141362-1/2, ATL)

did I come along talking about all those foreign, far places I had seen? Yet he made me go on telling him.

I had had some notion of sailing from Auckland to visit Robert Louis Stevenson at Samoa, for he had done me the honour to write me about some of my tales; and moreover I was Eminent Past Master R.L.S. Even to-day I would back myself to take seventy-five per cent marks in written or *viva-voce* examination on *The Wrong Box* which, as the Initiated know, is the Test Volume of that Degree. I read it first in a small hotel in Boston in '89, when the negro waiter nearly turned me out of the dining-room for spluttering over my meal.

But Auckland, soft and lovely in the sunshine, seemed the end of organised travel; for the captain of a fruit-boat, which might or might not go to Samoa at some time or other, was so devotedly drunk that I decided to turn south, and work back to India. All I carried away from the magic town of Auckland was the face and voice of a woman who sold me beer at a little hotel there. They stayed at the back of my head till ten years later when, in a local train of the Cape Town suburbs, I heard a petty officer from Simons Town telling a companion about a woman in New Zealand who 'never scrupled to help a lame duck or put her foot on a scorpion.' Then—precisely as the removal of the key-log in a timber-jam starts the whole pile—those words gave me the key to the face and voice of Auckland, and a tale called 'Mrs Bathurst' slid into my mind, smoothly and orderly as floating timber on a bank-high river.

The South Island, mainly populated by Scots, their sheep, and the Devil's own high winds, I tackled in another small steamer, among colder and increasing seas. We cleared it at the Last Lamp-post in the World—Invercargill—on a boisterous dark evening, when General Booth of the Salvation Army came on board. I saw him walking backward in the dusk over the uneven wharf, his cloak blown upwards, tulip-fashion, over his grey head, while he beat a tambourine in the face of the singing, weeping, praying crowd who had come to see him off.

Rudyard Kipling, *Something of Myself*, pp. 100–2.

The box seat (1891)

JOHN MACGREGOR

John MacGregor, who described himself as a surgeon-major in the Bombay Army, wrote an account of his 'roving and ranging' on a homeward voyage round the world in 1889. It was accompanied by a poem in ten cantos on the same subject titled 'The Girdle of the Globe'. He appears on the frontispiece in full Highland costume.

NEXT MORNING WAS my first experience of New Zealand whips, which New Zealand thinks is one of her specialties. But the roads were very heavy on account of recent rains, and our progress consequently was not very rapid. Do you know anything about the 'box seat'? Then you have never travelled in New Zealand. The box seats on each side of the driver are greatly affected by peripatetic globe-girdlers, and the knowing ones had engaged these two seats on the arrival of the train at Oxford the night before. Captain P., of the Ninety-fifth Royal Recruits, occupied one of these seats, and a lady of the land occupied the other. She was one of those who received honourable mention from Mr Froude in his 'Oceana,' and I found her very obliging; for, as the country was familiar to her, she exchanged her box seat for mine inside, so that I might be able to see the country to advantage.

The driver was frank and communicative, as all these drivers are. And as we drove through the forest I inquired about the Kauri pines described by Mr Froude when passing through the

'A sketch of a coach, with its cargo of fashionably dressed ladies and gentlemen', 1880s.
(G-1345-1/2, Making New Zealand Collection, ATL)

same place. But the driver shrugged his shoulders, for it was he who drove Mr Froude on that occasion, and he said that so far as he knew there was not a single kauri pine in the whole of that forest. Mr Froude also exaggerates the height of the trees when, after asking Lord E., he says that 'the gun is not made which would bring down a bird from such a height.' But any ordinary gun with the proper shot would take down any ordinary bird from the highest trees visible from the roadside, and except in extent the forest was nothing remarkable to see for any one who had previously roamed on the mountains afar.

I was disappointed in not seeing the kauri pines, which I had now no chance of seeing, as I had left them behind. I knew there was a plantation of them near Auckland. But why should I go out of my way to visit them? Was it in vain that I had so diligently read my 'Oceana'? And would I not see them in the ordinary course of affairs? It was only then I discovered that the handsome kauri pines are found in the forest near Auckland, and there alone. Yet, notwithstanding its occasional inaccuracies, 'Oceana' must have had an enormous sale, for I met with it wherever I went.

John MacGregor, *Toil and Travel*, pp. 55–6.

The Flora (1895)

MARK TWAIN

Mark Twain's visit to New Zealand took place as part of a lecture tour around the world in 1895–96. He arrived in Bluff from Hobart in November 1895 and travelled north: 'It was Junior England all the way to Christchurch'. Twain sailed from Wellington, after visiting Wanganui and Hawkes Bay, in early December.

'Mark Twain at the City Hall, Dunedin … A Sketch from the Stalls by W.M. Hodgkins', 1895. (A-212-024, ATL)

Sunday, 17th.—Sailed last night in the *Flora*, from Lyttelton.

So we did. I remember it yet. The people who sailed in the *Flora* that night may forget some other things if they live a good while, but they will not live long enough to forget that.

The vessel was extravagantly overcrowded. If the *Flora* had gone down that night, half of the people on board would have been wholly without means of escape. The owners of that boat were not technically guilty of conspiracy to commit murder, but they were morally guilty of it.

I had a cattle-stall in the main stable—a cavern fitted up with a long double file of two-storeyed bunks, the files separated by a calico partition—twenty men and boys on one side of it, twenty women and girls on the other. The place was as dark as the soul of the Union Company, and smelt like a kennel. When the vessel got out into the heavy seas and began to pitch and wallow, the cavern-prisoners became immediately sea-sick, and then the peculiar results that ensued laid all my previous experiences of the kind well away in the shade. And the wails, the groans, the cries, the shrieks, the strange ejaculations—it was wonderful.

The women and children and some of the men and boys spent the night in that place, for they were too ill to leave it; but the rest of us got up, by and by, and finished the night on the hurricane deck.

That boat was the foulest I was ever in; and the smell of the breakfast-saloon when we threaded our way among the layers of steaming passengers stretched upon its floor and its tables was incomparable for efficiency.

A good many of us got ashore at the first way-port to seek another ship. After a wait of three hours we got good rooms in the *Mahinapua*, a wee little bridal-parlour of a boat—only 205 tons burthen; clean and comfortable; good service; good beds; good table, and no crowding. The seas danced her about like a duck, but she was safe and capable.

Next morning early she went through the French Pass—a narrow gateway of rock, between bold headlands—so narrow, in fact, that it seemed no wider than a street. The current tore through there like a mill-race, and the boat darted through like a telegram. The passage was made in half a minute; then we were in a wide place where noble vast eddies swept grandly round and round in shoal water, and I wondered what they would do with the little boat. They did as they pleased with her. They picked her up and flung her around like nothing and landed her gently on the solid smooth bottom of sand—so gently, indeed, that we barely felt her touch it, barely felt her quiver when she came to a stand-still. The water was as clear as glass, the sand on the bottom was vividly distinct, and the fishes seemed to be swimming about in nothing. Fishing-lines were brought out, but before we could bait the hooks the boat was off and away again.

Mark Twain, *More Tramps Abroad*, pp. 209–10.

The loss of Letter III (1898)

CHARLES TREVELYAN

Charles Phillip Trevelyan, brother of the famous historian, accompanied Beatrice and Sidney Webb to New Zealand in 1898. Leonard Woolf described Trevelyan as typical of a Victorian elite-intellectual, liberal and international, passionately interested in history and politics. His visit to New Zealand reflects these interests and social connections.

Masonic Hotel,
Napier.
Monday, August 15

Letter III was such a good one. But alas! it is now floating down the Mohaka River, or more probably tossing on the Pacific billows. I have had a fine adventure. New Zealand is not an easy country to travel in yet. Last Monday we left Auckland for Wellington. We reckoned on spending two days at the volcano country and getting here yesterday. From Rotorua you drive the whole way, much of it through mountains, of which travel I will try to rewrite an account presently. Suffice it to say that yesterday Sunday we started in pouring rain through a terrifically steep and magnificent range of fern-clad mountains, expecting to get to Napier that evening. At about ten o'clock we drove down to an inn by the side of the Mohaka River. Last year the bridge was washed away, and since then the only means of crossing the river has been a heavy hollowed tree canoe, attached to a steel rope, which is driven across by the action of the water. There is also a rope cage with which sometimes the shepherds pull themselves across hanging and swinging from the rope. When we arrived we were told by the host, who also was the only man responsible for the canoe, that we could not get over. The flood ran too high and would swamp the canoe, he said. There were a lot of shepherds also waiting to cross with their horses. I offered to go with anyone of them to try it. The experienced ones would not dare. The daring ones could not steer. So there was nothing for it but staying till the water fell, and we sadly saw the coach, which waited us on the other bank, toil up the steep bank away. So there we were stranded. The inn was comfortable, and we spent the evening playing chess and reading and chatting on politics with the shepherds who are all keen politicians even as the Cheviot farmers. One indeed was a Geordie from the Tweed. All of them whatever their party and ourselves roundly cursed the government for leaving the main road across the country, one of the mail roads and the chief tourist route, for 18 months with no bridge. Won't we let the Liberal members know our minds when we get to Wellington! Last night it poured and poured and today it was a bit higher. So this morning early I decided, (with due dissuasion from Mrs Webb, anxious for justification in case I was drowned) to go over by the rope cage and leave them to come on when the floods fell, and to bring on the baggage. The crossing was of course impossible for the unathletic Webb or even the masculine vigour of Mrs Webb. The difficulty of the situation was first that the rope was fixed to the bank higher at the other end than our end, so that I should have to pull myself uphill so to speak, and secondly that the water was risen so high that, when the rope gave with my weight, I might reach the water; in which case the tearing current would probably make progress impossible. Our host fixed up a board with ropes attached to a pulley to hang only about 2 feet below the rope, the least possible space for me to sit in. My valise with a few clothes, third volume of Wilhelm Meister, the precious Letter III and my excellent razors was tied by a rope to the side of the board. I bade an affectionate farewell to the Webbs wishing them a speedy crossing, and mounted my car. I had about a hundred yards to go across the raging stream swollen high with days of rain. At first I got on easily enough, except that the rush of the water half a foot below me almost made me dizzy with its swiftness. About half way across when it became evident that I should not touch the water, I let go the rope which they had fastened on to drag me back in case I got into difficulties. Then the tug began. For about 40 yards I had to go hand over hand up hill, on a thin wire rope. It was lucky I had done plenty of the 'ladder' in the Harrow gymnasium. With several rests I struggled to the end, where there was a rope ladder hanging down ten feet to the landing, or rather where the landing should have been; for it was now covered by three feet of an eddying backwater. I now undid my valise with some difficulty as my hands were numb with wet and straining. At the last moment the knot slipped, and the valise plumped into the water. I was too fagged to get down quick and I saw it take two or three undecided twists in the shallow water and then shoot off into the current where it was whirled away to the Pacific at the rate of 30 miles an hour. So George may buy himself at my expense a new edition of the red Wilhelm Meister, and I shall have to read vol. III in the original without the crib on calm days in the Indian Ocean. After that I clambered down, floundered for a moment in three feet of muddy water and reached land safely; while the shepherds and Webbs on the other side could not forbear to cheer. I saw them turn back to the inn which must be their prison for 24 hours and may be for a fortnight. Then I tramped up the steep grade towards Napier, most rejoicefully in spite of the fact that it was five minutes before I could straighten out my fingers, obstinately crooked into stiffness by gripping. I soon met my coach coming down to see if we could get over this morning, and he turned back with me to drive me the rest of the 23 miles into Napier. On the way up the five miles of mountain from the river I met a tramp, whom I turned back on representation of what the river was like and how little work there was beyond it. He was an intelligent unskilled workman who had been at the goldfields near Auckland and many other industries. He had voted for Reeves in Christchurch and was sturdy and unembittered in spite of his tramps. He absolutely refused whiskey until the very end of the drive though it was in the buggy with us, and then only when he was nearly freezing with wet and cold. As I neared Napier it began to get a little clearer; but I still have little hopes of the Webbs crossing for a day or two. It gives you an idea of the size of New Zealand & greatness of its mountains and difficulty of communication. If they go back, they have the alternative of going all the way back to Auckland, three days driving and one railway day, and then reaching Wellington by one day's sea and one railway. So they will wait however long it takes. It is a pity they are not on their honeymoon. But they are still sufficiently devoted to enjoy some hours tête à tête a day. But I am afraid the meagre literature of the inn and my bag which Webb will ransack, will hardly fill in the interstices of more than 24 hours. Meanwhile I have been commissioned to get due information about the Harbour Board and Municipality of Napier, which I shall do tomorrow as well as see the great meat-freezing establishments where the millions of sheep are packed for England.

The Hotel here is comfortable, and all the people so deliciously English. Today the chief roadmaker was a Mac something with broad Scotch twang. The river had been renamed the Esk. The wayside innkeeper hailed from the Salisbury plain. All types of English gentlemen, commercial folk, valetudinarians, fathers of families sat down with me to dinner today. But this leads me to begin again my unlucky letter III, which is now in a Pacific grave.

Charles Trevelyan, *Letters from North America and the Pacific, 1898*, pp. 137–40.

An adventure (1898)

BEATRICE WEBB

Beatrice and Sidney Webb, famous socialist intellectuals and Fabians, came to New Zealand in 1898 as part of a world tour. They investigated local government, trades unions, and education. The story of crossing the Mohaka River is told by both Beatrice Webb in her diary and by her companion Charles Trevelyan in his letters.

The next day brought us an adventure. We started off at seven o'clock up a precipitous pass and then down again to the basin of the river we had to cross on our way to Napier. The night through I had listened to the rain pouring down on the corrugated iron roof, and throughout our drive the rain drenched us—driving itself under rugs and umbrellas and splashing up from the miniature torrents through which our horses scrambled. Trevelyan sang songs to keep up his spirits, and I spent most of my time half listening to the words and half wondering whether the singing was pleasant or not. He had sung songs all the foregoing afternoon and some of the notes of his voice had got on my nerves. Suddenly we came in sight of the river. On the opposite bank our special awaited us, and on the near side of the rushing rapids of muddy water a little group of men stood round the canoe. But alas! We soon discovered that none of these were boatmen, but only disconsolate shepherds, waiting until the salaried government ferryman chose to consider it safe to cross. He was a fair bearded blue-eyed slouching individual—the host at the riverside inn, whose cautious temperament and deficient nerve was reinforced by his interest in you as a guest. Trevelyan scolded and Sidney blandished; all in vain: he would not go by himself for a five-pound note. Whereupon Trevelyan tried to induce one of the shepherds to go with him, but was stopped by the driver across the bank shouting that anyone who understood the canoe could get across, but that if anyone tried who did not he would be a —— fool. So we all returned to the little inn and tried to be gracious to its inmates. There were four sheep drovers: one a pleasant spoken Northumbrian—the son of a tenant farmer, and like his father, his grandfather—all his ancestors—a staunch Tory. He did not approve of the government land policy—the Government had no right to take a man's land away—but thought Dick Seddon the ablest and strongest man in politics. Captain Russell was too much of a gentleman. He described vividly the work of mustering sheep and went into the details of sheep-driving—how he would have a job for a month and then be slack for another. In work he expected to make 15/- to £1 a day and usually took the contract of driving so many sheep to a station at so much a head, making good any losses. His companions, serious, responsible sort of men, listened silently as we all sat over our meals together. Three hands from the neighbouring station sat at the far end of our table and now and again joined in: they were all Seddonites. Two hours after dinner the hands were drunk; the drivers were as sober and silent as when they had sipped their tea with the plateful of mutton. Trevelyan was restless and, early in the afternoon, asked us whether we objected to his going on without us: he could, he thought, swing himself over in the cage attached to the wire rope by which the canoe was worked from one side of the river to the other. I assented cordially, for I reflected that if persons travel together they ought to feel free to break off the companionship if they chose, and that if he did so this time, we should feel freer to make exactly the arrangements that suited us in the future. Sidney was put out but did not express the feeling except to me. So early this morning Trevelyan, feeling himself somewhat of a hero, climbed into the cage: all the shepherds sitting on the iron rope to keep it taut. In three minutes he was splashing down on the other bank, having lost his bag overboard, but evidently delighted with the success of the exploit, and his escape from the tedium of a riverside inn.

A long walk up the mountain discussing the plan of our future local government investigation, then back to lunch with the four sheep drovers; a smoke and a long afternoon's talk with the manager of a large station who rode up early in the afternoon and took his place in the parlour with us—completed our day's wait by the Mohaka River. The next morning the flood was over, and four o'clock in the afternoon found us sipping a cup of tea over our bedroom fire at Napier. Fourteen hours railway journey to Wellington.

Beatrice Webb, *The Webbs in New Zealand*, pp. 29–31.

Travelling companions (late 1890s)

MRS ROWAN

Ellis Rowan (1847–1922) began collecting and painting the flora of Australia at the suggestion of her husband when her health was failing, and became an internationally famous flower painter, working in Australia, the United States, and the Pacific. She lived in New Zealand in the early years of her marriage and toured in the late 1890s to observe and paint the flora. Her book is based on her letters.

MAKING AN EARLY START by the coach for Napier, I found, alas! that the box seat had already been engaged by a little German doctor, as broad as he was long. 'Take great care of him for he looks very precious,' were Miss Gill's parting words to me.

It was a glorious day, the sky that intense blue which has no equal, and under the bright sun and the wonderfully clear air the colouring of mountain, sea, and forest was almost too vivid in its intensity. We halted half-way to change horses and have lunch at a little wayside inn, and the sun was just setting when the first whiff of the sulphurous air reminded us that our journey was at an end for that day. The little village of Ohinemutu was unusually active as we passed through, for native elections were going on, and the Maori women were resplendent in all the colours of the rainbow, with the inevitable pipe in their mouths. At the hotel all the old faces had gone, and at the table I saw a long row of strange people. There was a little, long-haired, carelessly-dressed, spectacled professor, with his kindly, homely little wife, a contrast to 'her ladyship' opposite, who eyed us through her glasses as if we were minute specimens, and quarrelled with her food until we were driven to wonder why she ever left the comforts of her own home, if she could not bear the ordinary trials of travelling. Her husband, a tall, military-looking Scotsman, bore all her complaints with the resignation of long habit. Next them sat an Irishman with a tread-on-the-tail-of-me-coat-if-you-dare expression that warned off intrusion and friendliness too; then a dear old Scots couple, who were full of tales about the early days of their settlement and the gradual growth of the colony. The tall English gentleman next I knew was a splendid specimen of the old-time squatter, one of those who have helped to make Australia what it is, and my heart warmed at the sight of him and

Margaret Ross and Sarah Ryan in a coach crossing a river on the way to Mount Cook, c. 1890.
(G-8248-1/2, Ross Collection, ATL)

his wife. Opposite these were two pretty American girls and their maiden aunt. The girls were full of life, and amused us all with their naïve and original sayings. The aunt was a very starchy spinster, of the 'prunes and prism' variety, with a mouth always in the first position. A British matron sat in silent dignity next her good-natured, wealthy, ship-owning husband, of whom she seemed proud, though she failed to imitate his urbanity. A rheumatic farmer carried a liberal sample of his own soil about his person; a man sat beside him who was afterwards so continually popping up again on our travels that he merits a more lengthy description.

He was my travelling companion of the day before, a little German Jew, a doctor by profession, and he was here partly for his health, I imagined, and with the most laudable desire for information was taking snap-shots and notes after the manner of the immortal Mr Pickwick, whom he resembled in another way—he was very fat. His credulity was unbounded,—he believed everything that was told him, and put it all down in his note-book with the utmost gravity. He carried an immense brown bag, and whenever he wanted anything out of it that thing was certain to be at the bottom; and to find it, the little man invariably turned out the entire contents upon the floor of any room or place where he might be; we thus became intimately acquainted with his belongings, and I could describe to a nicety his entire wardrobe, so often was it distributed into its component parts before my reluctant eyes. He was writing a book, he said, and I have often longed to see it, and its marvellous stock of traveller's tales.

The two English tourists wish they were elsewhere, and the newly-married couple coo and cast sidelong glances at each other, much to the amusement of two black-eyed amusing little children, daughters of a book-maker, who made his 'pile' on the last Melbourne Cup. The remainder of our neighbours wear no particular identity, and a long summer's day spent with them would not be a joy to look back upon.

Mrs Rowan, *A Flower Hunter in Queensland and New Zealand*, pp. 195–8.

A party in Rotorua (1901)

JOHN FERGUSON

Like so many young men, John Ferguson spent a year travelling the world with his brother Percy. They left Liverpool in April 1901 and arrived in Auckland in July. They went to Rotorua and visited the site of the Tarawera eruption, but otherwise remained near Auckland.

I HAVE MENTIONED BEFORE that Doctor Kenny has asked us to spend an evening at his house, so, meeting him one Saturday at the barber's shop (the only one in Rotorua), he asked us to fix the 14th, which, having no other arrangements for that evening, we did. That evening after our return from Wairoa we set out for the doctor's, quite expecting that we were to spend a few quiet hours with him alone. What was our surprise to find a party of seven men already assembled when we arrived, and amongst them three officers just returned from South Africa, and sent up to Rotorua to recover from enteric and wounds. Captain X——, just on fifty, might have been a man of thirty, he was so jolly and young in all his ways, in spite of all he had gone through in the war. After a smoke we were taken off to the drawing room, where another surprise awaited us. I had thought it was a bachelor's party, but here we found that the gathering was graced by members of the fair sex corresponding in number to the men. I was quite puzzled at first to know where they had all turned up from, for during our seven weeks at Rotorua we had hardly seen a skirt anywhere. It was quite a pleasure to meet such a muster once more. The worst part of it was we had to sit down and play progressive Luker! How I do detest cards, especially under these circumstances. Still, we both knew it had to be gone through, so settled down to our task as best we could. Thanks to our partners, who had any amount of conversation in them and were young and bright (and four of them certainly pretty), we soon felt happy, and I think we all paid more attention to conversation than the progressive Luker, for the time soon went and the bell sounded. I had moved round two tables, P—— three, and I was distinguished by a clean card; the others had obtained stars on

A party in Rotorua

Meeting house at the Spa Hotel, Rotorua, which was used as a dining room, c. 1900.
(G-8312-1/2, Auckland Star Collection, ATL)

theirs to show their moves. The two prizes were given out, and I came in for the second. I had not had a single match with me during the day when I wanted one for my pipe, so I thought myself fortunate when, having undone my very carefully packed parcel, I found my want well supplied. Dr and Mrs K—— were a delightful host and hostess, being musical, bright and jolly. We made music and songs afterwards, and there were some excellent voices amongst the party. The doctor's house, which we thought a very pretty one, was entirely built of wood, as they all are about here, but once inside, it was difficult to tell it from a brick one. Wainscoting from three to four feet high, of teak from the native woods, ran round the dining room walls, while electric light and bells were fitted throughout the house. The drawing room was every inch typically English. It was the doctor's birthday only a few days before this, so that the birthday cake was going round, and it fitted in nicely with mine. After the music was over we said good-bye to the ladies who had added so much to the enjoyment of the evening, and were then taken off by the doctor to have a smoke and a 'chin-chin', and the doctor's whisky was excellent, not like the frightful stuff they give you at the hotels in New Zealand.

Here, as well as in Australia, the true born and bred Colonial women, I notice (and one can't help noticing it) are far more active, energetic, and able to look after themselves than some of their sex in the old country. Life in the Colonies seems more independent altogether,—one learns to help oneself and this perhaps is one reason why the women, as well as the men, are so healthy-looking and finely-built; but now to go back to the 14th.

Midnight found us shaking hands with those whom we had met at the doctor's, outside his gate. The three officers had to walk to the Geyser Hotel, and to get there they had to go up to their knees in mud; the road was awful, but they had gone through greater hardships on the battlefield, so made light work of this. For a lantern they had procured an old beer bottle with a candle inside; the night was pitch dark, they stumbled off in one direction and we the other—our hotel was fortunately close by.

John Ferguson, To the Antipodes, the Orient and the West, pp. 90–3.

The Wanganui River (1904)

BEATRICE GRIMSHAW

Beatrice Grimshaw was born and brought up in Ireland. As a young woman she went to live in Papua New Guinea where she became the first white woman to ascend the Sepik and Fly rivers. She wrote many novels and short stories based in the Pacific and a number of travel books. In 1904 she visited the North Island of New Zealand. Grimshaw eventually settled in New South Wales.

New Zealand is not yet fully opened up—that was what the geography books said in my school days. The saying, like most geography-book information, slipped through my mind easily, and did not create any marked impression. The marked impression came later, when I went half round the world to see New Zealand, and discovered that I could not take train to just anywhere I chose. It seemed incredible, in a country as highly civilised as France or Germany, that coaches—not the ornamental tourist brand, run as an accompaniment to railways, but real Early Victorian coaches, with 'no frills on them' of any sort or kind—were the only means of transit, save boats, to a great part of the famous hot lake and river district of the North Island. One could go to Rotorua, the most remarkable collection of geysers and hot lakes, direct by rail from Auckland. But the lovely Wanganui River, the beautiful up-country bush, and whole duchies of hot-water and mud-volcano land, could only be 'done' by coach and boat.

A canoe on the Wanganui River. (C-2009-1/2, Cowan Collection, ATL)

This made the journey more interesting, on the whole, though it was a little amazing at first to leave the railway far behind, and strike out right into the early nineteenth century. One should have worn side-curls, a spencer, and a poke bonnet, instead of the ordinary tourist coat and skirt and useful straw hat, to feel quite in character with the mud-splashed coach, its six insides, two outsides, and four struggling straining horses; the days of wind and shower, the hurried meals eaten at lonely little wayside inns, and the nights spent in strange barrack-like, barn-like places, where the stable was of more importance than the house, and every one always arose and fled like a ghost at the early dawn of day.

But first, after the railway town and railway hotel were left behind, came Wanganui River, a whole day of it; nearly sixty miles of exquisite loveliness, viewed in perfect comfort from the canopied deck of a river steamer. The Wanganui has been called New Zealand's Rhine, but it no more resembles the Rhine than it resembles a garden-party or an ostrich farm. It has nothing whatever in common with Germany's great historic river but its beauty; and the beauty of the Wanganui is of an order very far indeed removed from that of the ancient castle-drowned streams of Europe which are strewn with records of dead and decaying æons of human life. Solitude, stillness, absolute, deathly loneliness are the keynotes of Wanganui scenery. Shut in by fold on fold of great green mountain peaks, scarp on scarp of fern-wreathed precipice, one can almost fancy that the swift little paddle-steamer is churning her way for the first time into solitudes never seen of man. Now and then a Maori dug-out canoe, long and thin and upturned at the ends, may be sighted riding under the willows, or gliding down-stream to the swift paddle-strokes of its dusky-faced occupant. At rare intervals, too, the spell of silent loneliness is broken by the sight of some tiny river-side settlement perched on a great green height—half a dozen wooden houses, and a tin-roofed church: the whole being labelled with some extraordinarily pretentious name. One of our passengers that day got in at London, and went on to Jerusalem; another was booked from Nazareth to Athens!

All New Zealanders are *not* Maories, despite the hazy ideas as to colour which exist at home. There is a little trifle of nine hundred thousand full-blooded white settlers, to compare with the few thousand native Maories still left, in the land they once owned from sea to sea. Still, the Maori in New Zealand is an unmistakable fact, and a most picturesque fact into the bargain. To see a family taking deck passage on the boat—handsome dark-eyed women, with rosy cheeks in spite of their olive skins, and beautifully waved black hair; bright elfish little children; dogs and cats and a sack or two for luggage—is an interesting spot in the day's experience, especially when some patronising passenger, accustomed to 'natives' in other countries, gets one of the delightful set-downs the Maori can give so effectively. For all their shapeless clothing and heavy blankets, hatless heads and tattooed lips and chins, the New Zealand Maories are very much 'all there'; and when the patronising saloon passenger struts up to one, and remarks: 'Tenakoe (good-day), Polly! You got ums nicey little fellow there, eh?' 'Polly' will probably reply in excellent English: 'My name happens to be Te Rangi, not Polly; and as for the child you are referring to, I believe it belongs to the lady in the yellow plaid sitting aft!'

At the end of the day comes an hotel, standing on a wooded cliff above the river, and looking down upon a long lovely stretch of winding water and high-piled forest. The night is spent here, and in the morning comes the coach, with its team of four fine satin-skinned bays, its many-coated driver, its portmanteaux on the roof, mysterious little parcels in the 'boot', and confidential letters in coachman's hat, for all the world like something in Charles Dickens. There is no bugle and no guard, and the coach itself is a high, long-legged, spidery thing enough, not even painted red, and though it is 'Merry Christmas' time, it is a warm summer day, with some prospect of thundery rain, but not the faintest of any typical Dickensesque Christmas weather. Still, the sentiment is there, so one may as well make the most of it.

Beatrice Grimshaw, *In the Strange South Seas*, pp. 338–41.

Crossing the Mararoa River (1904–05)

LUCY BROAD

Lucy Broad, a well-known temperance campaigner and member of the White Ribbon League, visited New Zealand and Australia in 1904 and 1905, meeting White Ribboners and campaigning for prohibition. She thought New Zealand was 'the most progressive country in the world at the present time'.

ARRIVED IN NEW ZEALAND I was met with the reiteration of the impossibility of meetings, and at this point I find this entry against January 13*th*, 'I wonder if the thirteen club is disastrous? NO, Providence rules. But as *talking* was no go I tried *walking*, hoping to get to Milford sound! Off on *Friday*, 13*th*, and my room was No. 13, and I had £13 in my pocket, worse luck, thought there should have been £14.' And this was what came of it. I had got over eighteen miles of the road to Lumsden, and arriving at the hotel where the stage changes horses I made some inquiries, and was told something about a river to which there was no bridge, but the man added laconically, 'he supposed I could cross it, people did.'

Now I have a decided idea that what people can do so can I, or at any rate I can try; so I proceeded; but I am bound to say I did not like the look of that Mararoa river. However, 'people did', so I ventured to wade, but the current was deep and strong in the centre, and I was washed off my feet, and I shall not soon forget the sound of the mad water swirling in my ears. But Providence was good to me, and I was washed towards the bank, and making a great effort, with my heavy skirts dragging me down, I was able to climb it; but only to find myself minus my cloak, umbrella, small bag, and one of a lovely pair of new walking shoes all gone down the river! I walked on by its side looking for my lost property, and praying for my little bag (which contained some valued papers), until my hurt feet pulled me up.

Then, as it was impossible to go on with my bare foot, and I dare not trust myself to the river again, I commenced to 'cooey' to the hotel at some field or so's distance. I kept this up for a great time, and the light was beginning to change and I to shiver, and I had turned away, feeling that come what would I must try the road, when the welcome sound of the splash of a horse's footsteps called me back. It was the man at the hotel, and as I rode across he remarked that he had no idea there was so much water on, it had risen a great deal since yesterday. When I told him of my losses he rode down the river to have a look, and my relief was great when half an hour later my little bag was handed into my room—it had hung on to a low branch some half a mile down stream.

Next morning the friendly people at the lonely hotel did their best to fit me up for the backward track, the slender boots of the lady of the house would not come near my feet, and the man's heavy ones were equally impossible, so at last I started with a cut-down gum boot, tied round the ankle, and of the sort that 'needs must fit because they were too big.' I had gone a short distance in this plight, when a buggy took me up for a lift, and the owner insisted on my putting on his own good spring-sided boot. I met this gentleman's wife in Sydney afterwards, and she told me that when her husband returned to his home at the big sheep station near by, he had to stand a lot of good tempered banter about the exchange he had made. But it was part and parcel of the out and out colonial kindness that one so often meets.

Well, I was told that I was by no means the first who had come to grief at this crossing, some having even been drowned there; and acting on these representations I wrote to the papers and pressed the need for a bridge. In a later issue a gentleman wrote supporting my claim, but adding that 'I should have been much better after my involuntary cold bath if I had carried a whisky flask and taken a stiff nip!' That was very good considering I am a W.C.T.U. worker, but happily experience shows that abstainers have the best of it in trials of strength and endurance, and so we can afford to laugh at the advocates of 'the whisky nip'; yet perhaps it would be well for me to learn to have less of the British element of *stick*. And here I may remark that my misadventure reminds one of the numbers of people who get swept away by that other current of strong drink, and the curious thing about it is that most of them like myself thought they should be able to get through all right. But the current is deeper sometimes than others or the powers of resistance are less, and so multitudes get drawn in. This being so, how earnestly we would recommend the new strong bridge of total abstinence, or better still the diverting the traffic by prohibition.

Lucy Broad, *A Woman's Wanderings the World Over*, pp. 120–3.

A sample menu (1906)

W. R. TRENCH

William Trench, the Vicar of Kendal, kept dogged notes of his itinerary, menus, and times of travel in his Notes from Sea and Land. *This visit to New Zealand was his second: he had visited first in 1867. The principal interest of his notes is in the Anglican Church.*

IT MAY INTEREST some of my kind readers to know exactly how well they 'do us' on one of the best, if not *the* best of the eastward passenger liners, so I give a sample menu of our 8.30 breakfast, our 12.30 luncheon, and our 7 o'clock dinner.

The second saloon of the liner SS *Ormuz*, from the *Orient Line Guide*, 1889. (B-K 402-6, ATL)

Breakfast.—Porridge. Fried Plaice. Chops and Steak [to order in 10 minutes]; Grilled York Ham and Chipped Potatoes. Scrambled Eggs; Fried Eggs; Omelettes à la Jardiniere [to Order]; Devilled Bones; Grilled Sheep Kidneys. Curry and Rice. Macaroni Fritters. Cold—Raised Pie and Roast Beef. Stewed Apricots and Rice.

Luncheon.—Bouilli Soup. Potted Lobster; Sardines. Cottage Pie; Welsh Rarebits. Cold— Roast Sirloin Beef, Horseradish; Galantine of Chicken; Melton Mowbray Pie; Cumberland Ham; Spiced Beef; Haunch Venison; Corned Ox Tongue; Roast Leg Pork. Roll Jam Pudding; Marmalade Turnover; Ginger Biscuits; Oat Cakes. Cheese—Cheddar, Gorgonzola, Gruyère.

Dinner.—Consommé à la Fleury; Potage Purée de Gibier. Red Mullet aux Fines Herbes. Sweetbreads à la Toulouse; Croquettes of Turkey and Ham. Roast Sirloin Beef, Horseradish; Corned Ox Tongue and Carrots; Roast Goose, Apple and Savoury Sauce. Delhi Curry. Cold—Cumberland Ham—Roast Fowl. Plum Pudding; Apple Tart; Coburg Cakes; Genoese Pastry; Laitances de Harengs au Diable.

Programme of Music.—March, 'Billboard' (*Klohr*); Waltz, 'Blue Bells' (*Waldtenfel* [*sic*]); Selection, 'The Geisha' (*Jones*); Valse, 'La Little D'Amour' (*Charmettes*); Dance, 'Merry Little Niggers' (*Bidgood*). March, 'With Might and Main' (*Man*); Waltz, 'Tougours Fidéle' [*sic* (*Waldtenfel*); Selection, 'Three Little Maids' (*Rubens*); Intermezzo, 'Day Dreams' (*Farban*); Two Step, 'Mosquitos Parade' (*Mackie*).

W.R. Trench, *Notes from Sea and Land by the Vicar of Kendal*, pp. 6–7.

Two whole males in Rotorua (1906)

E. WAY ELKINGTON

*E. Way Elkington spent seven years in New Zealand as a young man,
travelling with friends and working at a variety of jobs. His account is
a descriptive social geography as well as the record of his travels told in
a comic, mock heroic style.*

PRIOR TO LEAVING Hamilton I had wired to my friends in Rotorua to book us rooms at their
pension, and when our buggy drew up I saw them at the window, and with them at least a
dozen other men, women, and children. Afterwards I heard, from the one that played, that as
we jumped out of the buggy there was an exclamation of surprise from them all, and one girl,
expressing the general thought, cried: 'Why, neither of them is lame!'

We turned out to be the only two whole males in the establishment; every other man was
an invalid, or thought he was, which amounted to the same. The result was that we thoroughly enjoyed ourselves, and, needless to say, neither of us left the next morning—we stayed
there for about ten days, each day swearing that the next would be our last.

Rotorua is a seductive place, and when you once begin sight-seeing you don't feel inclined
to stop till you think you have done it thoroughly. I say *think* advisedly; for unless you are prepared to spend at least two months in the district, you cannot hope to see one half of the sights
and wonders of this curious corner of the world.

From Rotorua there are endless organised excursions of a delightful and, as the guidebooks say, 'an awe-inspiring nature'; and, need I add, there is the ubiquitous Cook's man ready
to be of service to the tourist. Though I have never 'cooked' a trip yet—and I hope I never
shall—I would recommend those who can afford such luxuries to do so in this place, as the
sights to be seen are all handy and you can enjoy them more safely when going the orthodox
route. Afterwards you can, accompanied by a guide, go back and visit those places in which
you were most interested.

One of the most pleasant things in travelling is to be lucky enough to come across nice
people. Fortune has generally favoured me in this respect, and at Rotorua it did not fail me.
The boarding-house at which we stopped was full of nice people, and, as I said before, being
whole and apparently in our right minds, we were, metaphorically speaking, received with
open arms. My two Sydney friends had been there a week and knew every one, and (I don't
want to seem boastful, but the fact was too obvious even for me not to notice it) every one
wanted to know us, and one girl (after being introduced) would not rest until I had declared
upon my oath that neither my friend nor I had sciatica, rheumatism or gout, that we were not

Sanatorium, Rotorua, c. 1930. (F-90815-1/2, ATL)

'on diet', and that we could both walk. A sigh of relief broke from her as I finished, but presently, when she left me, I saw her go to the matron and whisper something in her ear. I put her down straight away as a Doubting Thomas, but I found out afterwards that she had only been asking permission to have a dance that night. She had, I also learnt during our first waltz, been staying there two months with a rheumatic father, and that every man who had been there during that time had had some complaint, and all the while she had been dying for a dance.

E. Way Elkington, *Adrift in New Zealand*, pp. 75–7.

Cooped up on the river (1907)

ALYS LOWTH

Alys Lowth has been variously identified as an 'English tourist', a 'New Zealand Lady', and Mrs A. Adlam of the Transvaal. She seems to have been an Englishwoman who settled in South Africa and wrote several novels and travel books, including a novel set in the Transvaal and a travel book about Africa. Emerald Hours in New Zealand *is half way between a romance novel and a travel book for health travellers. Mrs Greendays is said to be 'suffering from a serious condition of nerves', and the narrator/heroine is 'fagged out after the arduous anxieties of an exam'.*

'ANYTHING,' cried Mrs Greendays in an agonised voice, '*anything* would be better than to be cooped up in this—this *fowl-house* any longer!'

'My dear!' expostulated her husband.

'I can't help it!' she retorted, almost in tears. 'I did not have ten minutes' sleep last night, and my head *aches* with the stuffiness of that hole they put us into! *What* a country! Fancy being able to get no better accommodation than this in a *town*,—the terminus of a railway,—and a town where they say that it is always raining! I would *never* have left home had I known that I should have to put up with such discomfort!'

'My dear!' exclaimed Captain Greendays once more. 'Do consider, Hilda! We have been travelling for nearly three weeks in almost perfect weather, finding comfortable hotels everywhere, and the very first time things go wrong—'

'The *first* time! What about Atia-muri?' interrupted Mrs Greendays tragically.

'Well, *nearly* the first time,' amended her husband patiently. '*I really* don't think we can complain when we have an occasional reminder that this country is new, *very* new, and—'

His voice died away as he followed his wife on her way to the landing stage, and Colonel Deane and I laughed involuntarily as our eyes met. It was about six o'clock in the morning; we had arrived at dusk the evening before to find it raining pitilessly and the only place in the shape of an inn a very wretched, third-rate boarding-house with not an apartment in the house bigger than a ship's cabin, excepting a bare and dreary dining-room. But all the rooms were arranged for two, and though we had wired for ours days before I should have had to share mine with some stranger if Mrs Greendays had not taken me in with her, while her husband and Colonel Deane, to avoid unknown room-mates, had shared another. When we asked for baths we were curtly told to go to the river if we wanted such luxuries, and in every way the proprietors seemed bent on proving their independence by being as offensive as possible. In the night the rain came down in torrents, it became very cold, and this morning the weather was worse instead of better than it had been, greatly to our dismay. So in spite of the uncomfortable lodging Captain Greendays had suggested waiting two days for the next boat in the hope of its improving, but Mrs Greendays had very promptly pooh-poohed the idea.

And therefore we were now picking our way through the muddy track and over a swampy strip of meadowland, to the launch.

'The old chap is quite right,' said Colonel Deane. 'And especially in this case, as it is only a few months since the railway was opened as far as this. People who wanted to avoid the sea-trip to Auckland from Wellington used to come up the river only as far as Pipiriki, then drive from there to Rotorua via Taupo, and then of course there was no need for hotels in this out-of-the-way place.'

'It does not take very many months to build an hotel!' I retorted.

'And one will be open in a few weeks!' he returned. 'You must not be unreasonable. I think that considering the rush that woman had last night,—half the people had never given her notice of their coming—she did it uncommonly well. We each had a bed and a good meal, and what more can travellers in the wilds expect? And Taumarunui has been very much in the wilds until just lately.'

'One is surely justified in expecting ordinary civility,' I said. 'But don't let us talk about the wretched place any more. Is it really always raining here?'

'Pretty often, I think. It is so surrounded by hill and forest, you see. But I have an idea that it is going to clear up before long.'

This was comforting intelligence, for at the moment the rain was coming down as if it never meant to stop, and the hills were quite hidden by a thick veil of mist. Mrs Greendays and I were pinned up in travelling rugs, for we had no macintoshes of our own and had firmly declined taking Colonel Deane's and Captain Greenday's, and in the walk to the river from the boarding-house our rubber-less shoes were soaked through and through. But we were not much better off on the launch than on the way to it. It was a tiny boat, very dirty, and with no covering or awning of any sort. The badly-painted seats were leaving great splotches of red paint on the clothes of those who had inadvertently sat on them, and even these seats were all occupied by earlier passengers when we arrived.

Luckily Captain Greendays espied an empty and unpainted bench on the upper deck, and seized upon it. There was just room for us all, and there we sat, in a row, cowering under our umbrellas, and huddled close perforce.

It continued to rain for an hour or so, but the mist cleared away from the hills soon after we started, and it was so fascinating to watch the kaleidoscopic changes as the windings of the river constantly altered the arrangements of their thousand peaks that I forgot all about the weather. I had even grown accustomed to the cold stream that was steadily trickling down my neck from Mrs Greendays's umbrella, when Captain Greendays broke the spell by hailing a passing boatman.

'You might find something to put under these ladies' feet!' he begged. 'Can't you spare that coil of rope?'

The man shook his head. The rope might be needed in shooting the rapids a little way farther down the stream.

'Then see if you can find a—sack—or a board—anything!'

The man went away, and presently returned with some narrow bits of wood from a broken candle-box, which he solemnly proceeded to place beneath our feet. We severally thanked him fervently for his well-meant effort and did not even smile until he had disappeared with a muttered word of acknowledgement for the tip slipped into his hand. Then Mrs Greendays broke into an irresistible laugh, and said:

'Well, Tom, if that was not a fowl-house we slept in last night,—and I still contend that it was *fit* for nothing else,—you can't deny that we resemble a lot of roosters now, perched up on this bench with one foot screwed round the ankle of the other, and only just a toe on the deck to balance by!'

'And very ruffled feathers!' assented her husband, with a rueful smile.

Soon after this we had some exciting moments as we shot the rapids. Then we had to pull into the bank to wait for the bigger launch. By this time the rain had ceased, and as we watched the other boat come labouring up the stream with a vast amount of puffing and immense volumes of black smoke issuing from her funnel, Colonel Deane jumped ashore and returned in two minutes laden with wild cherries and mint and some rata blossom, all dripping but delightful.

We hoped to find the larger boat more comfortable, but were sadly disappointed. It was a steam instead of a motor launch, five feet longer and fifty per cent dirtier than the other, for the smoke from the funnel rained soot all over us and completed the damage begun by the red paint of the other. And there was no way of escape unless one descended into the tiny stuffy cabin that the boatmen used as dining-room, smoking-room, and all too probably sleeping-room!

However, the scenery made up for all these annoyances. We could no longer see the hills, for we were in a deep gorge, with high densely wooded cliffs on either side of the river, which was continually winding round corners. The foliage was really lovely. The sombreness of the many pines was brightened by the lighter greens of birch and willow, with occasional dashes of rata-bloom. The tree-fern, growing to a tremendous height, had fronds six and eight feet long, and some of the other ferns were wine-red, bronze, and yellow. Many of the trees had smaller ones growing from their branches, and there were mosses in all the shades of green and yellow, with quantities of stag-moss growing like a carpet, so thick it was and long. And there were masses of feathery pampas grass, or *toi*, as the Maoris call it, and velvety reeds,

Passengers and crew aboard a steamer alongside a bank of the Wanganui River, c. 1900. (F-49536-1/2, ATL)

bushes festooned with snowy clematis, with all the sage, olive, and emerald tints of green as a background, and grey rocks jutting out, stained with patches of yellow, red, and silver moss and lichen.

It was so silent and so solemnly beautiful, like the centre aisle of a vast cathedral, that when the skipper blew a hideous blast from the steam whistle to warn the house-boat of our approach I wished that I had the power to instantly order his decapitation for contempt of sacred things.

But the others regarded this act of vandalism merely as a signal that the luncheon hour had arrived; there were sighs of relief and a stir among the passengers crouched in the bow of the boat among the luggage, and a few minutes later we swept round a corner into view of the houseboat that is moored halfway between Tamaranui and Pipiriki as an inn for travellers on the river.

Alys Lowth, *Emerald Hours in New Zealand*, pp. 37–40.

Three absolutely drunken young bush-cutters (1910)

COUNT FRITZ VON HOCHBERG

Younger brother of John, the third Prince of Pless, Count von Hochberg set out on his travels through the 'British Empire in the East and South and in Japan' in 1907 when he was 39. He spent a month in New Zealand, which he thought was the 'worst country for travelling'. Von Hochberg had an English wife, and his book was written in English. His progress through New Zealand and other places is aristocratic, with baggage and servants.

AT 10 A.M. WE STARTED. As a gentleman who came yesterday with us (he is English and a Jew, I'm sure) had taken the other box-seat, and it was so cold that I had to put on my fur coat, I sat with the servants and some other passengers inside. Inside means under the top held up by four iron bars, but unless you button the oil-cloth curtains down, it is quite open. Thank God nobody had this infernal idea, although it rained. There was just room for six *thin* people inside—The bush was pretty through which we drove—magnificent trees, covered with moss parasite ferns and creepers, and beautiful tree ferns in abundance. The road was

A coach with passengers, possibly on the West Coast of the South Island. (F-68821-1/2, ATL)

good, which was lucky, considering the stone-hardness of the seats. The utter non-existence of any flowered bush or tree or plant was a pity, and the trees and shrubs were all small-leaved, so that one missed the beautiful effects of a tropical bush, but it was lovely all the same, and delicious to see real trees and green again. One heard many birds piping, whistling and singing in a very pretty way.—At 11 a.m. we rattled over a road, where enormous pebbles out of the river had been laid loose on the road, into a wretched-looking village, where, to our dismay, we had to stop till 1 p.m. The mounds (one really could not call them hills) round about had been cleared of their trees, which gave the place, with its hideous buildings and its broad, cobble-thrown, straight road in the middle, an indescribably melancholy, desolate look under the low-hanging, grey clouds. Wandering along this cobble street, I was astonished to see what they have in these shanty shops of the bush. Panama hats, pine-apples, Singer sewing-machines, cottage pianos, mackintoshes, even plated and silver spoons and toast racks.

After a good lunch in quite a decent hotel, at a long table with several clerks and commercial travellers and cattle buyers, the coach pulled up in front. The inside this time was occupied by the servants and myself and three absolutely drunken young bush-cutters, one on my bench, two (the worst) on the opposite bench, squeezed in beside Lazarus, who faced me, his idiotic Indian face contorted with disgust, like an affected woman ready to faint. They

were a rough lot, I admit, and yelled and sang, laughed and spat and shouted, and were altogether not exactly pleasant mannered. But as there was no special to be had, we had to put up
with it. The road was abominable; the bush we drove through, and some very steep, hilly
country, with deep, narrow ravines and gullies, were very fine. I was cold and I was very glad
to have my fur coat on. It was lucky we were so packed, it steadied us. The bumping, too, had
the good effect of sobering the three bush-cutters by and by, and it was quite interesting to
see how they came back to sobriety, and how with it the expression of their faces changed.
Finally, after two hours, they were sobered enough to be ashamed of themselves, and the poor
young devils commenced to show me the different sorts of trees, and which sorts were valuable, and to take the greatest trouble in initiating me in the way of cutting bush, etc., etc., and
so a conversation started and I learnt a lot of things about the work and ways of how a bush-
cutter lives. Sober, they were neither stupid nor uneducated, and the red-haired youngster,
called by the others Paddy, was even very witty and amusing. He was Irish. At four we arrived
at Piperiki, where a large hotel is well situated on one side of a valley at the bottom of which
the Wanganui River runs. I was astonished to find how this valley reminded me of dear
Furstenstein. It might have been the very place, only the river is a little broader. After dinner
the English Jew (he was an elderly man) joined us (unasked), and expressed his astonishment
at my not being furious at having had to drive with what he termed 'drunken ruffians.' He
never offered me his box-seat though, so where else should I have gone? 'Oh no,' said Healy,
almost pointedly, 'he even says he enjoyed it.' 'It's awful and disgusting,' said the Jew, 'to see
young men make such beasts of themselves as these drunken devils.' I really could not help
pointing out to him that it was all very fine for him, a rich Londoner, to look down upon
these poor devils in contempt. When one thinks that the only possible lark and amusement
these poor young creatures have is in going for three to four days every six months into a
cobble-beaten, desolate village to—well, to get too much to drink; because certainly most of
them don't go in there to *get drunk*, one understands. They work hard the whole year round
in that God-forsaken wild place, away for months from any human being, except what they
call their mate (it appears they cut in twos), live in a small tent, and sometimes are so stiff
from the cold they can hardly get warm. I'm sure they would enjoy and prefer travelling comfortably first class, dining in smart restaurants and going to a play afterwards. After all, Paddy
was only nineteen years old. Once sober, they were really very gentle-mannered, and apolo-
getically nice too. Paddy pushed his friend in the ribs when the latter had spat on my coat by
mistake, and the poor devil got red in the face with confusion, and rubbed it off with his poor
sleeve at least for ten minutes. I really couldn't be angry. No, as I told the Jew, who thought
himself so superior with his well-stocked purse, I didn't mind *their* company, *they* were, as I
told him, naturally rough and vulgar without *any false pretences* and airs. I minded *pretending,
so-called educated* people much more!

Count Fritz von Hochberg, *An Eastern Voyage*, pp. 84–7.

Worth seven weeks' sea-journey (1910)

COUNT FRITZ VON HOCHBERG

Count von Hochberg and his travelling companion, an Englishman called Healy, set off to walk the Milford Track, which, unlike most places the Count saw in New Zealand, met his exacting aesthetic standards. He took eight hours to walk the twenty-two miles from Pompolona Huts to Sandfly Point in 'delicious solitude', leaving a querulous Healy far behind.

December 22nd.—We left at 7 a.m. in radiant sunshine on a steamer with a largish party. A conversation sprang up with my deck neighbours, and it came out that the lady, a pretty, slim, fair-haired young woman, had been in Germany for a year with her relations at their country place, Hermsdorf, near Görlitz, a place I continually pass through in the motor. At the beginning Lake Te Anau is not overwhelmingly pretty, but the more the steamer advances the prettier it gets. The hills both sides are thickly wooded, and the trees reach down, with their green branches, into the lovely green lake's waters, the foliage hanging partly over steep, wild cliffs and precipices. The undergrowth is one mass of loveliest ferns and thick mosses in every imaginable tint and colour, from silvery grey to bright greens, from yellow to reddish browns. On some of the trees a mistletoe grows, covered with bright red blossoms, like the flowers of the red bouvardia. The effect is really fine.—The hills rose steeper and steeper, and enormously high, snow-capped, pointed peaks stood out of the thick green woods, reflecting themselves in the beautiful lake.—From all sides silver-white cascades fell over rocks and mossy slopes noisily into the lake, sending a shower of white spray glistening in the sun.

We had a very good cold lunch on board, and after steaming along in this exquisitely lovely and grandiose scenery, we landed at 3 p.m. on the other side of the lake, and walked through a fairy wood for a mile to Glade House, a large Government rest-house.

Lake Te Anau covers some miles, and has many long arms, and at some places is so narrow one thinks the steamer can hardly get through, and the trees almost meet. Then one comes out into some picturesque bay or arm, surrounded by magnificent snow-tipped mountains, and everywhere luxurious vegetation and magnificent woods. Some of the hills are 6,000 feet high. To describe the woods we walked through seems to me almost impossible. They are too marvellously beautiful, almost unnaturally beautiful, so that one thinks oneself in an exaggerated stage scene, that some wildly fantastic artist has created and painted. The trees (unknown to me) are enormously high and thick, with brilliant green small foliage, looking like beech-trees in the early spring. A thick undergrowth is formed of all sorts of younger trees and shrubs and enormous tree ferns, and the ground is covered thick with velvety mosses of every form, variety, and colour, between which, out of which, on which every possible small fern grows in luxuriant masses and exquisite forms. Creepers with foliage like the banksia twist themselves from tree to tree, from branch to branch, and all this is thickly covered over with emerald green, silver-grey, golden-yellow, and reddish mosses, like magnificent velvets, and from the thinner branches, long, hairy, grey-green mosses and lichens hang in thick fringes everywhere. The effects of the sun and the light falling through this mossy, ferny thickness are exquisitely beautiful, and I've never, not even in Japan, of which it somehow reminds me, seen its equal. Everywhere the red-flowering mistletoe puts in its brilliant red note, everywhere cascades and brooks of water, clear as fluid crystal, murmur or ripple, and these glorious green high domes echo with the melodious calls and songs and whistles of birds. Alas! this unparalleled place has one awful drawback, making sketching an impossibility: the sand-flies! They are small, black, harmless-looking things, as small as a gnat, but as soon as you stop walking or sit down they are all over you, and their bites are a thousand times worse than mosquitoes. Of course I had gloves and a veil, but I was cruelly bitten all the same, for they crawled up my sleeves and into my collar and everywhere.

At Glade House we had tea. Our guide put 'the soft shirt' in the big bag he carries on his back, what we call a 'Rucksack', and at about 4 o'clock we started. The road led through those glorious woods, alongside a broad, clear, aquamarine-blue stream, rushing towards the lake, in which were trout of a size and quantity such as I've never seen. Continually I heard the sweet fluting note of the bell or poe bird, very much like the Australian magpie that enchanted me with its lovely, sweet, flute-like calls at Merton in the early morning. I had taken the lead, and before I realised it, had left my party far behind, and was all by myself.—Coming out of the woods into an open valley, towards big snow-peaked giants, I saw a magnificent avalanche come thundering down one of them, like a huge waterfall, and the evening star just appeared over the hills in the pale blue sky, where some thin rosy clouds were floating.

At 9 p.m. I reached Pompolona Huts, the first rest-house, where we were to stop the night, 12 miles from Glade House, and enjoyed my supper very much, beside a roaring wood fire. Healy and the guide arrived at 10 p.m. Healy complained about his feet.—The rest-house was crammed full, and we had to sleep ten men (and they really have only a flannel shirt that does for the five days) in the men's hut—a large room, where the bunks are all round the walls like berths in cabins, one on top of the other. There was *one washing-stand, one basin!* Challys, the hut manager, smiled when I told him to shake me when waking me up in time, because I slept so soundly and wanted to start early, and at 4 a.m. I understood his smile, for I was wide awake fighting with the infernal sand-flies. So I got up, and, thanks to the sand-flies, could use the basin first. 'I thought you wouldn't want any special calling,' said Challys, when he saw me, fully dressed, step into the dining hut to have my breakfast.—The Challys are both English, he and she, and uncommonly nice, civil people, and Government can indeed be con-

Count von Hochberg, a picture published in his book *An Eastern Voyage*, 1910.

gratulated on having got these charming people for their rest-house.—These huts are only built of wood, with a corrugated-iron roof, and have only the most absolutely necessary in the way of furniture, but everything is scrupulously clean, the beds good, barring the sand-flies.— The ladies' hut (containing ten bunks) is attached to the dining hut, on which other side are a room for the caretakers and a kitchen. Then there is a hut divided in two by itself, having ten bunks each, one for men, one for the guides.

We started punctually at 7 a.m., and the road commenced to go uphill almost at once, and was very rough. We were supposed to lunch at Beach Huts, and walk on to Milford Sound (22 miles). After half an hour's walk Healy shouted to me, very angrily (he was seedy that morning, and already weary, I think), 'Are you going to run all the time like that? Because if so, I shall turn round. My feet ache most awfully.' I explained to him I only wanted to cross the pass (4 miles' steep climbing) before the sun got too hot, and suggested to him to take it slowly, and not turn round, as it appeared a pity to me. But he retorted gloomily that he would get lost when he was alone, and that he did not care to cross the pass by himself. So I proposed to him to keep the guide, and let me walk on, to which he agreed.—I soon left them far behind, and was again absolutely by myself in this exquisitely beautiful scenery. I'm sorry to say that I enjoyed it thoroughly, and only regretted Healy was so off colour.—The woods were just as fine as yesterday, only, of course, with the morning lights and the dew glistening everywhere they looked totally different, though just as fascinatingly beautiful, and perhaps one heard even more birds. The narrow path soon rose in very steep zigzags up the hill, after crossing the rushing aquamarine stream by a narrow wooden bridge. The woods there came to an end, and up and up one climbed into the open, where the enormous snow fields, glaciers, and pointed snow-covered tops of these magnificent hills towered into the pure blue sky. The vegetation was lovely still.—Among thick mosses and many ferns, exquisitely beautiful, tall, white ranunculuses grew in enormous clusters on high stalks. In some parts the hillside was almost white with them. They call them here 'mountain lilies,' but they are undoubtedly a sort of ranunculus, by foliage and growth. The pure white flowers, with brilliant yellow many-petalled centres, grow in large clusters, and remind one very much of the anemone japonica, only they are fuller. Besides these there were an abundance of a pure white flower looking like primula japonica, and higher up quantities of large white star-like mountain asters, on longish hairy stalks.—The view up to the snow-covered mountains round one, and into the still shadowy wooded valleys, through which the green rivers rushed away into further bluish hazy valleys, was magnificent, and the cool wind from the glaciers most refreshing, the clear water delicious and icy cold. I had my little goblet with me and enjoyed many a good, clear, cool drink.

At 9 a.m. I reached the top of the pass, where snow still lay and from where I had a magnificent view down both sides, into many valleys and over many snow-peaked mountains. At first I thought of waiting there for H. and guide, but having got hot with the climb and the wind being icy cold, I thought it wiser to walk on, and so I commenced slowly to descend on the other side. After passing, hopping from rock to rock, several rushing little streams, where avalanches had broken away the bridges, leaving heaps of snow and broken wood, I came into wooded country again, and soon found myself in the green fairy cathedral.—No! Words can't describe these beauties. In some places the water trickled over the rocks and the mosses had formed regular brilliant green cascades through which thousands of diamonds of water-drops dript down all the soft, long, green, velvety slope, to gather underneath in a pure, clear, rocky basin, while on the sides of these moss cascades, slender, fine ferns and white flowers formed a thick yet dainty fringe, and all the glorious trees, the tree ferns, the moss-covered rocks, the moss-covered dead trees lying across the pass from rock to rock, formed a velvet-green arch, under which you walked, the wild river roaring over and between enormous boulders and rocks, whirling in transparent blue-green pools, and the small, white-sprayed cascades fell over the precipices, and there, above all, towering out of this magnificent green entanglement of mosses, ferns and huge trees, the snow-topped hills rose 7,000 to 8,000 feet high.

After an hour and a half of slow descent, for, despite the sand-flies, I had to stop continually and admire, everything seemed so full of the joy of life, I reached a place where a board pointed out to me 'The Falls Hut,' but having been told that we should lunch at Beach Huts, I walked on to where another board points to Milford Sound. But no Beach Huts came. About twelve I met a roadman (the only human creature I had seen since the morning), and he told me Beach Huts had been re-named lately 'Falls Hut,' on account of the Sutherland Falls near by, and that I was 5 miles away from them by now. So I thought I would just walk on, and so I did, through equally beautiful scenery.—Then the track (for the whole road was only a narrow bridle track) took me to a wide and wildly-rushing river, at least 30 to 40 metres across, if not more, but no bridge. There were two huge posts to which ten steps of a high wooden ladder took me up to a narrow wooden platform, and on the opposite bank I discovered a similar arrangement, and a heavy wire rope from one bank to the other and two thinner wires running over an iron wheel. I commenced to turn the wheel to see what happened, when from the thick branches overhanging the opposite bank's platform, a small brown box slid towards me, looking the size of a cigar-box. So I wheeled on. The thing came sliding towards me high in the air, dangling on the wire rope, at least 20 to 30 metres over the rushing river, and when I had got it close to me I saw it was a longish wooden box (I can't describe it otherwise), with a low wooden border round three sides of about 15 centimetres high, hanging from two iron girdles on that wire rope. The most primitive sort of an arrangement I had ever seen, just large enough to hold a slim man in a crouching, sitting position. As I saw there was no other way of getting across, and that the thing, though small, looked solid enough, I trusted myself in it, holding the one wire firm till I was well and safely seated in this swinging thing. I then let go the wire, and whiz! Down and along I shot right enough till half across the roaring river. I could see I was at least 20 metres above the river, but now the trouble began, for I had to pull myself up by the one wire to the opposite platform, and as easy as it had been to shoot down the one side, just as hard was it to pull myself up the other by the thin wire in that crouching position. My arms ached, but I held hard to the wire, for I knew well that if I had let go I should have whizzed back with enormous velocity to the middle of the river till—well, who knows when?—my party came up two to three hours later. So putting all my strength together I steadily pulled and pulled, and finally reached the opposite platform.

If the former walk were lovely, it was really nothing compared to the supernatural ideal beauty of the other side. The woods seemed still higher, still more majestic, the varieties of ferns still greater, the river wider and wilder, the scenery grander still and more fantastic. One waterfall especially (it is called the 'Giant's Gate,' I call it the 'Fairy Fall') will always remain unforgettable in my memory. Out of the dense, thick, green, moss-covered wood, climbing over the hill, a white waterfall thundering over a deep cavern in the rock, which was shaded from blue-black into a coppery brown, fell down not so very deep into a largish basin of absolutely sapphire blue, shading off into emerald green, and at the farthest borders into pure aquamarine blue, to run out of the pool a crystal, transparent, aquamarine river, between enormous rock boulders. The banks of the pool were shaded with magnificent giants of trees with moss-covered stems, and the silvery spray settling on millions of slender, graceful ferns and moss cushions shone and glittered in the sunshine, falling in through the opening above the pool, like thousands of diamonds. It would be impossible for a pen to describe so much beauty, such exquisite colouring, such harmony, scenery, poetry. The cleverest brush of an artist alone could render it, and then most likely people wouldn't believe it, but would say it was a fantastic, idealised landscape. And the delicious solitude of it all! There was nothing but the cool sound of that white spray falling down into the whirling sapphire pool, yet broken sometimes by the sweet fluting notes of the bell bird. I could not tear myself away for half an hour. I have never seen anything so exquisitely lovely and purely beautiful. It was worth all the seven weeks' sea-journey.

Count Fritz von Hochberg, *An Eastern Voyage*, pp. 103–11.

PART 5

The wilds of the antipodes

A poster advertising Shaw Savill Line's shipping service to New Zealand, c. 1930.
(Epj-E-SHIP-1930-02, ATL)

The Travellers' Rest (1909–10)

JAMES MACKINTOSH BELL

Geologist and geographer James Mackintosh Bell was director of the Geological Survey of New Zealand for six years before he moved back to Canada. The Wilds of Maoriland *is an account of New Zealand and the travelling he did about 1909–10.*

ABOUT SIX MILES from Awanui our track led from the uplands to lower ground, and here merged into a wider and definitely formed road. I have seen the knee-deep sloughs of mud which mark the streets of a Canadian prairie town after the melting of the winter's snow; I have been dragged by sturdy Russian ponies through the deep accumulation of liquid filth which so often covers the highways of a Siberian town even far into the summer, but never in any of my travels have I seen such a road as formed that six miles' stretch. There was not a dry spot anywhere; we were drenched to the skin, dead tired, and ever so hungry. We must reach a habitation of some sort before nightfall—now not far distant. I still marvel that our already tired ponies managed to drag themselves and us through such a quagmire,—up to their knees at every step, and frequently up to their withers, occasionally completely bogged, now panting, now shaking, and now being urged forward by active persuasion and even by imprecation. Fortunately for us, the brave little beasts stood the pressure well, and just as night was closing in, the lights of the 'Travellers' Rest' at Waipapakauri, some two miles beyond Awanui, came into view. How gladly we approached this haven, and—how gladly we left it next morning!

The inn-keeper, an evil-looking, one-eyed old man, gave us far from a ceremonious welcome, and after some *pourparlers*, led us up a narrow, almost vertical, flight of stairs to a single damp apartment—which alone was available for the three of us. It was so small as to be almost completely filled by a large and partially collapsed double bed, a diminutive single pallet, and a washstand, devoid of water and towels, but plentifully supplied with large cakes of brilliantly coloured and highly scented soap. The evening meal was no more cheery than our sleeping accommodation. Alterations in the dining-hall were proceeding, and part of one of the thin walls was removed, allowing full vent for the icy wind to play around us and waft doubtful odours from the whisky and beer bottles filled with decayed arum lilies, which gave a funereal aspect to the dismal scene. In vain we asked for the open fire—found in nearly every New Zealand habitation, no matter how humble—by which to warm ourselves and dry our soggy garments. There was nothing to do but freeze in our thin change of clothing intended for the milder weather near the North Cape, and send our wet clothes to the kitchen, whence our wretched meal had so recently emerged, and where they took a back seat far from the kitchen range among the malodorous garments of Maori and Croatian gum-diggers and the varied other human nondescripts always present at inns in the New Zealand back-blocks.

James Mackintosh Bell, *The Wilds of Maoriland*, pp. 17–19.

Marooned at Pompolona (1913)

STANLEY UNWIN AND SEVERN STORR

As a young man, the well-known publisher Stanley Unwin travelled around the world with his future brother-in-law, Severn Storr, to investigate bookselling conditions overseas. Both men kept a diary, and Two Young Men See the World *is a selection from their journals. They visited New Zealand in 1913 and walked the Milford Track.*

IT WAS A QUEER-LOOKING CROWD that sat down to tea that evening in the kitchen-dining-room at Pompolona, some of us collarless, in all kinds of scrap garments. It really might have been a fancy dress tea. Mrs Airey was clad in a blanket, Mr Airey had bare legs and feet. Johnnie, looking exceedingly dishevelled, with his scanty hair brushed back, sat next to Dr Wellbeck, whose enormous head was capped with a shock of shaggy locks. Then there was poor Spinney, whose mournful expression and doleful hoarse voice uttering cheerless complaints about the weather could but bring sallies of laughter from us all. Opposite to us sat a Mr and Mrs X—, who had been already weather-bound one day. They were a rosy-faced, middle-aged couple; he looked like a cross between a gorilla and a pig, a most extraordinarily ugly little man. At the other end of the long table sat Mr Challice, who had come over from Glade House on a tour of inspection, and, incidentally, to mend the telephone, which was to be the only source of excitement during our imprisonment at Pompolona. With him were two guides or tracksmen, and Mr and Mrs Graham. This last-named personage was a very bright little woman, an excellent cook and hostess, and our thanks are due to her for keeping our spirits so high.

The kitchen-dining-room at Pompolona had a wide, open fireplace; an array of pots and kettles stood on a high grid, or swung over the fire of damp logs from sooty hooks. Beneath the fire was the oven, where Mrs Graham manufactured her life-saving dainties, and on either side were piled sodden logs a-drying.

After our meals we would all sit round the fire in a semi-circle, discussing our chances of escape, or the cessation of the downpour, or we would write on what available paper we could collect, or read a number of third-class novels that had seen better days.

The gentlemen's sleeping hut was a few yards away from the main hut. It was a fairly airy

Walkers outside the Pompolona Hut on the Milford Track. (C-24334-1/2, ATL)

apartment, with two rows of bunks around three sides and another wide fireplace, a door, and a tin washing-basin and jug on the fourth side. The ten bunks were comfortable and clean enough, and the whole room was adorned with drying garments and paraphernalia of all kinds.

Tobacco was running short, and one cannot overestimate the companionship of tobacco during such an imprisonment as this. Our only moments of real excitement were when the telephone bell rang and we knew that we were in communication with the 'Outside World,' as Spinney mournfully called it. The 'Outside World' was only the accommodation quarters at Glade House, which is about five hours' steamer trip from Te Anau. This steamer only runs twice a week, and is the *only possible* means of communication with Glade House. Te Anau itself is fifty miles from Lumsden, the road between them being liable to heavy floods. Forwards, we were divided by impassable streams from the next huts at Quinton, and a telephone message told us that we could not go back, for the Clinton River at Glade House was nothing but a roaring torrent, having flooded its banks, and the boat that ferried us across was tied to the veranda posts!

Thus we found ourselves at the mercy of this incessant element, rain; entirely cut off, but fortunately with a solid roof above our heads and no lack of food for the moment; but there were thirteen of us all told in this hut—Ah! Thirteen, by Jove! Here's the reason for it all!

Stanley Unwin and Severn Storr, *Two Young Men See the World*, pp. 240–2.

On the Track (1914)

MARY HALL

A Woman in the Antipodes was Mary Hall's second travel book, written about a journey that began in New Zealand and Australia before returning home to London through Asia. Preferring 'Nature' to colonial towns, which 'as a rule do not appeal to Europeans', Hall walked the Milford Track and travelled the length and breadth of New Zealand from the Bay of Islands to Stewart Island.

AT THE BOTTOM of the steep incline we followed the direction of a sign-board, and turning sharply to the left, found the Quintin Huts in a little clearing in the midst of the dense beech forest.

We were quickly supplied with—I might almost say, 'buckets' of tea, and in the circumstances, what nectar it was!

We found a large party of men and four women travelling in the opposite direction, and staying here for the night, so that the huts were crowded to their utmost capacity.

We soon skinned off our rain-sodden garments, and obtained hot water for our ablutions. As this was not the Garden of Eden, the next difficulty was, how to replace the discarded apparel. The contents of our haversacks gave us but slight encouragement: however, with a little ingenuity, we managed to clothe ourselves sufficiently for a mixed company. The collar and sleeves of my night garment just peeping out from a drapery of blankets looked quite 'shirty'. But for a little sameness, the supper party that night might have been an impromptu fancy dress affair.

The local colour was well in evidence, as with the material at hand it was difficult to avoid a resemblance to the Maori costume. In conversation we discovered that among these 'Maori chiefs' was a distinguished editor of a well-known Auckland paper, the youngest M.P. of the Dominion, and doubtless others equally renowned, but whose identity remained hidden beneath the incognito.

False modesty had no show that night, as we sat brazen-faced watching our clothes drying on a line drawn across the open fire-place. The unmentionables of a strange gentleman might have been seen in close proximity to the corsets of a lady unknown to him, and an interesting contrast was created by the hobnobbing of something white and lace-trimmed with a pair of weather-beaten gaiters.

It was also a curious study of human nature to notice how each owner of the various articles would surreptitiously contrive to get his or her property uppermost, and nearest the fire.

At one moment your boots might be in a decidedly advantageous spot; and at the next absolutely effaced by a monster pair of masculine foot-gear; or your stockings would be pushed aside, perhaps six deep, and certainly as wet as when they were first placed there.

But if other things were lacking in the huts, there was never a dearth of firing, and before we were ready to leave again, everything was dried.

The sleeping-shed that night was a study. In the first place, there were eleven of us for ten bunks, so two of the youngsters had to dovetail into one; and such is the advantage of youth, that next morning they were able to aver that they had had a very good night.

In this particular hut a little privacy was ensured by a curtain hung around the table on which were two washing basins. As each one finished washing, any soiled water which was not on the floor was emptied out of the window, and the basin was soon in use again.

Those of us who were not moving on that day did not hurry to get up, but lay calmly watching the difficulties of the others. Various garments seemed to have gone astray during the night, and much searching was necessary to restore them to their rightful owners.

The continuous downpour soon made it apparent to the energetic section of our party that they too would be obliged to remain for the day. The walkers going in the other direction, among whom were two guides, after a lengthy deliberation decided to try their luck. We watched them depart, and then settled down to pass the time as best we could.

The caretaker of the hut dried up the bedroom—not before it was desirable—as until it was done I found goloshes the most suitable bedroom slippers. We all helped to make the beds, and fortunately the two youngsters had secured a bunk each for the night, by placing their belongings on them. We had scarcely finished getting the place a little more comfortable, when it was reported that the other party had turned back.

In a few minutes, four miserably wet and dripping creatures were disrobing, and the room again became a pond. To add to the discomfort, one of the quartet began to wash her clothes, and instead of putting each article as she finished on the floor, she calmly dumped it on to the nearest bed. The prospective occupant was close at hand, and mildly hinted to the lady that as they were rather damp, she would be just as pleased if she put them on her own.

The return of these people proved to us that the terror we had felt the previous evening in crossing the Roaring Creek was not without justification. They were all experienced walkers and climbers, and capable of waging a successful war with the elements in their wildest moods, but even they had to submit to defeat, and wait a more favourable opportunity.

One of our number had increased the weight of his load by a pack of patience cards, and with them we whiled away the time by playing bridge. When tired of that we picked up one of the coverless magazines or books lying round, and were lucky if we found a complete article or story to fill up the interval until the evening meal. Everything was done to the melancholy accompaniment of falling rain, and the noise of rushing water. Nevertheless the hut that night resounded with laughter and good-humoured prattle.

Women walking along the Milford Track, c. 1930s–40s. (C-23305-1/2, New Zealand Free Lance Collection, ATL)

Two of the other ladies present regarded our party, I fear, with some disapproval. The appearance and general demeanour of these travellers was certainly incongruous in relation with their surroundings. They were ladies—distinctly gentlewomen—who could be pictured with an English rectory background, and I am afraid that the conduct of a member of our company pained one of them so deeply that in consequence she passed a sleepless night: nor could our humorous friend be held entirely blameless, although I must confess she reduced most of us to a condition of helpless mirth.

Conversation had turned on the subject of two having to share one bunk. The jocular woman in question was at the moment behind the curtain: she divested herself of her skirt, and darting out arrayed in tweed knickers, shirt, and with her transformation front pulled down over her chin to simulate a beard, she struck a mannish attitude with her hands in her pockets, and exclaimed: 'Who will share a bunk with me tonight?'

Truth to tell, this sally was received with shouts of laughter, the perpetrator's extraordinary appearance being quite sufficient to send everyone into a fit of hilarity, with the exception of the rectory ladies, who hastily retired to bed in pained silence; and after a while we all settled down to sleep.

Mary Hall, *A Woman in the Antipodes*, pp. 25–8.

All about Auckland (1914)

G.L. MORRILL

G.L. Morrill, pastor of the People's Church, Minneapolis, wrote a number of books of travel and religion under the pseudonym 'Golightly'. South Sea Silhouettes features many photographs of naked or semi-naked young Pacific women, and is written in a racy colloquial style. He came to New Zealand with his wife and cousin in 1914.

THE 'ATUA' ENTERED the Hauraki gulf, slipped by Rangitoto mountain, with its volcano cone, and steamed into Waitemata harbor to Auckland. In spite of the hard and ugly names the Maori natives called these places, they are very beautiful.

Docked at last, we bade good-bye to the good ship and officers, our floating hotel and servants, and started for the 'Waverly,' a novel named hotel. About to take mine ease in mind inn, I learned that the Easter holidays began at three o'clock, and the banks would be closed for ten days till after the races. I needed money, and plenty of it, for if I failed to get my Cook draft at once my goose would be cooked.

I hurried and crowded in just before the bank closed, and was told point-blank that although I had given good gold for my American Express checks to Cook in San Francisco, and had received a draft on the Bank of New Zealand for English gold, the government would pay out no gold. It was war-time and I must take pounds of their paper or nothing at all. I took it, although I knew if any of the 'paper' was left over when I reached Australia it would be discounted. Australian and New Zealand banks think very little of each other's daily news or bank paper. Like the ancient Jews and Samaritans they have as little dealing with each other as possible. Fifteen minutes later and I would have gone begging, and been in an excellent mood to preach a new sermon, on the bank steps, from the text, 'The door was shut.' Here was another argument against the incestuous union of church and state that Easter or any other church day should close business and bank doors. Henry VIII didn't go quite far enough in his divorce ideas of church and state, though he did go the limit and more when it came to women and wives.

We rode over town in a double-decker car, having acquired the ship habit of sitting on deck. Auckland has over 100,000 souls who look, dress, act, think, work, eat, drink and live much alike. The houses, too, are built on one pattern, and are as homely as many of the owners. There is no place like their homes of small wooden boxes with an iron lid on them. As if ashamed of human nature's journeyman carpenter work, that had traveled so far from art ideals, nature has tried to cover up the angles with vines and roses. Viewed as a trellis the house frames are very satisfactory.

That night I asked the hotel clerkess if there was a vaudeville show in town. She was tall and pretty, but before answering, rose to full height, looked at me in an injured innocence kind of way, and said, 'My word! you are in New Zealand. Auckland is a respectable city—there is a play at the Queen's opera house.' I begged her 'pawdon', thanked her, and went up hill to the op'ry. It looked very ordinary outside. I put down twelve shillings for my party and was given six metal cart wheels which the ticket taker took at the door and rolled into a tin box. The so-called 'opera' was a good first-class second-class vaudeville show, such as you can get home for half the price.

There was little applause, but the dreary silence was broken every few minutes by the thump and dump of the big cart wheel tickets. It was the usual song, dance, juggling variety bill. The bill that made the hit was the 'Kaiser Bill', for he was often referred to, and in a way that made all good English soldiers and sailors shout.

After the performance we went in a dive. I am sure it was, because the word 'dive' was written in big, bold letters over the door. I knew there were dives but didn't know they labeled them that way. We took a chance, and entering found it was only a restaurant. In the United States it is often reversed, what is advertised as a restaurant is frequently a dive.

G.L. Morrill, *South Sea Silhouettes*, pp. 124–5.

Landing difficulties (1923)

ALMA M. KARLIN

A young Austrian who had just published a novel, Alma Karlin decided to travel, and in 1919 she set out on what was to become an eight-year journey around the world. Her book records the 'purely personal aspect' of her travels: her difficulties with money, travelling alone, dangers and misfortunes, ill health. Karlin visited New Zealand in 1923 and stayed, lecturing and writing for newspapers, for several months.

IT WAS SUNDAY AFTERNOON, and the passengers, who had suddenly appeared in silk dresses which seemed to me rather superfluous, were pressing past the passport official, behind whom I could see the rising terraces of Wellington. The official asked me what my nationality was. I answered, and handed him my passport.

'The passenger list says British!'

I told him that I had showed my passport to the agents, but then remembered that the clerk had been more concerned with the innocent exterior than with the guilty interior, and I calmed down His Honour by telling him that. He was polite, but full of regrets. He could not let a foreigner go ashore, and on Sunday there was no one there who could deal with such a difficult situation. An American man—a descendant of the great nation—had no better luck, and so I felt rather more resigned to my fate. That evening we drowned our sorrows in drink, he in whisky and soda and I in ginger beer.

If grey hair is caused by cares (my hair is still brown, which makes me doubt the assumption), the passport examinations I had to go through would have been enough by themselves to turn mine grey. Oh, ye gods! At the far end of the world, to think of their making such a fuss over such a small person! And besides, a person who was politically as little dangerous as a child of the prince whose subject I was and of whom no one there had ever heard! I must hand over a photograph (the official consoled me by saying that it could be as ugly a one as I liked, and so I picked out the most horrible one I could find in my case), and then I had to fill out a long questionnaire, change my money (at a loss) from Australian into New Zealand money, and after all this deposit ten pounds so that, in case of need, they would be able to get rid of me again. As I had my letter of credit with my remaining three hundred yen in my pocket, I gave him the cash I had changed without making any fuss, and depositing my luggage I set out contentedly into the town. But when I went to a bank to cash my letter of credit I was told that they had no connections with Japan and therefore could not deal in yen.

So there I stood in the street, in a strange country, with only three shillings as working capital!

Alma M. Karlin, *The Odyssey of a Lonely Woman*, pp. 441–3.

The Hotel St George (1930)

LADY ANGELA ST CLAIR ERSKINE

Lady Angela St Clair Erskine, author of a book of memoirs in the 1920s, was the daughter of the fourth Earl of Rosslyn. She was passionate about fishing and country life, and her trip to New Zealand in 1930 to see the country and to fish came about because her doctor recommended a sea voyage after illness. Fore and Aft is her idiosyncratic account of that trip.

The St George, where I stayed in Wellington, is the most up-to-date hotel in New Zealand. It has an American air to it. There is a bathroom to each room, a 'cupboard grille' in every bedroom door, and clam chowder and sweet corn figure on the menu. It has at least seven floors, and strikes one as immensely high in comparison with all the other buildings. In view of earthquakes these are of more modest dimensions, mostly not more than two stories high and built of timber. Brick and stone do not stand shocks, but apparently steel and concrete will.

I never saw anything so lovely as the flowers in the sitting-rooms of the St George. On every table were huge bowls of lilies, dahlias, gladioli, chrysanthemums, huge zinias; in fact all our own lovely autumn flowers. They were beautifully arranged as if human hands had hardly touched them. I found afterwards that the manageress attended to them all herself. This art of arranging flowers seems to be a gift bestowed upon the New Zealander. Wherever I went I found flowers in lesser or greater quantities, but always well arranged and with the colours perfectly blended.

My first morning on shore was spent with the hairdresser, the chiropodist and the manicurist. In the afternoon I wandered round the town, which is not particularly interesting or beautiful. You could not help being struck at once by the politeness and intelligence of the inhabitants.

Hotel St George, Wellington, c. 1920s–30s. (G-100922-1/2, New Zealand Free Lance Collection, ATL)

Just as the best rooms are to be found at the St George so is the best cooking to be found there. At dinner I was introduced to a native dish, toheroa soup. Toheroas are found and dug out of the sand beyond the Bay of Islands. They are used either fresh or from tins, and the soup is quite delicious. The Prince of Wales, I heard, liked it so much that he left an order for regular supplies to be sent over to him. It can now, I am glad to say, be bought in this country. Oysters from Stewart Island are the biggest I have ever seen, and cost about shilling a dozen! A popular New Zealand way of using them is to serve the whole in a sauce, with fillet of beef.

I did not care much for any of the other kinds of fish that I got out there—always excepting the rainbow trout from Taupo. Trout is not allowed to be sold in New Zealand. This law prevents the fishing being commercialized.

Everywhere in New Zealand the quaint custom prevails of having to fetch your own fish from the fish-monger!

Parlourmaids do all the waiting in the New Zealand hotels, and the 'head waiter' is also a woman. They were efficient and looked very clean in their white uniforms, and I found all the servants in New Zealand most obliging. I had heard so much of the independence of the domestics in the Antipodes that I was prepared for a good deal of discomfort. I experienced none, unless perhaps it was having to dine at six or six-thirty. You soon get used to it, and the early dinner hour enables the servants to get their work finished by eight-thirty. Even so, considerable latitude is allowed to the visitor, more especially to the fisherman. If I came in late I never had any difficulty in getting what I wanted to eat.

The hotel servants all belonged to a Union, to which they subscribed sixpence a week, but I gathered that there are very rarely any disputes. Private employers are inclined to complain about the six-thirty dinner, but it must be remembered that very few people keep more than a couple of servants, and that the day starts early in New Zealand!

I saw Mrs Sinclair-Thompson talking to a very grand-looking lady, and found out afterwards that she was interviewing a cook. She volunteered that as she would be working for English people, she would have no objection to serving dinner at 7.15.

In the evening I went to the 'flicks.' There are several good picture houses in Wellington, and their news bulletin is excellently presented. Smoking is not allowed, but apparently this restriction does not affect the attendance, as they are usually packed. There are no movies on Sundays.

Lady Angela St Clair Erskine, *Fore and Aft*, pp. 137–9.

The wettest walk in the world (1931)

MARIE BYLES

After finishing her law degree and saving hard, Marie Byles left Sydney on a mountain climbing trip around the world. New Zealand was her next mountaineering destination, and she climbed extensively in the Southern Alps, conscious of following in the steps of Freda du Faur, another Sydney mountaineer.

Beech trees on the Milford Track. (F-21068-1/4, ATL)

THE NEXT DAY DAWNED, or rather failed to dawn, amid the heaviest downpour of rain I have ever experienced. It seemed as if the heavens were emptying oceans of water upon the earth, turning the whole of the mountain-sides into one continuous waterfall and the footpaths into one continuous river. The Sutherland Falls were a mere trickle in comparison with the smallest of the falls that plunged from the mountain-tops into the valley below.

We ascertained by telephone that the party leaving Milford that day for the return trip had already left. Obviously, if the weather were good enough for them it must also be good enough for us. Accordingly out we went into the storm and lightning, the whole twenty-five of us, men and women, young and old, the last class including at least three people over the age of sixty.

For six miles we tramped along raging mountain torrents instead of footpaths. This is no exaggeration. Once, indeed, I seriously wondered if we had not missed the path and taken to the bed of the stream instead, for the water was terribly swift and the ground underfoot very rocky. However, we presently emerged on some 'dry' ground where the water was only ankle deep, so apparently we had not missed the way. The monotony of the paddle was relieved at frequent intervals when we came to a roaring river across the path. Generally the water came nearly to our waists, and we held hands to steady ourselves in the precarious transit. Once we reached a deep pool that came to the armpits of the man, who kindly carried the girls across. Still we went on, with the heavens pouring themselves upon us, the lightning flashing all round, but the thunder was drowned in the voice of the storm.

At length we reached the boatshed at the head of Lake Ada, an uninviting tin hut with a mud floor. Again the telephone was with difficulty brought into operation and informed us that the party from Milford had been forced to go back because the boat could make no headway against the swift current of the swollen river. The voice at the other end suggested that we should also go back. This was no doubt an excellent suggestion, but easier to give than carry out. Two miles or so we ploughed our watery way backwards, and then met a river that we simply could not get across. Clearly we were marooned and must make the best of one night in the boatshed at least, and perhaps more. When we regained it, one far-seeing man cheerfully suggested that the first thing to do was to take a stock of the provisions that were waiting transportation to Quinton, and apportion rations right away. However, a more practical lady, who started making a fire, got in first. The provisions were eventually found to consist of sweet biscuits, a leg of bacon, and some tinned nectarines. If you should ever have the pleasure of entertaining any of our party I would suggest that you do not offer them sweet biscuits!

The dry clothes of the party were pooled, and in due course everyone appeared arrayed in fancy dress. The more respectable appeared in pyjamas and night-dresses, while some were reduced to bathing costumes and improvised brown-paper overalls. One lady shone gloriously in an orange kimono and put the rest of us to shame. The dripping garments were hung up on the rafters, the most personal and intimate clothing of both the men and the women appearing quite unashamedly among more presentable and outward articles. In turn the clothes were dried before the weakly-burning fire, and when dry, or more or less dry, they were held up to public auction.

Was the party downhearted? No! Indeed, to judge by the noise you would have thought it was engaged in a picnic under the blue skies. There proved to be several sweet singers, and they whiled away the time by giving us appropriate musical items.

Marie Byles, *By Cargo Boat and Mountain*, pp. 253–6.

Bare, brown country (1932)

ARDASER SORABJEE N. WADIA

Ardaser Sorabjee N. Wadia wrote a number of travel books, including The Call of the Southern Cross, *about his visit to Australia and New Zealand in the early 1930s. A Parsee, Wadia was a professor of English and history in Bombay before becoming a well-known travel writer. He also wrote a number of books explaining different religions.*

AFTER STAYING A DAY at Christchurch, I left for the famous Mount Cook in the heart of the New Zealand Alps. This was another long motor-drive, and it was most tedious in parts. The first part up to Timaru was fairly enjoyable, but thereafter we entered bare, brown country till we approached the snow region. This bare, brown country with bare, brown hills stretching out for miles and miles was as much a revelation as a disappointment to me. From travel-books and picture-magazines I had imagined New Zealand to be one endless stretch of lovely green country, thickly wooded and highly cultivated, where smiled eternal spring from year's end to year's end. Instead, I found undulating plains and high rolling downs covered with short, stubby, dried grass, the eye-tiring monotony of which would have got on my nerves were it not relieved here by a cluster of cottages and there by a clump of trees. Especially was this the case in the South Island, where again and again I felt as if I were carried on a magic carpet back to my native land of India, so very brown and parched the country looked at times. But this short, stubby grass that makes great parts of New Zealand so attractive, provides an ideal food for sheep which, like us men, thrive best on simple diet and rigorous climate. When taken to the more fertile parts of the country and put on the richer diet of green pasture-lands, the sheep soon lose their fine tone, become flabby, and their wool in consequence, coarsens.

A New Zealand Railways poster advertising Mount Cook, 'The height of happiness', 1927. (F-126075-1/2-CT, ATL)

Travelling, like life, is often a study in contrast. When we reached Mount Cook late that evening, we realized the truth of that saying. For barely an hour before we were rolling up and down the dreary brown monotony, and now as if by magic we were transported right into the midst of a glistening white world with snowy ranges towering above us wherever we turned our eyes. The Hermitage Hotel was an acme of comfort and forethought. The Mount Cook Motor Company, which runs it, has set itself an ideal of hotel-keeping which is worthy of being followed in all other parts of the world. Its primary objective was not merely to look after the comfort of its guests, as is the case with most hotels in the world, but to bring them together and entertain them so as not to have a dull moment hanging on their hands from the time they came down to breakfast in the morning till they retired pleasantly tired at night. This ideal of hotel-management is indispensable in snowland, where one's activities depend entirely on the moods of nature.

Ardaser Sorabjee N. Wadia, *The Call of the Southern Cross*, pp. 117–19.

PART 6

Scenic New Zealand

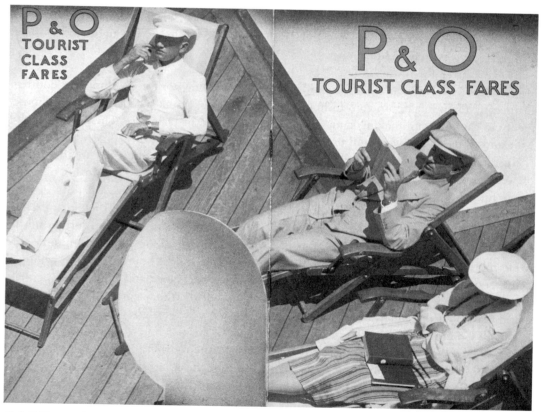

P & O Tourist Class Fares, a booklet cover from 1936. (C-23510-1/2-CT, ATL)

They do love New Zealand! (1930)

BOHUMIL POSPISIL

*An experienced journalist and travel writer, Bohumil Pospisil visited
New Zealand in 1930 for ten months with a free railway pass from
the government. His book was first published in Prague in Czech and
then translated by Pospisil and published in New Zealand.*

On the western coast is the prosperous port of New Plymouth, of 16,000 inhabitants. I
rather liked it, as the town covers the hills. Here is the beautiful Pukekura Park with its water-
mirrors, fine ferns and palm-like trees. The tramway conveys the comfortable one to the
bathing beaches. Quite near are several historical spots. Nearly every hill and small island has
traces of Maori fortifications and some pas are well preserved.

To the local Rotary Club I had to talk about Czechoslovakia. The hospitable Rotarians and
the Hotel Albion fed me well. Two or three Fish and Oysters Saloons, belonging to Jugoslavs,
also treated me with grand portions.

'Kako zshivem!' How are you?

'A dobro, hvala Bogu! Ima kutchu, ima leba i zaradim novace. A shto ima dobro u
Dalmaciu? Tamo ima dobro vino-nishta, vishe. Rada malo.' Thank God, fine! I have a house,
plenty to eat and I am making some money. What is good in Dalmatia? There is wonderful
wine and that's all. No work and no money.

Inside the nice, inlaid white-tiled saloons which were always crowded was an atmosphere
of well-being. And they were doing well indeed. One of them invited me to his nice and
tastily furnished house. Will they return Home? Why? They do love New Zealand!

These fish and oyster restaurants of the Jugoslavs I have seen mostly in the North Island.
Here and there I found one even in the South Island, but near Auckland and further north,
live most of the Jugoslavs, or rather Dalmatians, with their fish saloons. They seem to be able
to do more with little money than the Britishers, working longer hours and more willingly,
being good business people as evidenced by the nice appearance and equipment of their
restaurants. They have not forgotten their Slav origin and when they got hold of me I had to
talk much about the conditions in Europe. Naturally we talked politics, the paramount subject of all Continental talks, till our tongues got sore.

I mentioned having been well fed at the hotels. In the morning, porridge into which I
could pour cream till the meal was fairly swimming in it; steak or eggs, fried sausage or ham
and eggs followed the entrée of fish; scones or buns spread with butter and honey, and some
fruit. Added to that coffee or tea, fresh white, brown or toasted bread—in short a fine choice.
Butter, milk, cream, bread, scones and tea on the table for liberal use!

In the better class hotels the choice was still richer: I managed usually in the following fashion: first porridge into which I poured cream and chucked in a substantial piece of butter; then some meat; a few scones covered with butter; with my coffee I crunched toast; with the second cup I washed down some cake or brown bread covered with honey; I left the table by taking a couple of bananas, or an apple or an orange, though before porridge, I had sometimes a compote. For the foundation I preferred boiled plums, knowing their important function in digestion. And when I fancied something extraordinarily tasteful I simply said to the smiling white-robed waitress: return, please! In the better hotels and boarding-houses I was wakened up with a cup of coffee at my bed. Needless to say that in such cases I had to make rational arrangements with my stomach, because the grand breakfast was followed by so-called morning tea or tiffin which took place about 10 a.m., and I had to reserve some space in my inside for the 1 p.m. lunch.

Lunch: fish or some mysterious mixture the name of which I could not catch at first from the inquiring waitress. Hors-doo?—she did not mean a horse cutlet—which stood for hors d'ouvre [*sic*]; soup; meat with cooked vegetables like potatoes, carrots, etc, beetroot, pickles, cauliflower, cabbage; every vegetable was in its special dish which circulated round the table or everybody was served with his own series of portions; then followed pudding or jelly; compote, sweets, cheese, fruits, nuts. The inevitable mountains of bread, toast, scones, cakes, butter, honey, jugs of milk and cream, tea or coffee were on the table as a matter of course.

The dinner was similar and usually richer.

Then no wonder that a New Zealander wonders in Europe why every piece of bread costs so much, every bit of butter so much, every cup of coffee two crowns.

Bohumil Pospisil, *Wandering on the Islands of Wonders*, pp. 49–51.

Visiting the blow-hole (early 1930s)

S.E.G. PONDER

Author of several books about being a soldier and travelling in Asia, Major Ponder came to New Zealand on leave while being transferred from Hong Kong to Malta in the early 1930s. His book aims to amuse, not to instruct, the reader, and is highly personal.

I arrived at Wairakei in the late afternoon, to find the place consisted of a small bungalow type of hotel standing in a large and charming garden. There was no other habitation for miles and miles.

A porter appeared, removed my baggage, saw that I was in the Service, and instantly greeted me as a loving and long-lost brother. Surprised and embarrassed I thought he was going to embrace me, but it seemed that he owned a brother who was serving in the Queen's Regiment. Did I know him? Had I heard of him? Where was he at that time? This porter, however, was not at all upset when I was forced to admit that I had never heard of his brother. For the remainder of my stay this army-minded myrmidon stalked me, and, when caught, I was forced to listen to songs of brother-praise and to intimate family details.

Another servant, attached to the hotel, showed me to my room, and he, except for shabby clothes, might have been a young colonel in a crack cavalry regiment, for he had that air stamped all over him. I tried to get him to talk, but he shied away with a suspicious agility. My bedroom should have belonged to a tweeny maid at home. The wallpaper would, at least, have sent her into ecstasies of pleasure, but it revolted me.

At tea, in the tiny sitting-room, I found a large family of sightseers and an unattached young man. The young man grinned at me, eventually, and asked if I would like a swim in the swimming bath of the hotel. I said I should like one very much and unsuspectingly allowed myself to be led down a garden path to where a few cubicles had been built on the edge of a swiftly flowing steam whose bed and sides had been enlarged. There was also a dam and a sluice gate, and the water was a dirty grey in colour.

My companion warned me that the water was likely to tickle my skin. We removed our clothes and I dived in to find the water almost unpleasantly hot. I swam about and then sat at the bottom of the sluice gate and allowed the water to pour down over my back—a particularly sensuous sensation. It was then I began to experience the effect of this alum-impregnated water. In no time at all I was feeling as if a million fleas were feasting with rapturous enjoyment upon my person—I could have torn lumps out of my flesh with my finger-nails.

My companion laughed loudly and said it was good for me. And that I should become used to it. He may have been correct, but I fled to a shower having normal water and so felt a little better.

I returned to the hotel, and, when in the sitting-room with the family and a whisky and soda, the plump and amiable proprietress came into the room and asked if any of us wished to go out and visit the blow-hole after dinner. Somebody asked why after dinner when it would be quite dark. Surely we should not be able to see anything at such a time? The woman, however, assumed an air of mystery and stated that it was far more beautiful at night and that we must leave it all to her. We did.

At eight o'clock a motor car came to the front door of the hotel, and four of us, including a woman, squeezed ourselves into it, for it was a small car and was driven by the colonel-like manservant. As soon as I got into the car I nearly came to grief, for, having been asked to be the first to get into the back seat, I emerged again with some suddenness on the far side, the

From an advertisement for Wairakei, 1930s, showing the hotel and Geyser Valley. (C-24006-1/2-CT, ATL)

off-side door not having been properly fastened. This put everyone, except myself, in a good humour, and we started off with a jerk which nearly made me swallow my tongue.

A Maori guide stood on the running-board, and clung to the side of the car as we fled out on to the road and tore madly up a slight hill and down the other side. Two miles down this road the car stopped; we were told to get out and that we must walk for some distance across a desolate piece of moorland.

The guide, with a lantern, led the way through the dark night and we crowded close behind him, for he began to tell us something about the blow-hole. By those who know, it is considered to be the safety-valve for the whole of this portion of the Thermal Regions, and should it ever become blocked up in any way, then upheavals of awful magnitude would take place. The Maoris have always known of its existence, and, according to them, it has never ceased its activity, nor has it shown any signs of flagging, the fierce pressure of steam given out remaining constant. They regard it as a god, and it was considered, and still is so, extremely unlucky for travellers, passing nearby, not to go and pay their respects to it, bad luck of the most shocking variety having befallen those in the past who have failed to carry out this duty.

As we drew near to the spot there came the sound of a deep, heavy roar which grew in power every moment until it was actually deafening. By this time I was thoroughly intrigued, and wondered if the actual sight was going to come up to expectations—such things rarely do.

We came at last to where a narrow path with a wooden hand-rail to one side led steeply downwards. The whole world was now filled with tearing, rushing sound. The guide halted at the top of the pathway and said we had arrived. There was certainly no doubt that we had done so, but, as it was a Stygian-like night, we could see nothing—only hear. The noise of escaping steam under gigantic pressure was almost terrifying, and it set our nerves on edge. We howled to the guide to turn on his powerful torch and let us see this horror, which we could only hear. He did so. There, a few feet below, was a tiny round hole, level with the ground, and about nine inches across; and from it a vast stiff, and almost steady, column of steam tore up into the upper air to vanish beyond our vision. A terrific and awe-inspiring sight.

After a few moments gazing in fascinated wonderment the old Maori led us down the path and we stood within a few feet of the hole. I punched my walking stick into the column, and it was nearly torn from my grasp, so great was the pressure.

The woman of our party refused to come anywhere near the hole, and, beckoning the guide, she asked him where all the steam came from. The Maori, who was old and wizen and quite without a sense of humour, looked at her to see if she was trying to pull his leg, and then said it came from an ever-boiling lake far below her feet. I felt, from his manner, as he turned away, that he would have liked to have told her if she did not believe him she had better dig down and see for herself.

Not far from the blow-hole was a pile of battered petrol cans, and the Maori, picking these up one by one, flung them into the steam. In a flash they soared upwards into the blackness of the night, to descend a minute later many yards away, where they hit ground with nasty, suggestive crashes.

When the cans were exhausted the guide took a large piece of sacking and soaked it thoroughly in petrol, after which he hung it on the end of a long pole and set alight to it. When it was burning fiercely he thrust it into the stream. The result was as unexpected as it was alarming. The sack was instantly torn into tiny, burning fragments which soared up, turning the column of steam into a fiery, writhing, burning pillar. I cannot remember seeing anything quite so wonderful: it was indescribable in its awe-inspiring beauty. The woman ran away, giving squawks of terror as she did so, and not without cause, for I myself was considerably shaken by the sudden and terrible weirdness of it.

The sacking burnt out at last, the night closed down again, and we went silently back to the car and so to bed.

S.E.G. Ponder, *Sun on Summer Seas*, pp. 103–7.

Glorious Manapouri (1945)

FRANCES AHL

Frances Ahl's book was intended to 'bring a knowledge of New Zealand to the American people'. Her sixth book, it is less an account of her travels than a potted history–travel guide. Ahl visited New Zealand twice in the 1940s.

FROM THE TIME I left Lumsden, I wondered why the bus was labelled Te Anau instead of Manapouri. Later when we reached a particular fork in the road and one sign read Te Anau and the other Manapouri, I just could not understand why the driver was not taking the route that led to the latter. Finally I asked, 'Aren't you going to Manapouri?'

'After Te Anau,' he replied in a matter of fact tone of voice.

When I heard the newlyweds, seated just behind me, remark to some of the other passengers that they were booked for Te Anau because they could not get accommodations at Manapouri, I at once thought to myself yes, it was just as the Government Tourist Bureau had warned—reservations must be made well in advance.

And so I inwardly rejoiced at my good fortune—more than seven thousand miles from home and soon I would be sojourning in a comfortable hostel on the very shores of beautiful forest-clad Lake Manapouri, undoubtedly the loveliest body of water in all New Zealand. How tragic I thought that young lovers, but a few hundred miles from one of the most romantic sights in their own native land, were denied the privilege of hotel accommodation because they had carelessly neglected to heed the warnings of their own official travel service.

If any reassurance of my enviable lot was at that particular moment necessary—and I hasten to assert positively that it was not—had I not that very morning checked each and every coupon with the Invercargill office and learned that everything was in good order.

A bit puzzled that I was the sole passenger when the bus left Te Anau, I was still too full of eager expectation to realize that anything could be wrong.

'Will I be able to get a taxicab to take me to the hotel at Manapouri?' (I had been thus advised to query of my driver).

'I go right there. I live there.'

Silently I drank in the sheer beauty of the scenery—the impressiveness of the rugged mountains, their glistening silvery crests and peaks surging up to the blue heavens. How I loved the open stretches of forest through which the car was winding. But soon my thoughts were interrupted by the driver.

'Do they know you're coming? Do they expect you at Manapouri?'

'Yes! Here are my reservations for two nights—August 20 and 21.'

'You're right—that's tonight and tomorrow night.'

A sharp turn in the road, and I was peering in the distance for a somewhat sumptuous hotel—four or five stories at least—something akin to the beautiful chateau at Lake Louise in Canada or some of the lovely hotels in Lucerne, Switzerland. If Manapouri really is to New Zealand what Lucerne is to Switzerland, should it not have big hotels—rustic if you wish, but spacious and comfortable?

Soon we stopped at the gate of a low, rambling, one-storied house. The bus driver, without a word, carried my two bags to the front porch and before I knew it was on his way to complete his delivery service some few miles down the road.

Meanwhile, I was greeted by one with the appearance of a farmer, who had just finished milking the cows, rather than of a hotel manager.

'And what can I do for you?'

'I have reservations from the Government Tourist Bureau for two nights here.' And I opened my purse and took forth my coupons.

'Right you are. I forgot all about you until this morning … But come right in …'

And as he continued talking he walked across the living room and showed me down a long narrow corridor to my room.

Somewhat puzzled, I began to survey my surroundings—twin beds unmade, the soiled sheets and pillow slips of the previous month yet to be removed; a dresser in one corner and a table with white china wash bowl and pitcher in another; no running water or electric lights; no semblance of any clothes closet but a few crude hooks on one wall; two small windows opening onto a rough wooden porch; and a door that refused to lock.

'We aren't much for business around here. I'll reckon that door hasn't been locked for 33 years.'

'Where are all your guests?'

'Guests! Oh, we haven't any now. We've been closed for several months.'

'How about your housekeeper?'

'Well, now since my sister is away I guess you'd call me the housekeeper; what gets done around here … but I don't worry very much … you just run along now and enjoy yourself. I'll see to making up the beds after I get a fire in the grate.'

'Do you have a cook?'

'I'm cook, too … I haven't thought about dinner yet, but we'll have something to eat after a while. Run along now and take a walk down to the lake before dark; don't worry, just leave everything to me, I'll get affairs under way presently. You just have a good time … You came all the way from America to see Manapouri.'

This was Manapouri, I pondered. Manapouri, with its 'most comfortable hostel;' glorious Manapouri, where one should spend at least two days and take pleasure in the full beauty of the

Dominion's loveliest lake with its numerous forest-covered inlets, its maze of inlets and bays; and above, the lofty mountain ranges with their massive snow-capped peaks towering over all.

The day's end was rapidly approaching. Lumsden, the nearest town, was some 50 miles away.

With bags again on the porch, I waited the return of the bus and its driver. To go back to Lumsden was unthinkable. The only available transportation was the government service car. One stranded traveler was not sufficient to move such a large vehicle so many miles. In fact, the driver was not permitted to leave Manapouri for any destination off schedule without first having received the consent of his superior.

Telephone calls and seemingly endless delays followed. At long last a reservation was secured at the Te Anau Hotel and the driver was allowed, for the price of a chartered bus, to take me there.

Frances Ahl, *New Zealand Through American Eyes*, pp. 110–14.

The tour group (1953)

RAY DORIEN

Ray Dorien, a novelist and travel writer, wrote a series of 'Venturing' travel books, including one on Australia. She spent five months touring New Zealand in the early 1950s. Dorien also wrote a romance novel set in New Zealand, Flower of Delight *(1957).*

IN NELSON I WAS JOINING A TOUR, the only way in which I could see the places on my programme. On the quayside I was collected by the guide whom I shall call 'George'. He had been patiently watching the gyrations of the steamer and thinking, no doubt, of the breakfast he was missing. We went to the Metropolitan Hotel where the rest of the party had been staying.

Still, this time there was breakfast, which I enjoyed, in spite of the waitress' habit of shouting the orders loudly through the hatchway!

I had been placed at a table by myself, with my back to the other guests who were to be my companions on tour, and I wondered what they thought of my back, and I wondered too what they were like. In the lounge, immediately afterwards, I found out, for two pleasant, little, elderly ladies introduced themselves as from Milton, a farming town south of Dunedin. They knew and loved the names of every bush and flower.

'And this is Miss Nelson from Australia,' they introduced a fair girl with a love of roaming, and a passion for taking photographs. 'And here is a country-woman of yours.'

Brochure from the 1950s for Newmans coach tours. (C-24007-1/2-CT, ATL)

Miss Dobson was plump and enthusiastic. She had shaken the dust of wartime England from her feet, and was now happily settled in the North Island. She said she had arranged her social groups to her satisfaction.

'I only wish I'd come to New Zealand when I was a girl,' she declared. 'I keep telling Mr Brown what a good thing it would be if he brought his family out here.'

Mr Brown was another of these ubiquitous English business-men, this time from the Midlands, who was looking for opportunities of expansion in New Zealand.

'I like the idea of giving my six children bacon and eggs for breakfast every morning,' he said with his jovial laugh. 'And they could have riding and swimming, cheap fishing and shooting. But when I think how many towels our factory can turn out in one morning, why, the population of New Zealand would be running about dressed in towels all their lives! Afraid it's not big enough yet.'

He sighed as if he regretted the fact.

'If I had had an independent income, I would like to have settled in Timaru,' he went on 'Fine schools, and there's a grand beach for swimming. You can get to the Southern Alps and Mount Cook, and there would be mountaineering and winter sports for the children.'

This was where I asked him if he were acting as high pressure salesman for Timaru, which I heard was a most delightful town on the East Coast.

'You could do a guid deal worse than settle there,' said an elderly Scotsman, firmly.

I made a mistake in calling Mr Laird a Scotsman. He was a New Zealander of over forty years establishment, and he was proudly showing his new country to his brother and sister-in-law from the old one. They had the typical fairness of skin, the light grey of hair and the blueness of eye characteristic of their race. They were polite but reserved, and I found out later that they were hiding the fact of their home-sickness. They thought the New Zealand scenery at its finest when it reminded them of Scotland—as it often did. Occasionally they would admit—with reluctance—that the New Zealand scenery was on a slightly larger scale.

'It's the finest country in the world,' insisted the brother-in-law. 'Next to Scotland, of course. More chances for men here,' he continued with that touch of accent which persisted in spite of his forty odd years away from Scotland. 'Let a man know his job thoroughly—I don't care what it is,' he said. 'Let him stick to it, and get known for doing it. And I reckon in ten years he'll get where it would take him twenty years in the Old Country.'

'And we have a honeymoon couple,' continued the lady from Milton with that unquench-able feminine interest in romance. 'You'll see them later.'

There was time for shopping before the coach started, so I went across the street to buy some of the noted Nelson apples. The Chinese salesman wanted to know my age and other personal details. Perhaps it's an old Chinese custom! There are some Chinese shopkeepers in New Zealand, descendants of the trading or gold-mining early settlers.

In the South Island one sees very few Maoris. In the days before the white man came the

Maoris used the South Island for seeking the precious green-stone—*pounamu*—for their axes and ornaments. They were afraid of the mountainous region in the south where their fearful Gods dwelt. They gave the highest mountain the name of 'Aorangi', the Cloud-piercer. Now it is the more familiar Mount Cook.

I had to hurry back to get myself into the coach with the rest of the party for a drive of exploration round Nelson.

The young honeymoon couple were delightful in matching brown slacks and check flannel shirts. They seemed almost like twins, both being dark-eyed and dark-haired. The young man had been in the Pacific Islands during the war, and was interested in the world at large, which could not be said of some of the New Zealanders one met. Contentment is no doubt a virtue, but contentment with oneself and one's own country can degenerate into something not quite so pleasant.

I found myself placed in the front seat, as I was the newcomer, with a farmer from Auckland beside me. At least, he had been a farmer. He poured scorn on any romantic and sentimental notion of life on a farm. He said that I had simply no idea of the difficulties. Animals, however delightful to look at, needed to be looked after constantly. During the week-end the farmer had to do the work for which he paid his help, and during the busy seasons he had to pay dearly for extra labour. For his part he had given up the job thankfully, and had taken up a position in a town where he had some freedom.

I was not quite prepared for his freedom in the use of my Christian name, although I should have remembered that this was an old New Zealand custom. We argued about it.

I said, 'But if everybody calls everybody by their Christian name, what is there left for my friends to call me?'

And he said, 'Darling is good enough for you.'

I thought I had better study the scenery, and admired the great palms in Anzac Park.

Ray Dorien, *Venturing to New Zealand*, pp. 59–63.

The People's Palace (1955)

TOM HOUSTON

In 1954 Tom Houston took up a challenge from the Duke of Edinburgh to graduates to work 'his way round the world on £5'. Sponsored by the Daily Mail *for weekly articles, he set out just before Christmas for New York. Shortly afterwards he married, and by May Houston and his wife Caroline had reached Wellington, where they worked for a time before continuing to Australia.*

THE SHIP TURNED into Cook Strait between the two islands in the beauty of late autumn evening. The outer harbour of Wellington extends for about six miles and is encircled by hills, and as their silhouette encroached upon us lights came out all along the perimeter.

By the time we landed in 'Windy Wellington', however, the rain was falling in fits, and in plastic mackintoshes we bore the two battered suitcases to the gangway, past Miss Holiday Camp sitting on the rail with her legs crossed while a posse of photographers tried to get her likeness in the dull morning light, past several of our friends barely recognizable in suits and coats and hats, and down to a warehouse where customs' benches were roughly aligned. Knowing no one in the Dominion, with £2 5s 0d between us and with the urgent consideration that five months of my original nine month time limit were now gone, every minute that passed and every person we met had a special significance.

Sailors on the *Rangitiki* had said that non-union dock-labour was highly paid in Wellington, with a possible £25 a week if overtime was plentiful. Within an hour of landing the harbour authorities promised me work starting at eight o'clock the next morning.

'Have you been a wharfie before?' they asked.

'No.'

'Wharves and wharfies in New Zealand—docks and dockers in England—waterfront and longshoremen in America. It's all the same. You're big enough to earn your pay.'

Meanwhile Caroline had made a number of telephone calls and discovered a room of sorts, although accommodation was less easy to find than work. To British subjects New Zealand offers a wonderfully free opportunity, from the moment that we showed our passports at the customs not one person, including many later employers, asked for any document or reference whatsoever, and the longest columns in the newspapers were always the situations vacant; but the faces of the men at the wharf grew sad when they were asked about bed-sitting-rooms for £2 or £3 a week.

'You won't find it,' said one man. 'I don't want to discourage you, but I can tell you that you won't find that in Wellington. The People's Palace would be your best bet, in my opinion.'

The People's Palace replied that they charged £1 a day for each person.

'And that's without meals, mind you,' said the wharfie. 'The landlords are exploiting the housing shortage, I reckon. You see, Wellington can't grow any bigger, itself,' and he pointed to the line of hills surrounding the port. 'Across the bay you might find it cheaper, I wouldn't say myself, but you might, you know.'

'Why don't they build upwards, skyscrapers?'

'It'll be a long time before they start using the American ways here. If you go to Sydney, mind you, you'd find it different, but not in New Zealand, not for a long time.'

The quiet manner and kindness with which he answered our questions made us aware of the extraordinary affinity between the people of New Zealand and of the United Kingdom, and that comparison was rapidly strengthened, when, after scribbling some names and addresses on a scrap of paper, with one at least more hopeful than the People's Palace, a truck driver gave us a lift to the centre of Wellington, where the shops and buildings, the pedestrians and the cars, might well have belonged to any preponderantly grey and nineteenth-century English provincial town, like Bristol without the old part, or Reading without red brick.

Hotels and boarding houses were so full that we were lucky to find a damp, eight-by-eight foot room for seven guineas a week, which included a toast and tea breakfast. By paying another ten shillings access to the community kitchen was permitted, and an immediate cash deposit of five shillings secured the loan of a key for our room. The landlord was a Syrian.

'You've come to the right country,' he said proudly. 'All one class of people. Nothing but middle class here'—only he pronounced it 'muddle', and muttered 'nothing but muddle class' several times before opening a colourful golf umbrella to protect himself while walking ten yards to his new Jaguar, and driving off down the street.

So we began life in New Zealand, and bought at a local store sufficient food for two or three days, as well as two plastic mugs (5d each), a tin-foil cake dish (11d) which could be used as a plate or frying-pan, and a small saucepan (2/7). These were our only utensils for ten days, except for one or two trophies from the *Rangitiki*, pilfered in the wake of various souvenir hunters.

Tom Houston, *The Five Pound Look*, pp. 179–81.

The view from Viet Nam (1961)

TRINH KHANH TUOC

In 1961 Trinh Khanh Tuoc came to New Zealand as a Colombo Plan student. At 17 he was the youngest of the first large group of Vietnamese students who came to New Zealand to study. He studied chemical engineering at Canterbury. Our New Zealand Experience is not a travel book but a discursive book about the experiences of Colombo Plan students.

Later:

Wellington is not unlike Dalat in many ways. From the terminal, one can see small clusters of houses clutching to the side of a hill. The air was fresh with a chilly wind. It was a cloudy Saturday afternoon. They sky was blanketed by a large grey cumulus that oppressed our mind as well as the atmosphere. Hardly a gay welcome.

We were met by an official who described himself as a student officer and, along with many other young foreigners, we were taken to the city. By that time it was darkish, round seven, and the streets were bare, the city deserted. I only saw two people on the way. We stopped at a hostel called the Y.M.C.A. It was, we were told, not the normal procedure to put students there but there was only one vacancy at the usual boarding house or hostel—the Colombo Plan Hostel. I am staying at the Y.M.C.A. on the third floor, above an interminable series of steps. My room is shared with somebody but I haven't met him yet. It looks gloomy with a pearl bulb throwing a weak light on to my bed, in the corner. There is only one table for the two of us. We, the five of us, were given dinner somewhere, among other students of other races. Each of us received ten pounds for temporary expenses, then we returned to our residence.

I am back at the hostel now but before going in I had a good look. It is an old grey building flanked by two smaller but no brighter ones.

My room has a window overlooking what appears to be a precipice. There is certainly no light out there. It started to drizzle but it stopped almost immediately. The moon then came out, a tiny scythe unable to brighten the night. It looks just as lost and lonesome as I. The wind is wailing now, very plaintively. One always has the impression that it is not really the wind that cries, it's the call of a beloved one that it carries. I tell myself that I am crazy, that this is just a bad dream, that I am going to wake up in our cosy, familiar, crowded room, away from this coldness and this solitude. I would like to scream to liberate this oppressing sadness and reverse the course of time. I seem to discern beyond that window two eyes watching me, silent, a gaunt figure. Mother's long black hair that I used to pull playfully.

This is a nightmare. Maybe sleep will free me from it. In any case I feel dead tired, may be just plain dead, and my eyes are slowly closing.

Khanh

Saturday, March 25

Dear Father,

Do you remember reading somewhere that New Zealand has a small population? That was what I was thinking during my first encounter with Wellington because the streets were deserted and I only saw two Maoris who were running. They did not look like the ones in the slide we saw; they did not wear grass skirts nor were they tattooed. But the whole place was so empty that I was already asking myself: 'If this is the Capital, what's a small village in this country?' I got the answer today. We were in the empty streets at about seven last Saturday. In the afternoon there had been a big rugby match. By that time everyone was home for dinner or preparing for the pictures at eight.

The past week has been a flurry of activities: opening bank accounts, taking identification cards, sightseeing, matriculating, shopping.

We were taken to the External Aid Division where we were told of life in New Zealand for more than an hour. But the speaker was shouting so fast that I did not catch much. I can only remember him saying: 'You must learn to eat mutton.'

Groups of us were then taken shopping by a student officer. I didn't buy much because there were so many of us that he couldn't advise each of us individually. It was becoming hopeless when we went to a function of the United Nations Association. I met a very friendly chap who asked me all sorts of questions on my first impressions, my experiences on flight, my hopes. I was hampered by my lack of English vocabulary, so the conversation progressed very slowly. Then, after a good hour, I asked him where he came from and guess what? Viet Nam! No need to tell you how glad we were. Ever since, Van—that's his name—has been with us five, tipping us on the local customs, explaining the thousand and one new things on the way, introducing us to his friends, playing the guide with infinite patience.

Tomorrow, we are starting on an English course at the university. Let's hope it helps. At the moment, it's a torture. It took me half an hour to get a glass of water in a restaurant yesterday. The written English is not bad, but the spoken one is impossible to understand.

Please do write a note of thanks to Van. But for him our morale would not be so good.

Khanh

Trinh Khanh Tuoc, *Our New Zealand Experience*, pp. 86–9.

Tuataras on the Brothers (1962)

GERALD DURRELL

Gerald Durrell came to New Zealand in 1962 to look at conservation work and make television programmes about conservation for the BBC. He spent six weeks in New Zealand travelling to conservation sites and filming.

AS WE GOT NEARER to the larger of the Brothers we could see that it rose sheer out of the sea, the cliffs being some two hundred feet high. On top of a flat area at the edge of the cliff crouched what appeared to be a baby crane looking, as cranes always do, like a surrealistic giraffe. The launch headed for the cliffs below the crane and we could see a group of three people standing around its base; they waved vaguely at us and we waved back.

'I suppose,' I asked Brian, 'that that crane's the way they get supplies on to the island?'

'It's the way they get everything on to the island,' said Brian.

'Everything?' asked Jim, 'What d'you mean by everything?'

'Well, if you want to get on to the island you've got to go by crane. There is a path up the cliffs, but you could never land on the rocks in this sort of weather. No, they'll lower the net down in a minute and have you up there in a jiffy.'

'D'you mean to say they're thinking of hauling us up that cliff in a *net*?' asked Jim.

'Yes,' said Brian.

Just at that moment the skipper of the launch cut the engines down, and we drifted under the cliff, rising and falling on the blue-green swell and watching the breakers cream and suck at the jagged cliff some twenty-five feet away. The nose of the crane appeared high above, and from it dangled—at the end of an extremely fragile-looking hawser—something closely resembling a gigantic pig net. The crane uttered a series of clankings, groans and shrieks that were quite audible, even above the noise of the wind and the sea, and the pig net started to descend. Jim gave me a mute look of anguish and I must say that I sympathised with him. I have no head for heights at all and I did not relish, any more than he did, being hauled up that cliff in a pig net slung on the end of a crane that, from the sound of it, was a very frail octogenarian who had been without the benefit of oil for a considerable number of years. Chris, wrapped up in his duffel coat, and looking more like a disgruntled Duke of Wellington than ever, started Organising with the same fanatical gleam in his eye that Brian always had in similar situations.

'Now I want you to go up first, Jim, and get the camera set up by the crane so that you can film Gerry and Jacquie as they land,' he said. 'I'll go up next and get shots of the launch from the net, and then Gerry and Jacquie will follow with the rest of the equipment. Okay?'

'No,' said Jim. 'Why should *I* have to go first? Supposing the thing breaks just as I get to the top? Have you seen the rocks down here?'

'Well, if it breaks we'll know it's unsafe and go back to Picton,' said Jacquie sweetly.

Jim gave her a withering look as he reluctantly climbed into the pig net, which had by now landed on the tiny deck of the launch. The skipper waved his hand, there was a most terrifying screech of tortured metal, and Jim, clinging desperately to the mesh of the pig net, rose slowly and majestically into the air, whirling slowly round and round.

'I wonder if he gets net-sick as well as sea-sick?' said Jacquie.

'Sure to,' said Chris callously. 'To the best of my knowledge he gets sea-sick, train-sick, car-sick, plane-sick and home-sick, so I can't see him escaping being net-sick as well.'

Jim was now about halfway up, still twisting round and round, his white face peering down at us from between the meshes of the net.

'We're all *mad*,' we heard him yell above the sound of the sea and the infernal noise the crane was making. He was still yelling presumably insulting remarks at us when the net disappeared over the edge of the cliff. After a pause it reappeared again and was lowered to the deck, where Chris stepped stoically into it. He stuck his nose and the lens of the camera through the mesh of the net and started to film the moment he was lifted from the deck. Higher and higher he rose, still filming, and then suddenly, when he was poised halfway between the launch and the top of the cliff, the net came to a sudden halt. We watched anxiously but nothing happened for about five minutes, except that Chris continued to go round and round in ever diminishing circles.

'What d'you think has happened?' asked Jacquie.

'I don't know. Perhaps Jim's jammed the crane to get his own back on Chris.'

Just as I said this the crane started up again and Chris continued his majestic flight through the air and disappeared over the cliff edge. We discovered later that Jim had set up his camera and tripod in such a position that Alan Wright could not swing the crane in, but Alan was under the impression that Jim had to be in that particular position, so he kept Chris dangling in mid-air. It was only when he saw Jim leave the camera, find a convenient rock and, squatting on it, take out a bar of chocolate and start to eat it, that he realised that he had been keeping Chris dangling like a pantomime fairy to no good purpose, so the camera and tripod were removed and Chris was swung in, demanding vociferously to know why he had been kept suspended in mid-air for so long.

The net was sent down once again, loaded up with our gear, and Jacquie and I reluctantly took our seats.

'I am not going to like this a bit,' said Jacquie with conviction.

'Well, if you get scared just close your eyes.'

'It's not the height so much,' she said, glancing upwards, 'it's the strength of that hawser that worries me.'

'Oh, I wouldn't worry about that,' I said cheerfully. 'I expect it's been carrying loads like this for years.'

'That's exactly what I mean,' she said grimly.

'Well, it's too late now,' I said philosophically, as the crane started its banshee-like screech and we zoomed up from the deck of the launch at the speed of an express lift. The wide mesh of the net gave you the unpleasant impression that you had been rocketed into the air without any support at all, and as you revolved round and round you could see the waves breaking on the jagged rocks below. The launch now looked like a toy and, glancing up, the top of the cliff appeared to be a good deal higher than Everest, but at last we reached the cliff edge and were swung in and dumped unceremoniously on the ground.

As we disentangled ourselves from the net and equipment, a stocky man who had been operating the crane came forward and shook hands. He had a freckled face, vivid blue eyes and bright red hair.

'I'm Alan Wright,' he said. 'Pleased to meet you.'

'There were moments,' I said, glancing at the crane, 'when I began to wonder if we should ever meet.'

'Oh, she's all right,' said Alan, laughing, 'she just maithers a bit when she's got a load on, that's all.'

We got the equipment up the final slope to the lighthouse on a sort of elongated trolley, drawn up the hillside by a cable and winch. The others decided to walk up but I thought it would be fun to ride up on the trolley and so I perched myself on the camera gear. We were halfway up when I glanced back and suddenly realised that—potentially speaking—this was every bit as dangerous as the trip in the net, for if the hawser that was hauling the truck broke, the truck, weighted down with equipment and myself, would run backwards down the rails and shoot off the edge of the cliff like a rocket. I was glad when we ground to a halt by the lighthouse.

When we had got the gear safely installed in the one wooden hut which we would all have to share as bedroom and work-shop, I turned to Alan eagerly.

'Tell me,' I said, 'did you manage to get a Tuatara for us?'

'Oh, aye,' he said casually, 'that's all right.'

'Wonderful,' I said enthusiastically. 'Can I see it?'

Alan gave me an amused look.

'Aye,' he said. 'Come with me.'

He led Jacquie, Chris and myself to a small shed that stood not far from the hut we were to occupy, unlocked the door and threw it open; we all peered inside.

I have, at one time and another, had many zoological surprises, but, offhand, I can never remember being quite so taken aback as when I peered into that tiny shed on the Brothers. Instead of the one Tuatara I had expected, the whole floor was—quite literally—covered with them. They ranged from great-grandfathers some two feet long to babies measuring some six inches. Alan, glancing at my face, misinterpreted my expression of disbelieving delight for one of horror.

'I hope I haven't got too many,' he said anxiously. 'Only you didn't say what size you wanted or how many, so I thought I'd better catch you a fair selection.'

'My dear fellow,' I said in a hushed whisper, 'you couldn't have done anything to please me more.'

Gerald Durrell, Two in the Bush, pp. 71–5.

Incredibly dull (early 1960s)

SARAH MUSSEN

On an impulse Sarah Mussen left England for Australia and worked her way around the Pacific for two years. In New Zealand she worked as a rouseabout in a Maori shearing gang and as a waitress and fruit-picker.

'YOU HAVEN'T GOT GLOW-WORMS in England, have you?' asked Derek one Saturday as we were eating breakfast.

'I'm not sure,' I said. 'I've never seen any.'

'We'll take you to the Waitomo Caves. We took Joy's mum and pop there last month; they thought the glow-worms were marvellous. So did the Queen.'

'How do glow-worms work?'

'Well, they have sticky lighted tails which they dangle down like fishing-rods to catch moths and flies. Fascinating.'

'We'll take you today,' said Joy. 'We can wait outside.'

'Be sure you look at the bench outside the caves,' said Derek. 'It's got "Johnson" carved on it.'

'Monument to posterity,' explained Joy. 'Mum and Pop did it. Wonder the Queen didn't carve her name too.'

'Or get the lady-in-waiting to.'

When Derek had polished the car and Joy and I finished the week's washing we drove to the caves. Derek and Joy sat on the bench outside while the cave-guide led about twenty tourists, including myself, inside. 'These caves are government property,' he said. 'You must not photograph, smoke, talk, or touch the rocks. Noise upsets the glow-worms and sweat dis-

Opotiki, 1959 (M.H. Wevers)

colours the stone.' A bearded man peered at us round a pink stalactite. Was he a caveman? No, explained the guide, he was the resident electrician.

We stumbled through caves, passages, and grottoes, down a flight of steps, and arrived at a jetty beside a black, glistening river. We climbed into a small boat and, the guide pulling overhead wires, started gliding along the underground river. It was like crossing the Styx to Hades; we could hear only the creaking of the boat, the slow movement of the water, see only the heavy blackness. Then suddenly we were in a vast grotto, glowing with myriads of tiny lights, luminous joints shimmering in fantastic patterns. They reflected on the water around us; we were floating in a new galaxy of stars.

Each weekend Derek and Joy took me for a drive through the Auckland countryside. 'Do you realize,' said Derek when we passed a lunatic asylum, 'that New Zealand has the largest proportion of loonies in the world? Said so in yesterday's paper.' We drove through the exotic bush on the Waitakere Mountains, and Derek pointed out kauris, and punga palms, and nikau palms which looked like umbrellas turned inside out. We never got out of the car, unless to buy a bag of chips at a beauty-spot kiosk. Joy and I munched them greedily, but Derek just nibbled one or two chips before waving the bag away. 'No more for me,' he'd say, 'I'm full as a family po.' He was more figure-conscious than most women, and each day at breakfast gave us the readings of his bathroom scales.

On Sundays we usually visited Derek's relatives: his dad, who taught me rhyming slang ('Just going up the frog and toad, I'm out of coffin nails. Here comes my thud and blister ... some tit for tat she's got. Hey, look at that sheila—what Manchester cities! They beat Sabrina's! Pass the bung-hole and belly-varnish, please. Quick, quick, I've got the back-door trots!'), and his mum, who was so hygienic that she never wore new clothes without washing them first. She dedicated each day of the week to a different part of her anatomy: Monday, manicure; Tuesday, shampoo; Wednesday, liquid diet; Thursday, massage; Friday, facial.

Derek's gran, a fat old lady wearing a rusty black dress and bobble-trimmed carpet-slippers, was the family's *enfant terrible*. 'You know what Derek said to me?' she once remarked, stroking the white beard sprouting from her chin. 'He said, "You'll love listening to Sarah, such a queer voice." He's right too. She still hasn't got the twang.'

Derek's cousin Sandra, who worked in an office, was very shy. Her round face crumpled into embarrassed dimples whenever we spoke to her, and she would agree with anything we said.

'Terrible weather, isn't it?' Derek would say.

'I'll say,' said Sandra.

'Good film we saw last night, wasn't it?'

'I'll say,' said Sandra.

Derek's dad couldn't stand anyone who was silent for too long. Sometimes he would turn on Sandra, shouting: 'Shut up, for Christ's sake! Can't hear myself speak the way you gabble on.'

As Derek's relatives lived in Mount Roskill, we were always nipping in and out of one another's houses. Mum's and Dad's and Gran's houses were square and wooden, very similar to ours except that inside they had black scallop-edged blinds instead of plastic venetians, and aspidistras instead of cacti.

Living with Derek, Joy, and their relatives, I found myself sharing their sense of security, their bland confidence in the future. Wherever I went in New Zealand people seemed to have the same illusion of security. Nothing that happened outside their two islands was real to them. Kennedy, Khrushchev, South African negroes, Tibetan refugees, were people who might have been living on another planet. I never heard anyone talk of bombs, radioactivity, shelters, or war, topics that haunted people in Europe, America, and even Australia. And no one in New Zealand seemed to have any particularly inspiring ideas, beliefs, or ambitions. The New Zealander, geographically and mentally, was in a backwater, soothing but enervating, relaxing, but after a time incredibly dull.

Sarah Mussen, *Beating about the Bush*, pp. 109–11.

Rain in Fiordland (1968–69)

ERIC HISCOCK

Eric Hiscock, author of instructional sailing books and several sailing travel books, and his wife Susan sailed from England to New Zealand in their boat Wanderer IV *in 1968–69. Hiscock had already circumnavigated the world twice in his previous boat* Wanderer III *and was well known in New Zealand waters.*

ALL NEXT DAY it rained and blew and we sympathized with our companions whose strings of pots were probably being smashed up by the sea outside. By evening three more boats had joined our raft, and again we invited all hands, twelve of them this time, for drinks aboard— a jolly party which lasted for five hours. Nobody showed much interest in listening to the weather forecasts, for no doubt they got their weather long before the meteorological office at Wellington heard about it; but they did listen, as did we, to the reports given every six hours from lighthouses—that evening Puysegur Point was recording 45 knots.

In those parts a north-west gale usually shifts to the south-west, and may then blow even harder, and our cove would be no good then. So the following evening as the wind started to shift, it was decided that we should all return to Beach Harbour. When we weighed we found, just as we had feared, that our anchor had fouled *Towai's*. By the time we had cleared hers and dropped it again it was too close to the shore to be of any use to her, and we, with the wind blowing us broadside on into the cove, were in an awkward position. Peter, who was already under way, quickly sized up the situation and returned to tow us out stern first and then went back to give *Towai* a pluck. I felt my seamanship had not been of the best.

During the night the gale blew itself out, and at daybreak everyone put to sea to salvage what remained of their pots, and bait and lay new ones. *Da Vinci* was the last to go, and her skipper came over to tell us that the sea had now gone down a lot. Before leaving he went to poor little *Flora* and pumped her out.

It was a windless and gloomy morning; for much of the time patches of drizzle hid the iron-bound coast from us as we motored north against a short, steep sea, which presaged wind to come from that direction soon, and rolling heavily in the beam swell. Twice, when visibility improved for a little while, we could see *Towai* working close inshore, apparently among the breakers. We had hoped to reach Doubtful Sound, 20 miles to the north, but had not covered half that distance when the expected wind sprang at us from dead ahead, and progress became so slow and wet that we turned to starboard, and with the wind then on the beam reached into near-by Daggs Sound. In the drizzle this looked dark and forbidding, but it is shorter

Opotiki Beach, 1959. (M.H. Wevers)

than most, and at its head only 8 miles from the sea we came to what appeared to be a well-sheltered anchorage in Jacobs Creek surrounded by mountains which half hid the sky. The glimpses we had of *Towai* near the coast that day brought home to us the dangers of the fisherman's life, and we were relieved to see her come in some hours later, anchor further down the creek and pick up a shoreline.

That night it rained in typical Fiordland fashion (a fall of 30 inches a month is not unusual), and towards dawn we were disturbed by a roaring which we thought must be wind in the trees; but when day reluctantly broke we discovered that the noise came from waterfalls created by the rain, dozens of them, their silver threads streaking the rugged sides of the mountains. So hemmed in were we, and so dark was the day, that we needed the saloon lights on until mid morning. Caddy weighed and came over to tell us that the wind outside was blowing at 35 knots, and that if it freshened any more it could scream where we lay. He invited us to raft up with him and his neighbours, scarlet *Isobel* and rusty little *Star of the Sea*. All had haunches of venison lashed in the rigging; one gave us a big cut of this for our 'tea'; another gave us boysenberries and ice-cream from her freezer.

The following morning was foggy, but at first light the fishermen went about their business: *Towai* to work the coast back to Breaksea where, all being well, she would spend the night; *Star* to work north to Doubtful, and *Isobel* to fish the seaward side of Secretary Island. We felt a little lonely when they had gone, the more so as the fog thickened to keep us there among the invisible waterfalls for three more hours. Even then it did not clear, but lifted just enough to let us see the shoreline underneath. We crept out to sea under power, and found it clear there but with no wind—the all-or-nothing pattern of weather to which we were growing accustomed—so we motored north to Doubtful where, we had been told, Blanket Bay on the south-east side of Secretary Island offered the best berth. There is a tiny islet in that bay which had a refrigerated depot where crayfish tails could be left to be collected by a small seaplane summoned by radio-telephone; the fishermen found it more profitable to use that expensive form of transport than to make the long, usually stormy, trip round Puysegur Point to dispose of their catch at Bluff. We had just anchored and picked up the shore-line, when down came the dainty little plane to make a graceful landing and taxi to the island to load her cargo. A cheerful young man from the islet came off by speedboat to ask if we had any letters to post, which we had, and a few minutes later the plane was in the air again, heading inland up the deep chasm of the sound for Te Anau, the nearest town some 50 miles away; we watched the silver speck diminish and fade out of sight.

Eric Hiscock, *Sou' West in Wanderer IV*, pp. 168–70.

Magical transport facilities (1973)

J.B. PRIESTLEY

The British novelist J.B. Priestley visited New Zealand in 1973 with his wife, the archaeologist Jacquetta Hawkes, in order to prevent a decline into a 'fat-lazy-fireside old codger'. He described his book as 'about a visit to the country', not a book about New Zealand, full of detail of people he met, things he did, sketches, conversations, opinions, and impressions.

WE LEFT FOR QUEENSTOWN about the middle of the morning. The road alongside Lake Pukaki was still rough going but didn't seem as bad now as it had done the evening before. The truth is of course that all of us exist in two different places at one and the same time. There is the place outside us, the one on the map, the solidly objective one; there is the place inside us, the one within the mind, the psychological place. (The essential self, once it understands the situation it is in, has some power of choice as to where it should live in this interior country of the mind and if necessary can move from a bad psychological place to a good one.) Many a man rich enough to own four beautiful houses cannot enjoy them because, in the interior country he carries around, he has chosen to exist in a slum or a miasmic swamp. We all have bad places in the mind, and the trick—not easy, I admit—is not to identify ourselves with them but to move out of them. I realize that this is *As-if* reasoning, the sort of thing that most philosophers pounce upon to denounce; but if we can remember to act upon it, then it will work in a rough-and-ready fashion and release us from much misery, which is something most philosophers cannot do. So while the road round Lake Pukaki was just the same as it had been the evening before, we found it endurable because we were now living in a much better psychological place.

I wish I could remember, in geographical terms, where we stopped for lunch; but I can't, not even after staring at two fairly large-scale maps. So here I am, at the other end of the earth, remembering this tiny sketch of a hamlet with affection but unable to give it a name. It consisted of a small tearoom, enclosed within a rose-garden, and a neighbouring general store: and that was all. If there were any houses near by, I never saw them; never a glimpse of one. Just the tea-room and the store, but also some extremely pleasant friendly women apparently in charge of everything. We ate sandwiches and scones (with jam and cream), and drank cold milk laced with whisky. This is a particularly good drink late at night, but there is nothing wrong with it at about 1.20 p.m. on a warm day. After lunch, Jacquetta wandered next door to see what they were selling there. She was so pleased with the store and (her note) 'the very nice young woman' who was looking after it, she came back to suggest that I should take a look at it, which of course I did. It was a real store, containing almost everything that sensible people—as distinct from those with more money than sense—could want to support a satisfactory existence. So far, so good; but now we came to *abracadabra*, illusion, the magical part. The nice young woman had said to Jacquetta, 'The schoolchildren should meet anyone so famous as your husband,' which made no sense to her and none to me when she reported it, for there were no schoolchildren in the store, none in the tearoom, none in the road outside so far as we could see. So we dismissed this odd remark and I stayed a little longer, exploring the darker corners of the store. Then, taking my leave, I halted, dumb with amazement, in the doorway.

There, facing me in a compact group, were about 20 schoolchildren, magically transported from the unknown. There too was their schoolmaster, who proceeded at once—just as if he and I had already set it up between us—to introduce me and to tell the children they could ask questions. They were, I fancy, mostly between 10 and 12 years of age, and were very shy. So was I, for that matter; and was probably still gaping goggle-eyed at them. The only person who wasn't shy was the schoolmaster, who was brisk and commanding after the manner of his kind. (My father was a schoolmaster.) When the questions finally came, they were almost the same question—*What was it like to write?*—or—*to be a writer?*—just as if repetition didn't worry them because each child felt he or she was asking a private question, the others ceasing to exist for a few moments. I found it rather hard going and so, I suspect, did everybody else except the schoolmaster, who continued to be brisk and commanding but probably unwilling now to give any of us good marks. But I never had time to explain to him that I was still lost in wonder at the inexplicable, almost necromantic presence of these children, a class conjured out of air. There may have been a moment—though I won't swear to this—when I fancied that if I turned round I might discover that the store and the tearoom had vanished. However, Jacquetta's note is more sensible than anything I am writing here: 'Somehow this little break represented the best of New Zealand.' True enough; well said; but there might have been a reference, however brief, to the magical transport facilities of the local education authorities.

J.B. Priestley, *A Visit to New Zealand*, pp. 59–61.

The Bruce Mountain Folk Museum (late 1980s)

P.J. KAVANAGH

Poet and novelist P.J. Kavanagh came to New Zealand at the end of the 1980s in search of his family's past. Kavanagh's great-grandfather settled at Patumahoe in 1866, and his grandfather and father grew up in New Zealand. Kavanagh's travels through New Zealand attempt to 'put a larger past in some sort of order'.

FISH-HAWKS HOVERED above the river. There were rags of cloud over the dark hills, as though the hills smoked, and a black squall over the heads, the entry to Wellington Harbour. I was to remember this later.

The hills were smooth but wrinkled, like the skin of a green elephant, or as though they were a plaster-relief map made by a too pedantic modeller. The clear light caught every fold and convexity. They had the appearance of smoothly grassed-over spoil-heaps, which in a sense is what they are, being volcanic. The sides of the steep Hutt Gorge were grown with delicate light-leaved bushes among darker ones, and this gave the wildness the appearance of a planned Victorian shrubbery. On the other side, in the plain, came grid-plan Masterton, a quiet place. I seemed to remember seeing an early letter by my medical-student father in which he expressed gloom at the thought of returning to practise medicine in Masterton, and I saw what he meant. His father did not live anywhere even as mildly populous as Masterton, but miles further along the road, at Pahiatua, nearer his patch of responsibility. Today that little township seems almost wholly given up to the sale of second-hand cars—they line the road there (perhaps, before, it was second-hand horses)—but the Reynold's Tavern is, I was told, a hundred years old, so he would have known that. Perhaps he even lived in it. It must have been a lonely life.

The loneliness of rural New Zealand, and that country's sometimes surreal attitude to the past, was made even more manifest when I was seduced by a roadside sign, not near any habitation, pointing towards 'The Bruce Mountain Folk Museum'. I followed where it pointed, along a track, myself followed by hopping white-backed magpies which seemed to have no fear of man, and came upon a hillside farm where the lone farmer—at least, no one else was about—stopped milking his real cows and, in silence, switched on a machine in a shed that mechanically milked a black-and-white mechanical cow. He sat on a milking-stool and watched my face while it did so. He followed me as I politely wandered round the shed looking at dusty horse-ploughs, old Ovaltine tins and metal advertisements for Virol. To what comments I could think of making he did not reply, but put a record on a wind-up gramophone and played an early monologue by an old-time English comedian, Sandy Powell, still attentively watching my face. Conceivably he was a little mad; I had no way of knowing, since it was my first rural contact in that place. Not quite the first, but the owner of the Reynold's Tavern had been no more communicative.

It was when I turned off the main road into my grandfather's district, towards Pongaroa, that I was hit for the first time by the full force of the picture-postcard, travel-poster overwhelming beauty of New Zealand. He must have traversed the place, up and down, hundreds of times, but of course he never mentioned its outstanding characteristic, tranquil beauty, mile after mile of it. It is an almost paradisal place. There are willows and poplars, probably imported; most of the native trees are dark and evergreen, in different tones and shades, which contrast with the brilliant emerald of the sometimes conical fields above them. These trees astonish in their variety of shape and tone. There are fir-like trees and yew-like trees, of great girth, and pohutukawa trees with grey bark, and palms, and lighter-coloured shrubs, like the tora; these are at the foot of the sheep-cropped, smooth and rounded, Irish-green pastures they give way to. It is the contrast between the various dark greens and the bright green fields that is exquisite, the perfect weedless turf on a succession of little ex-volcanoes; so perfect, that if it were not for the spectacular white of the sheep penned in corners, you might imagine the whole place, extending for dozens of miles, was an ingenious millionaire's golf course, with very short but glassily rippled fairways, and with tees and greens on mown plateaux and in moulded scoops. Even the sheep are exquisite, white, not grey, and of a particularly cuddly kind, Romneys, the sort that have curly fleece over their faces through which they peer. When you meet these on the road, being driven, you are not expected to wait but to point your car through them, and, unstartled, they mildly give way.

Occasionally, very occasionally, there is a white-painted 'smiling homestead', each one many miles from the next. My grandfather must have had access to all of these, and known the families in them. For him it may have been an isolated life but not a lonely one; although (I suppose) a kind of policeman, he was also there positively to help. It is good to think of him travelling those valleys and slopes, given their present beauty by the hand of man, for which soft loveliness the word now could be the Scottish 'douce', and of him having a hand in the clearing and settling and the justice of part of what is, after all, the point of New Zealand.

P.J. Kavanagh, *Finding Connections*, pp. 171–3.

London from the Routeburn (1992)

PAUL THEROUX

American travel writer Paul Theroux visited Australia and New Zealand on a book promotion tour shortly after separating from his wife, an experience that coloured his impressions of Oceania. He began in New Zealand, visiting major cities and walking the Routeburn Track, before moving on to another part of 'Meganesia', Australia.

WALKING ALONG THE RIDGE of the Harris Saddle, I had a clear recollection of the London I had left, of various events that people talked about: a steamy affair between a literary editor and one of her younger assistants; of a famous widow, an obnoxious Ann Hathaway type, who gave parties—drinkers jammed in a room full of smoke—that people boasted of attending. I saw people—writers—talking on television programs, and partygoers smoking, and snatching drinks from a waitress's tray, and shrieking at each other, and talking about the literary editor and her younger lover, and then they all went home drunk.

From this path blowing with wild flowers and loose snow these far-off people seemed tiny and rather pathetic in their need for witnesses.

'Bullshit!' I yelled into the wind, startling Isidore until he discerned that I was smiling.

I needed to come here to understand that, and I felt I would never go back.

Walking these New Zealand mountains stimulated my memory. My need for this strange landscape was profound. Travel, which is nearly always seen as an attempt to escape from the ego, is in my opinion the opposite. Nothing induces concentration or inspires memory like an alien landscape or a foreign culture. It is simply not possible (as romantics think) to lose yourself in an exotic place. Much more likely is an experience of intense nostalgia, a harking back to an earlier stage in your life, or seeing clearly a serious mistake. But this does not happen to the exclusion of the exotic present. What makes the whole experience vivid, and sometimes thrilling, is the juxtaposition of the present and the past—London seen from the heights of Harris Saddle.

Leaving the others behind I started the long traverse across the high Hollyford Face—three hours at a high altitude without shelter, exposed to the wind but also exposed to the beauty of the ranges—the forest, the snow, and a glimpse of the Tasman Sea. It was more than three thousand feet straight down, from the path on these cliffs to the Hollyford River on the valley floor. The track was rocky and deceptive, and it was bordered with alpine plants—daisies, snowberries and white gentians.

Ocean Peak was above us as I moved slowly across the rock face. It was not very late, but these mountains are so high the sun drops behind them in the afternoon, and without it I was very cold. The southerly wind was blowing from Antarctica. As the day darkened I came to a bluff, and beneath me in a new valley was a green lake. I was at such a high altitude that it took me another hour to descend the zigzag path.

Deeper in the valley I was among ancient trees; and that last half-hour, before darkness fell, was like a walk through an enchanted forest, the trees literally as old as the hills, grotesquely twisted and very damp and pungent. A forest that is more than a thousand years old, and that has never been touched or interfered with, has a ghostly look, of layer upon layer of living things, and the whole forest clinging together—roots and trunks and branches mingled with moss and rocks, and everything above ground hung with tufts of lichen called 'old man's beard.'

It was so dark and damp here the moss grew on all sides of the trunks—the sunlight hardly struck them. The moss softened them, making them into huge, tired, misshapen monsters with great spongy arms. Everything was padded and wrapped because of the dampness, and the boughs were blackish green; the forest floor was deep in ferns, and every protruding rock was upholstered in velvety moss. Here and there was a chuckle of water running among the roots and ferns. I was followed by friendly robins.

It was all visibly alive and wonderful, and in places had a subterranean gleam of wetness. It was like a forest in a fairy story, the pretty and perfect wilderness of sprites and fairies, which is the child's version of paradise—a lovely Disneyish glade where birds eat out of your hand and you know you will come to no harm.

I began to feel hopeful again about my life. Maybe I didn't have cancer after all.

Paul Theroux, *The Happy Isles of Oceania*, pp. 16–18.

At Cape Reinga (1991)

KATE LLEWELLYN

Australian writer Kate Llewellyn spent two months travelling in New Zealand and the Cook Islands in 1991. Her impressionist diary gives a record of her travels.

AT CAPE REINGA there is a lighthouse in the wind. Below, the waves tossed like something in a dream. The coast is raging wild; the wind blew my feet aside. We passengers crouched by a shed and ate our picnic lunch. Unless you held the plastic wrap down, the coleslaw blew away. I've never seen a wilder place than this. We walked down to the lighthouse but half-way there the wind made me turn back. I thought I could be blown into the bay. It's a fitting end for New Zealand; the hills, the sloping cliffs, the wild and dangerous day. Maori people's spirits, we were told, go here and then down to the roots of a nearby tree and slip away to the place from where they came. The Maoris found this land in the ninth century. In some places I have seen great log canoes with seats across them for oarsmen. One sits at Russell, nameless, drawn up on the sand. Its bow is carved and it's painted brown with a black band round the hull.

Today I saw kiwi birds in a night house near Kaitaia. A man and his wife built this and with a torch she led us in. The birds were pecking in the gloom. One egg was laid last year and now the birds are mating as it's spring. The egg is the largest for its layer's size of any bird alive. It's up to 20 per cent of its body weight while a domestic hen's is only five. When I asked, the man said that this egg wasn't fertilised. So they blew it. No wonder the bird is so rare.

There were glow-worm caves there so in I went, stared into the dark, saw light, came out and walked along a forest path among native trees all named with little placards at their base.

Everything is north here. Northlands is the name, North Cape, North Island, the family name of North. I feel I've been north.

The bus took us along the beach for an hour or two. I hate drivers who swerve buses on wet sand and laugh as their contents swirl around. Half-buried cars lay rusting in the sand where they'd been bogged. Children drove the bus with the driver's help.

At Awanui we got out. I had a local beer. At Kerikeri they grow kiwi fruit on poles, and lots of citrus fruit. We pulled up at a stall. This stall, the view at Cape Reinga and a small museum in a house we visited were the best things that I saw today. Well, the things that I liked most. The couple who grew the fruit stood there smiling, handsome, decent, worthy. They could be on a stamp that said 'New Zealand'. They had cut up fruit and put it out on plates for visitors to try. I was grumpy and reluctant to get out at yet another stop but I did. I ate some fruit and bought some mandarins—utterly delicious. I thought that they were

Cape Reinga, North Island. (Penny Griffith)

cumquats but they were deeply sweet. Clementine mandarins is their name. I got kiwi fruit as well and climbed back into the bus a better woman than the one who had staggered out. I wished that couple well. No sprays are used—all their fruit's organic. They had rare fruit as well. Tamarillos among others. I hope they make a million. Yet I fear they'll only struggle, times being as they are.

One town we went through has 60 per cent of its population unemployed. That's how bad it is here. But that's not the case all over the country, it's just worse, I think, in the far north.

Back in this seat of luxury [Paihia Hotel], I got into the bath and groaned with pleasure. Down to dinner once again to try more of the local fish. And mushroom soup with bacon. But again, no bread. All nations have their habits but do these people not like bread? And, no, I don't want focaccia with olives on it, thanks.

I have each night a marvellous man to serve me. He's local and is half Maori or some attractive mix. He is the best wine waiter I have had and his manners are impeccable. He told me when I asked that he'd been travelling and had just come home.

One day, if I know anything, he'll own the town. Isabelle, another waiter, kept asking if I'd like a heater brought. I told her not to bother but she brought it anyhow. It's these little kindnesses that touch the visitor; manners of a subtle kind. Tomorrow night the dining room's booked out as the fishing people meet. The chef said I could come and he'd cook me something separately but I think I'd best go out.

Kate Llewellyn, *Lilies, Feathers and Frangipani*, pp. 19–21.

Boomtown Rotorua (1996)

JOHN RUCK

After thirty years away, former journalist John Ruck returned to New Zealand and set off on a journey of discovery in the manner of Austin Mitchell, as the title of his book suggests.

ROTORUA WAS A LOT SMARTER than we remembered it. In the '50s and '60s it seemed a down-at-heel sort of town, notable mostly for its sulphurous odour. Its tourist attractions, based on thermal activity and Maori concerts, seemed to have changed little in decades. Yes, they were cheap, and yes, they looked and felt it. Once you had seen the hot pools and the geysers and the trout springs, there seemed little incentive to return.

Now it had sprouted a bigger variety of attractions than the average tourist's timetable, or wallet, could possibly cope with, particularly if he or she is adventurous and energetic. New hotels and motels had lifted its choice of accommodation to an international standard. Shops and restaurants were brighter and more numerous. New terracotta paving and planters graced the streets. A new (or newly refurbished) park beside Lake Rotorua attractively tied lake and city into one vista for the first time.

Less adventurous than younger fry, we skipped the more hair-raising attractions, choosing instead to ride a gondola, scoot down a luge, sample the hangi at a posh hotel, take a launch trip and, of course, revisit our quota of pools and geysers. At one of the city's farm shows, we laughed with the tourists at an elderly Japanese gentleman clinging to the back of a (fortunately docile) bull, but not at what he represented: more than half a million Asian visitors to Rotorua in a single year. Total tourist numbers in the year that we visited topped 1,205,000, a 38 per cent growth in three years.

At Whakarewarewa we joined a file of Asians inspecting something different: New Zealand's most exclusive school. It admits no more than nine pupils at any one time; it has a staggering staff ratio of one tutor to three pupils; and it operates without a single cent of government funding. Further, it actually pays its pupils while they take its three-year course.

It is tourism that keeps the carving school of the New Zealand Maori Arts and Crafts Institute in business. The whole institute, in fact, is funded by the visitors who watch the weavers and carvers at work, and then go outside to view the hot springs and geysers.

Clive Fugill, who as master carver is head of the school, might be described as a purist. He started carving as a schoolboy, was one of the school's first pupils when it opened in 1967, and has been there ever since. Like the Latin master who enjoys teaching the language because of, not in spite of, its strictly structured grammar and syntax, he teaches strictly traditional carving and will brook no lesser variation.

The reason is that to pre-European Maori the carver was an historian. With no written language, they relied on carvings as a visual record of their history and genealogy. To produce authentic carvings, Clive Fugill's pupils must master a great deal of theory: Maori language, protocol, genealogy, and tribal history. This last is an endless subject because of the ancient tribes' constantly changing pattern of alliances, intermarriages, treacheries and wars.

These days the carvers use steel tools instead of the stone adzes of their forefathers. Pupils at the institute start with a 44-piece set of European woodcarvers' tools and regrind the chisels into different profiles. First-year student Henare Peters showed us his set, starting with the nearly flat No. 2 gouge and getting progressively more rounded up to No. 9. Then there are the V chisels used for cutting out spirals; I lightly stroked the end of one with a forefinger, but quickly desisted; it was sharper than a razor blade. The mallets used to tap the chisels, however, are of the old-time Maori pattern: a long, rectangular block of wood, shaped to a handle at one end. The European type, with a head mounted on a separate handle, is too heavy for delicate work.

In pre-European times, different tribes' carving was in quite distinctive styles. One Northland tribe, for example, produced figures with pear-shaped heads, often cocked to one side, and sinuous curved or twisted bodies—in marked contrast to the full-faced, rectangular, blocky figures mostly seen elsewhere. 'We stick to the ancient, tribal styles,' Clive Fugill told us. 'Regional styles crept in about the 1950s when steel tools first became available, but these carvers weren't taught properly, and from our perspective we see a lot of inferior work.'

Not, apparently, as inferior as most of the work on sale in souvenir shops, which Clive Fugill describes as rubbish. 'It's big business, it's quick turnover, it's cheap and it's nasty.' But there is another trend: serious collectors wanting the genuine article—especially small pieces they can carry in their suitcases, but also including such things as wall panels at perhaps $1,200 each. This quickening of interest from tourists is a boon to graduates of the school who go on to sell their art in much the same manner as studio potters. One Christchurch studio carver, for example, has built up to a staff of six.

Meanwhile, it may say something about racial separateness in New Zealand that in 66 years neither Fay nor I had ever set foot on a marae. Now we remedied that by visiting Rakeiao marae and the Rangi-a-Tea cultural group.

We had been to Maori concerts before, of course. Most were notable for the zest of the performers—and also for their amateurish air: much prompting and much repetition 'toru ka wha' ('three, four') as the leader tried to maintain unison among the choristers.

This evening had most of the familiar ingredients, starting with that Rotorua institution, the humorous Maori bus driver. This one's name was Wyn, he told us as he steered our 'waka' to the marae, and his surname was Lotto; I can only wish him luck. And of course there were action songs, haka, stick games, long poi and short poi, canoe songs and—perhaps, inevitably, the pakeha New Zealander's favourite Maori song, *Pokarekare Ana.*

Unusually, we even had a chance to join in. Rawinia Mitau-Ngatai, the group's leader, showed us how to do actions of the canoe song *Uia Mai Koia*. Then 50-odd tourists, trying hard and with a good deal of laughter, showed her how not to. Well, some of us got some of it right.

John Ruck, *The Cross-leased Chardonnay Cellphone Paradise*, pp. 61–3.

Acknowledgments

My thanks and acknowledgments to: Creative New Zealand for an initial grant, which led to the work in this area; the Marsden Fund for a grant to the History of Print Culture Project; Brian Opie and HUMANZ; Penny Griffith; the History of Print Culture Project Steering Committee; Margaret Calder, Alexander Turnbull Librarian, and the staff of the Alexander Turnbull Library and the National Library, particularly Barbara Brownlie (Ephemera Collection), Marian Minson (Drawings and Prints), Joan McCracken (Photographic Collection), Shay Turnbull (Cartographic Collection), Susan Bartel (Promotions Manager, Heritage), and the staff of the National Library Gallery; the endlessly helpful staff of the Alexander Turnbull Library reference desk; Linda Cassells, Peter Rose, and Cathryn Game of Oxford University Press; and my friends and family.

I and Oxford University Press are grateful to the Alexander Turnbull Library and the National Library of New Zealand/Te Puna Matauranga o Aotearoa for permission to reproduce the illustrations.

Sources

The editor and publisher would like to thank copyright holders for permission to reproduce copyright material. Every effort has been made to trace the original source of all material contained in this book. Where the attempt has been unsuccessful the editor and publisher would be pleased to hear from the author or publisher concerned to rectify any omission.

Ahl, Frances, *New Zealand Through American Eyes*, Christopher Publishing House, Boston, 1948, pp. 110–14.

Arnold, Thomas, *New Zealand Letters of Thomas Arnold the Younger with Further Letters from Van Diemen's Land and Letters of Arthur Hugh Clough 1847–51* (ed. James Bertram), University of Auckland/Oxford University Press, Auckland, 1966, pp. 47–8.

Ballou, Maturin M., *Under the Southern Cross: or, Travels in Australia, Tasmania, New Zealand, Samoa and Other Pacific Islands*, Ticknor & Co., Boston, 1888, pp. 286–8.

Barton, B.H., *Far from the Old Folks at Home*, Privately Printed, 1884, pp. 334–7.

Bell, James Mackintosh, *The Wilds of Maoriland 1877–1934*, Macmillan & Co., London, 1914, pp. 17–19.

Bird, Isabella L., *The Hawaiian Archipelago: Six Months among the Palm Groves, Coral Reefs and Volcanoes of the Sandwich Islands*, John Murray, London, 1875, pp. 6–11.

Boultbee, John, *Journal of a Rambler: The Journal of John Boultee* (ed. June Starke), Oxford University Press, Auckland, 1986, pp. 36–40.

Broad, Lucy, *A Woman's Wanderings the World Over*, Headley Bros., London, 1909, pp. 120–3.

Brown, Henry, *Diary During a Trip Round the World*, Torquay, 1874, pp. 152–5.

Brown, W. Towers, *Notes of Travel: Extracts from Home Letters Written during a Two Years' Tour Round the World 1879–81*, Printed for Private Circulation, [London], 1882, pp. 80–5.

Butler, Annie R., *Glimpses of Maori-land*, Religious Tract Society, London, 1886, pp. 68–70.

Byles, Marie Beuzeville, *By Cargo Boat and Mountain: The Unconventional Experiences of a Woman on Tramp Round the World*, Seeley, Service & Co. Ltd, London, 1931, pp. 253–6.

Carter, C.R., *Life and Recollections of a New Zealand Colonist Written by Himself*, Printed by R. Madley, London, 1866, pp. 94–101.

Chapman, G.T., *Chapman's Travellers Guide through New Zealand: A Picture of New Zealand, Geographical, Topographical and Statistical*, G.T. Chapman, Auckland, 1872, pp. 93–5.

Colman, Russell J., *Trifles from a Tourist*, For Private Circulation, Norwich, 1887, pp. 61–2.

Crawford, J.C., *Recollections of Travel in New Zealand and Australia*, Truebner & Co., London, 1880, pp. 30–2.

Dilke, C.W., *Greater Britain: A Record of Travel in English-Speaking Countries During 1866 and 1867*, Macmillan & Co., London, 1868, pp. 330–2.

Dorien, Ray, *Venturing to New Zealand*, Christopher Johnson, London, 1953, pp. 59–63.

Durrell, Gerald, *Two in the Bush*, Collins, London, 1966, pp. 71–5.

Elkington, E. Way, *Adrift in New Zealand*, John Murray, London, 1906, pp. 75–7.

Fell, Alfred, *A Colonist's Voyage to New Zealand Under Sail in the 'Early Forties'*, first published 1926; republished Capper Press, Christchurch, 1973, pp. 26–8.

Ferguson, John, *To the Antipodes, the Orient and the West*, Private Publication, 1903, pp. 90–3.

Froude, James Anthony, *Oceana, or, England and Her Colonies*, Longmans Green & Co., London, 1886, pp. 262–3 and 282–4.

German Lady, A [Miss Muller], *Notes of a Tour through Various Parts of New Zealand Including a Visit to the Hot Springs*, Lee & Ross, Printers, Sydney, 1877, pp. 12–14 and 23–7.

Gordon Cumming, C.F., *At Home in Fiji*, William Blackwood & Sons, Edinburgh and London, 1881, pp. 180–2 and 223–7.

Gorst, J.E., *New Zealand Revisited: Recollections of the Days of My Youth*, Sir Isaac Pitman & Sons, London, 1908, pp. 11–15.

Grimshaw, Beatrice, *In the Strange South Seas*, Hutchinson & Co., London, 1907, pp. 338–41.

Hall, Mary, *A Woman in the Antipodes and in the Far East*, Methuen & Co., London, 1914, pp. 25–8.

Head, H.S., *The Journals and Letters of Hugh Stanley Head Edited by His Mother*, Rankin, Ellis & Co. Ltd, London, 1892, pp. 37–40.

Henley, Frank, *Bright Memories*, For Private Circulation, Torquay, 1887, pp. 87–93.

Hingston, James, *The Australian Abroad: Branches from the Main Routes Round the World*, Sampson Low, Marston, Searle, & Rivington, London, 1879, pp. 341–5.

Hiscock, Eric, *Sou' West in Wanderer IV*, Oxford University Press, London, 1973, pp. 168–70.

Hochberg, Count Fritz von, *An Eastern Voyage: A Journal of the Travels of Count Fritz von Hochberg through the British Empire in the East and Japan*, J.M. Dent & Sons, London, 1910, pp. 84–7 and 103–11.

Houston, Tom, *The Five Pound Look*, Travel Book Club, London, 1957, pp. 179–81.

Jameson, R.G., *New Zealand, South Australia and New South Wales: A Record of Recent Travels in These Colonies*, Smith, Elder & Co., London, 1842, pp. 300–3.

Karlin, Alma M., *The Odyssey of a Lonely Woman*, Gollancz, London, 1933, pp. 441–3.

Kavanagh, P.J., *Finding Connections*, Hutchinson, London, 1990, pp. 171–3.

Kennaway, William, *Biscuit and Butter: A Colonist's Shipboard Fare—The Journal of William and Lawrence Kennaway London to Lyttelton 1851* (ed. R.C. Lamb and R.S. Gormack), Nag's Head Press, Christchurch, 1973, pp. 96–8.

Kennedy, David, Jnr, *Kennedy's Colonial Travel: A Narrative of a Four Years' Tour Through Australia, New Zealand, Canada, &c*, Edinburgh Publishing Company, Edinburgh, 1876, pp. 175–7 and 191–3.

Kipling, Rudyard, *Something of Myself*, Macmillan & Co., London, 1937, pp. 100–2.

Lambe, J.L., *Twelve Months of Travel*, Printed for Private Circulation, 1888, pp. 120–4.

Little, W., *Round the World: Notes By the Way by a 'Commercial'*, Heckington, n.d. (c. 1875), pp. 90–3.

Llewellyn, Kate, *Lilies, Feathers and Frangipani*, Angus & Robertson, Sydney, 1993, pp. 19–21.

Lowth, Alys, *Emerald Hours in New Zealand*, Whitcomb & Tombs Ltd, Christchurch, 1907, pp. 37–40.

MacGregor, John, *Toil and Travel*, T. Fisher Unwin, London, 1892, pp. 55–6.

Marjoribanks, Alexander, *Travels in New Zealand*, Smith, Elder & Co., London, 1845 (republished Capper Press, Christchurch, 1973), pp. 24–2.

Markham, Edward, *New Zealand or Recollections of It* (ed. E.H. McCormick), R.E. Owen, Government Printer, Wellington, 1963, pp. 29–32.

Maudslay, Alfred, *Life in the Pacific Fifty Years Ago*, George Routledge & Sons Ltd, London, 1930, pp. 159–62.

M.E.M., *My First Voyage Around the World*, Privately Printed, Buxton, 1889, pp. 11–12.

Montrésor, Frederick, from *Leaves from Memory's Logbook* (ed. C.A. Montrésor), W.H. Allen & Co., London, 1887, pp. 61–4.

Morrill, G.L., *South Sea Silhouettes*, M.A. Donohue, Chicago, 1915, pp. 124–5.

Morton, H.B., *Notes of a New Zealand Tour*, New Zealand Herald Office, Auckland, 1878, pp. 11–12 and 13–15.

Mundy, G.C., *Our Antipodes: or, Residence and Rambles in the Australasian Colonies, with a Glimpse of the Gold Fields*, 3rd edn, Richard Bentley, London, 1855, pp. 262–7.

Mussen, Sarah, *Beating about the Bush*, Jarrolds, London, 1963, pp. 109–11.

Nesfield, Henry W., *A Chequered Career: or, Fifteen Years' Experiences in Australia and New Zealand*, Richard Bentley & Son, London, 1881, pp. 59–63.

Nicholls, J. Kerry, *The King Country: or, Explorations in New Zealand: A Narrative of 600 Miles of Travel through Maoriland*, Sampson Low, Marston, Searle & Rivington, London, 1884, pp. 94–7.

Partington, James Edge, *Random Rot*, For Private Circulation, 1883, pp. 336–9.

Payton, E.W., *Round about New Zealand: Being Notes from a Journal of Three Years' Wanderings in the Antipodes*, Chapman & Hall Ltd, London, 1888, pp. 77–83.

Ponder, S.E.G., *Sun on Summer Seas*, Stanley Paul & Co., London, 1936, pp. 103–7.

Pospisil, Bohumil, *Wandering on the Islands of Wonders*, Coulls Somerville Wilkie Ltd, Dunedin, 1935, pp. 49–51.

Power, W. Tyrone, *Sketches in New Zealand with Pen and Pencil*, Longman, Brown, Green & Longmans, London, 1849, pp. 2–4.

Priestley, J.B., *A Visit to New Zealand*, Heinemann, London, 1974, pp. 59–61.

Richardson, J.L.C., *A Summer's Excursion in New Zealand, with Gleanings from Other Writers*, Kerby & Sons, London; William Roberts Exeter, London, 1854, pp. 159–61.

Roberts, J. Herbert, *A World Tour, being a Year's Diary Written 1884–85*, Printed for Private Circulation, [J.H. Roberts], Liverpool, 1886, pp. 466–7.

Rochfort, John, *The Adventures of a Surveyor in New Zealand and the Australian Gold Diggings*, David Bogue, Fleet Street, London, 1853, pp. 18–20.

Rowan, Mrs, *A Flower Hunter in Queensland and New Zealand*, Angus & Robertson, Sydney, 1898, pp. 195–8.

Ruck, John, *The Cross-leased Chardonnay Cellphone Paradise*, Harper Collins, Auckland. 1996, pp. 61–3.

Sail, C.R., *Farthest East, and South and West: Notes of a Journey Home through Japan, Australasia, and America by an Anglo-Indian Globe-trotter*, W.H. Allen, London, 1892, pp. 178–82.

Sala, George Augustus, *The Land of the Golden Fleece* (ed. Robert Dingley), Mulini Press, Canberra, 1995, pp. 121–4.

Schwartze, C.E.R., *Travels in Greater Britain*, Printed for the Author by Cassell & Co., London, 1885, pp. 124–7.

Scott, Henry, *Reminiscences of a New Chum in Otago in the Early Seventies*, Timaru Herald Co., Timaru, 1922, pp. 11–12.

Senior, William, *Travel and Trout in the Antipodes: A Traveller's Sketches in Tasmania and New Zealand*, Chatto & Windus, London, 1880, pp. 195–9.

[Smiles, Master], *A Boy's Journey Around the World* (ed. Samuel Smiles), John Murray, London, 1871, pp. 205–8 and 216–17.

St Clair Erskine, Lady Angela, *Fore and Aft*, Jarrolds, London, 1933, pp. 137–9.

Talbot, Thorpe, *The New Guide to the Lakes and Hot Springs*, Wilson & Horton, Printers, Auckland, 1882, pp. 6–8.

Theroux, Paul, *The Happy Isles of Oceania: Paddling the Pacific*, Hamish Hamilton, London, 1992, pp. 16–18.

Tinne, J. Ernest, *The Wonderland of the Antipodes: and Other Sketches of Travel in the North Island of New Zealand*, Sampson Low, Marston, Low & Searle, London, 1873, pp. 15–17.

[Trench, W.R.], *Notes from Sea and Land by the Vicar of Kendal*, Titus Wilson, Publisher, Kendal, 1906, pp. 6–7.

Trevelyan, Charles, *Letters from North America and the Pacific, 1898*, Chatto & Windus, London, 1969, pp. 137–40.

Trinh Khanh Tuoc, *Our New Zealand Experience: Some Aspects of Overseas Students' Life in New Zealand*, Caxton Press, Christchurch, 1968, pp. 86–9.

Trollope, Anthony, *Australia and New Zealand*, 2nd edn, Dawsons of Pall Mall, London, 1968 (first published 1873), pp. 321–2, 335–8, and 483–5.

Twain, Mark, *More Tramps Abroad*, Chatto & Windus, London, 1897, pp. 209–10.

Unwin, Stanley, and Severn Storr, *Two Young Men See the World*, George Allen & Unwin, London, 1934, pp. 240–2.

Wadia, Ardaser Sorabjee N., *The Call of the Southern Cross: Being Impressions of a Four Months' Tour in Australia and New Zealand*, J.M. Dent & Sons, London, 1932, pp. 117–19.

[Wallis, Mary Davis], *Life in Feejee, or, Five Years Among the Cannibals*, by a Lady, William Heath, Boston, 1851, pp. 19–21.

Webb, Beatrice, *The Webbs in New Zealand 1898: Beatrice Webb's Diary, with Entries by Sidney Webb* (ed. D.A. Hamer), Victoria University Press, Wellington, 1974, pp. 29–31.

Wenz, Emile, *Mon Journal*, Typographie E. Plon, Nourrit et Cie, Paris, 1886, pp. 135–7 (extract translated by Lydia Wevers).

Wilson, Edward, *Rambles at the Antipodes: A Series of Sketches of Moreton Bay, New Zealand, the Murray River and South Australia, and the Overland Route*, W.H. Smith & Son, London, 1859, pp. 83–5.

Wirth, Philip, *The Life of Philip Wirth: A Lifetime with an Australian Circus*, Troedel & Cooper, Melbourne, 1934, pp. 49–51.

Woulden, Henry, 'Henry Woulden's Letters', from Thomas Bevan, *Narrative of a Voyage from England to New Zealand*, Smith, Elder & Co., London, 1842 (?), pp. 23–5.

Index